Understanding Political Science Statistics Using Stata

This manual walks students through the procedures for analysis in Stata and provides exercises that go hand-in-hand with online data sets. The manual complements the textbook, *Understanding Political Science Statistics: Observations and Expectations in Political Analysis*, by Peter Galderisi, making it easy to use alongside the book in a course or as a stand-alone guide to using Stata. Ellen C. Seljan demonstrates how to run commands in Stata for different kinds of research questions and shows the results of the analyses, using lots of annotated screenshots from Stata version 12 (but compatible with all versions, including Stata Small). Students will be guided through standard processes replete with examples and exercises to ready them for future work in political science research.

The diverse group of data sets provided include subsamples of both the 2008 and 2012 American National Election Studies, a Eurobarometer survey, single-year and longitudinal congressional district files, the 2012 Comparative Congressional Election Study, and a comparative, crossnational country file. Versions with reduced case numbers and variables are also included that are compatible with Stata Small.

This manual (and a parallel SPSS manual) are available as stand-alone products or packaged with the textbook *Understanding Political Science Statistics*, and data sets are available at www.routledge.com/cw/galderisi.

Ellen C. Seljan is Assistant Professor of Political Science at Lewis & Clark College.

Peter Galderisi has taught political science methods and statistics for more than three decades, and is currently a lecturer and local internship director in the Political Science Department at the University of California, San Diego. Previously, Galderisi was a Professor or Visiting Professor at Utah State, UCLA, UC Santa Cruz, and Cal State Fullerton. He specializes in U.S. political parties, campaigns and elections, American political development, interest groups, and election law.

Understanding Political Science Statistics Using Stata

A Manual with Exercises

Ellen C. Seljan
with Peter Galderisi

NEW YORK AND LONDON

First published 2015
by Routledge
711 Third Avenue, New York, NY 10017

and by Routledge
2 Park Square, Milton Park, Abingdon, Oxon, OX14 4RN

Routledge is an imprint of the Taylor & Francis Group, an informa business

© 2015 Taylor & Francis

The right of Ellen C. Seljan to be identified as author of this work has been asserted by her in accordance with sections 77 and 78 of the Copyright, Designs and Patents Act 1988.

All rights reserved. No part of this book may be reprinted or reproduced or utilized in any form or by any electronic, mechanical, or other means, now known or hereafter invented, including photocopying and recording, or in any information storage or retrieval system, without permission in writing from the publishers.

Trademark notice: Product or corporate names may be trademarks or registered trademarks, and are used only for identification and explanation without intent to infringe.

Library of Congress Cataloging-in-Publication Data
Seljan, Ellen C.
Understanding political science statistics using stata : a manual with exercises / Ellen C. Seljan with Peter Galderisi.
pages cm
1. Stata. 2. Political statistics. 3. Statistics—Computer programs. I. Galderisi, Peter F. II. Title.
JA71.7.S45 2015
320.0285′555—dc23
2014034873

ISBN: 978-1-138-85068-2 (pbk)

Typeset in Adobe Garamond Pro
by Apex CoVantage, LLC

Printed and bound in the United States of America by Publishers Graphics, LLC on sustainably sourced paper.

Contents

Acknowledgments

Stata software is developed and owned by Statacorp: http://www.stata.com/.

The 2008 and 2012 National Election data were made available through the American National Election Studies Organization.

The American National Election Studies (ANES; http://www.electionstudies.org). The ANES 2008 Time Series Study [data set]. Stanford University and the University of Michigan [producers]. These materials are based on work supported by the National Science Foundation under grants SES-0535334, SES-0720428, SES-0840550, and SES-0651271; Stanford University; and the University of Michigan.

The American National Election Studies (ANES; http://www.electionstudies.org). The ANES 2012 Time Series Study [data set]. Stanford University and the University of Michigan [producers]. These materials are based on work supported by the National Science Foundation under grants SES-0937727 and SES-0937715, Stanford University, and the University of Michigan.

Any opinions, findings, and conclusions or recommendations expressed in these materials are those of the author(s) and do not necessarily reflect the views of the funding organizations.

The 2008 and 2008–2012 congressional district files contain information made available from the following:

The Daily Kos (originally found in the Swing State Project) for results for pre- and post-redistricted estimates of presidential votes within each district: http://www.dailykos.com/story/2012/11/19/1163009/-Daily-Kos-Elections-presidential-results-by-congressional-district-for-the-2012–2008-elections.

The Federal Election Commission (http://www.fec.gov) for information on voting and campaign finances.

Keith Poole (University of Georgia) for party unity and DW-Nominate scores.

George C. Edwards III (Texas A&M) for Presidential Support scores.

The American Conservative Union (ACU; http://www.conservative.org) for ideology scores and seniority data.

The U.S. Census Bureau for 2007, 2010, and 2012 estimates of demographic factors. These data were compiled using their FactFinder program with the American Community Survey 3-Year Estimates (http://www.census.gov/acs/www).

The Cook Political Report and POLIDATA for the Cook PVI scores.

The Clerk of the U.S. House (http://clerk.house.gov/member_info/electionInfo/) for verification of voting data.

Lindsay Nielson, David Todd, Jordan Hsu, and Soren Nelson (University of California San Diego) for assistance with updating these data.

Eurobarometer 69:2, *National and European Identity, European Elections, European Values, and Climate Change, March–May 2008.*

Permission provided by the Office for Official Publications of the European Communities. Eurostat, http://ec.europa.eu/public_opinion/archives/eb/eb69/eb69_annexes.pdf, ©European Communities, 2008.

CCES2012: 2012 Cooperative Congressional Election Survey.

Permission provided by the Principal Investigators of the Comparative Congressional Election Study (CCES) study. Stephen Ansolabehere, 2012, "CCES Common Content, 2012," http://hdl.handle.net/1902.1/21447 CCES [Distributor] V2 [Version].

CROSSNAT

Data and permissions provided by the following:

The International Institute for Democracy and Electoral Assistance (http://www.idea.int/uid/).

The World Bank.

The Heritage Foundation's Index of Economic Freedom (http://www.heritage.org/index/). Terry Miller, Anthony B. Kim, and Kim R. Holmes, *Index of Economic Freedom* (Washington, DC: The Heritage Foundation and Dow Jones & Company, 2014), http://www.heritage.org/index.

Freedom House (http://www.freedomhouse.org).

CHAPTER 1

CONTENTS

General Overview

1.1 INTRODUCTION TO USING STATA FOR DATA ANALYSIS

Stata is a statistical software package that allows people with limited programming skills to conduct sophisticated data analysis. The following will serve as a brief primer and guide to the use of Stata/IC.

There are several ways for students to acquire the Stata/IC software. These options are listed in order of descending price.

1. Purchase a full, perpetual student license (US$179). This is recommended for those individuals who will wish to continue using Stata on an extended basis.
2. Purchase an annual (US$98) or six-month student license (US$65).
3. Use Stata in an equipped computer lab on your campus (free).

Additionally, reduced pricing may be available through Stata 13 GradPlans™. Check the Stata website to find out whether your school participates in this program: http://www.stata.com/order/students/.

Different versions of Stata have varying data capacities and prices. The most common version, Stata/IC, will allow you to analyze moderate-sized data sets, with up to 2,057 variables and unlimited observations. Users requiring a larger data capacity should purchase version Stata/SE. Users with minimal data requirements (under 99 variables, 1,200 observations) may purchase Stata Small. Note that the **EURO69.dta** file exceeds this capacity.

Stata File Types

There are three different types of Stata files with which you'll be working. Each type of file has a unique filename extension, the suffix separated from the base filename by a dot. Each of these files will open with, and only with, the Stata program.

*.dta: This denotes a saved Stata data file. This contains the data (spreadsheet), labels, and missing value parameters that are set up. In the following examples, the files that you will use are **ANES2008A.dta** and **congress2008.dta**.

*.do: This denotes a "do-file" (i.e., a file that contains instructions for a particular analysis). This file will include any commands needed to access, manipulate, or analyze your data. I recommend that before you exit Stata, you save and label each do-file that you create using a name (before the period) that reflects the analysis you are conducting, adding a number to the end indicating which run or attempt it was. For example, "agevote1" could denote the set of instructions used on a first attempt to analyze voting by age groups. Stata will automatically add the .do suffix (creating the file agevote1.do). You can then save this for future use on your hard drive. The computer doesn't care what name you use, but I find it easier to follow my work if I choose names that coincide with my analyses.

*.log: This denotes an output file, also known as a "log file." These files will record both your commands and the resulting output. Any program, including a text editor, can read this file type. You should also be aware of the default output file (.smcl), which can only be read by Stata. All instructions in this manual will recommend the .log file type for output files.

Examples will mainly be derived from the **ANES2008A.dta** and **congress 2008.dta** data files. This will allow your instructor to use the other files for class exercises. Several suggested exercises appear at the end of each section or chapter. One set of exercises will carry through a common, progressive theme for ANES2012A.

Executing Procedures

There are two primary methods to operate Stata. You can either type code directly into the Command box or a do-file or use the pull-down graphical user interface (GUI) menus. There are pros and cons for both of these options.

1. Executing Procedures through the Command Box

Pros:

- You can easily visualize the logical progression of your analysis from file retrieval, to data manipulation, to analysis.
- It is more time efficient.
- You can easily save your codes in do-files for later retrieval and replication of your analysis.

Cons:

- There is a greater learning curve for acquiring proper syntax in your commands.
- Some procedures with a multitude of optional customizations, such as formatting graphics, may require a significant level of syntax memorization.

2. Executing Procedures with Pull-Down Menus

Pros:

- Partially eliminates the need to learn a programming language.
- Provides a clear visualization of the array of options available within each procedure.
- You won't have to worry about making simple syntax errors (e.g., putting a comma in the wrong place).

Cons:

- Clicking through the multiple menus of options that are associated with each procedure can be time intensive.
- It is harder to keep track of what you have been doing and to replicate your procedure.
- You still must be familiar with some Stata syntax, such as how to formulate a proper logical expression.

The choice is yours. Those interested in acquiring data analysis skills to be used beyond the classroom are encouraged to execute procedures using the Command box. The following pages will demonstrate how to use this code-driven format, show the results of analyses, and then present a sample of the use of the pull-down menus. All examples will use screenshots taken from analyses run on a Windows 8.1 platform using Stata IC/12.

Application Overview

When you open Stata for the first time, you will notice five discrete components of the application—the Toolbar, the Review box, the Results box, the Variables box, and the Command box.

The Toolbar

The Toolbar provides easy access to some of the most commonly used application features. From the toolbar, you can open and save files. You can also create log files or do-files. You can edit or simply browse an open data file by clicking on either the Data Editor (read and write) or Data Browser (read only) buttons. Finally, the toolbar is an easy way to search Stata's many help files. After a search, you can quickly navigate to an open file using the "Viewer" button.

The Command Box

The Command box is where you enter code to be executed. Commands should be entered one at a time. Press the return key to enter your command. Pressing the "page up" button on your keyboard (alternatively, holding down the fn key and pushing the up arrow on an OS-X laptop keyboard) will allow you to quickly retrieve previous commands.

The Review Box

The Review box will keep a running list of all commands executed (both those done by code or by use of the pull-down menus). This list of commands can be sorted by order of execution or alphabetically by clicking on the relevant header. You can also search for specific commands using the search box. Correctly executed commands are displayed in black, while commands with errors are displayed in red. A single click on any command will enter that command into the Command box automatically.

The Variables Box

The Variables box lists all variables in an open data set. This list can be sorted by the order that the variable appears in the data, by the variable's name, or by a "label" given to a variable to describe its contents. You can also search for variables by name or label using the search tool. Clicking on the blank first column of any variable will enter that variable into the Command box automatically. Alternatively, you can select and enter multiple variables at once. To select a block of variables, hold down the shift key while clicking on the first and last variable in the block. To select a set of variables that does not appear sequentially in your data set, hold down the command key (OS-X) or Ctrl key (Windows) while selecting multiple variables. As before, clicking on the first column of the Variables box will insert selected variables into the command line.

The Results Box

The Results box displays output from all commands. All output is searchable by clicking the magnifying glass in the top right corner of the Results box. Correctly executed commands and the resulting output will display in black. Red text denotes an error message and is generally followed by an error code, in blue. The blue text is a hyperlink and will take you to further information about the specific error you have encountered.

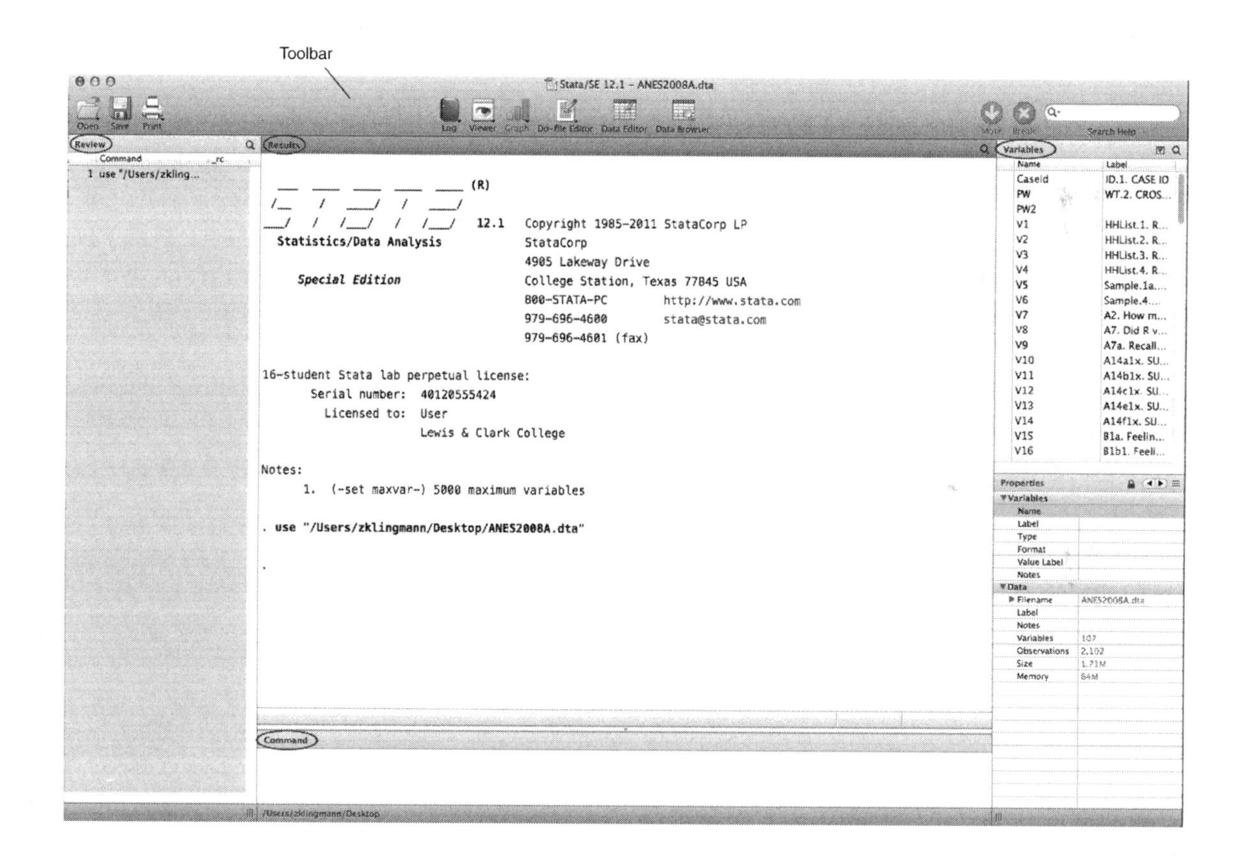

1.2 FIRST STEPS

Downloading Data Files

All data sets will be available on the Routledge Press website. A password will be provided for each student who purchases a version of the manual. I suggest you download these files directly to your desktop or a USB drive.

Protecting Data Files

Students often make a simple mistake when transforming data and then saving the original data file with the errors included. One way to avoid this problem is to set your original data files to "read only." Alternatively, one can save your altered file under a slightly different name (say anes2008a_2.dta rather than anes2008a.dta) so as to differentiate the altered from the original version.

Windows

Locate the file and right-click on it. On the bottom of the listed menu, click on "Properties." A new window will open. In the "General" tab, go down to the section on "Attributes" and check the "Read-only" box. Click "OK." From this point on, even if you try to change the original data file, you will be prevented from doing so. You can always create an altered file under a different name, but your original file will remain as is.

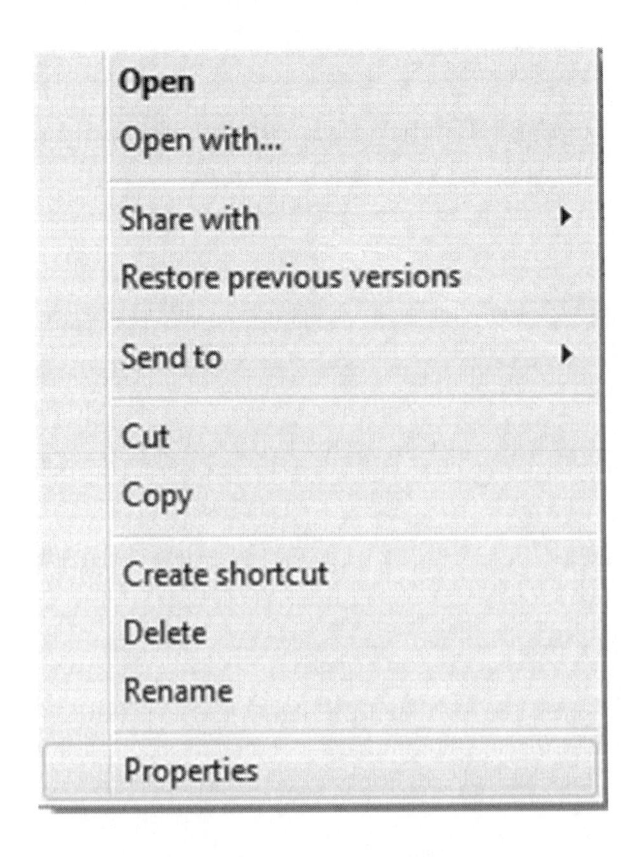

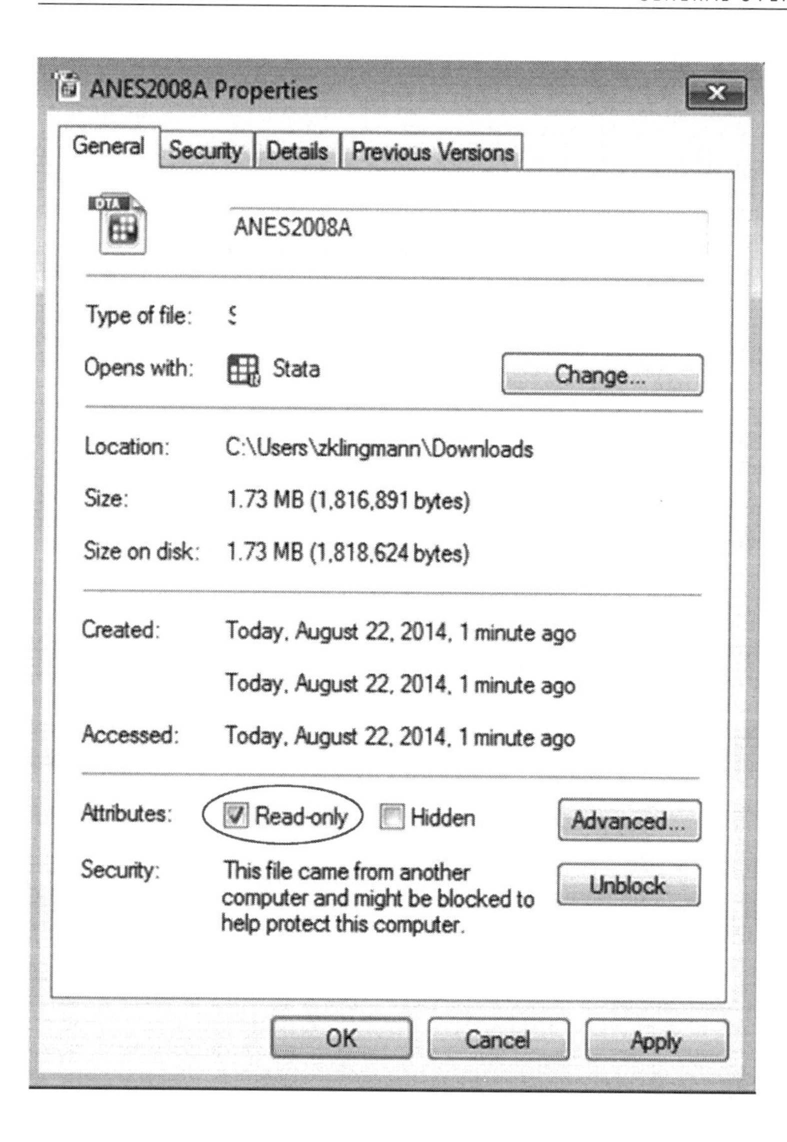

OS-X

Locate the file and right-click on it. Click on "Get Info," and a menu will appear. On the bottom of that menu, you will find a section called "Sharing & Permission." When displayed in full, this section will list the user accounts that have access to the file and the details of their permissions. To prevent editing your file, change all privileges from "Read & Write" to "Read only." From this point on, even if you try to change the original data file, you will be prevented from doing so. You can always create an altered file under a different name, but your original file will remain as is.

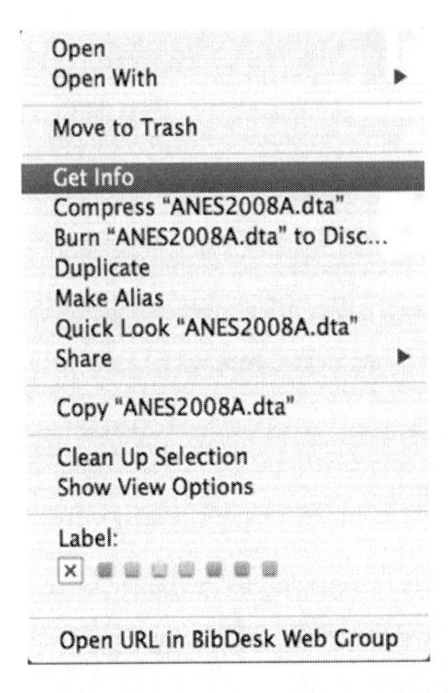
Open
Open With
Move to Trash
Get Info
Compress "ANES2008A.dta"
Burn "ANES2008A.dta" to Disc...
Duplicate
Make Alias
Quick Look "ANES2008A.dta"
Share
Copy "ANES2008A.dta"
Clean Up Selection
Show View Options
Label:
Open URL in BibDesk Web Group

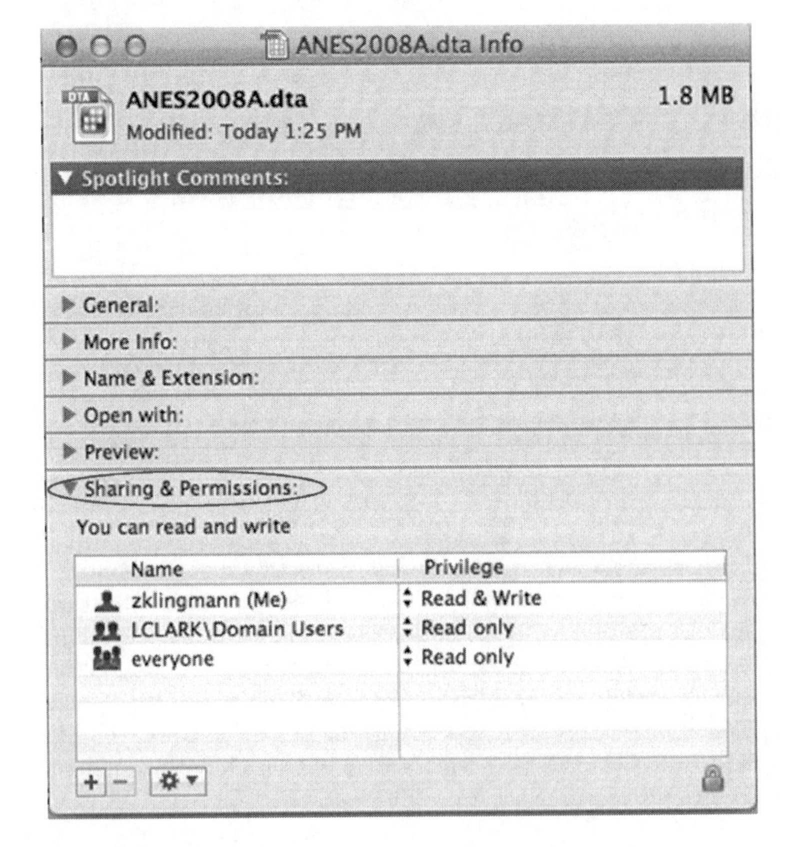
ANES2008A.dta Info
ANES2008A.dta
1.8 MB
Modified: Today 1:25 PM
Spotlight Comments:
General:
More Info:
Name & Extension:
Open with:
Preview:
Sharing & Permissions:
You can read and write
Name
Privilege
zklingmann (Me)
Read & Write
LCLARK\Domain Users
Read only
everyone
Read only

Do-Files

Do-files are documents used to record your commands. The easiest way to open a new do-file is through the toolbar (click on "Do-file Editor"). Alternatively, the command **doedit** will open a blank document. Do-files can be saved using the save button on the do-file's toolbar, the "File" drop-down menu, or standard keyboard shortcuts (command-s in OS-X or Ctrl-s in Windows).

Start, End, or View Log Files

Open Do-Files

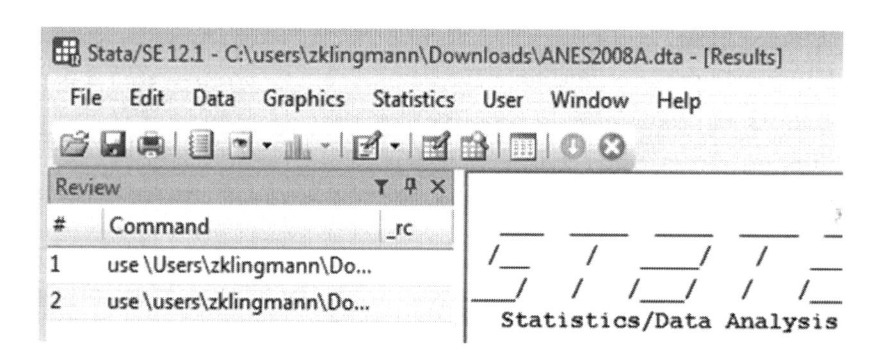

There are two methods of executing commands from do-files: "run" or "do." The primary difference between these two options is whether or not the commands and results are presented in the results box. Commands executed with "run" will be silent, whereas complete output, including any errors encountered, will be presented with the "do" method. For beginners, I recommend always running do-files with the "do" option.

To execute an entire do-file, simply click the "Run" or "Do" buttons on the do-file's toolbar. Alternatively, to execute only a portion of the commands in a do-file, first highlight those commands and then click the "Run" or "Do" buttons.

Do-files are an important way to keep track of how you have manipulated and analyzed your data. This can be an important backup in case of computer failure or accidental deletion of data. If properly maintained, they will allow yourself and others to replicate work in full. There is no "undo" option in Stata, so I always recommend keeping a complete do-file. It is also always a good idea to insert comments into your do-files as a way to make notes for future reference. To do so, simply start any line of text with an asterisk (*).

When do-files are run, all comments will be ignored and will not interfere with command execution.

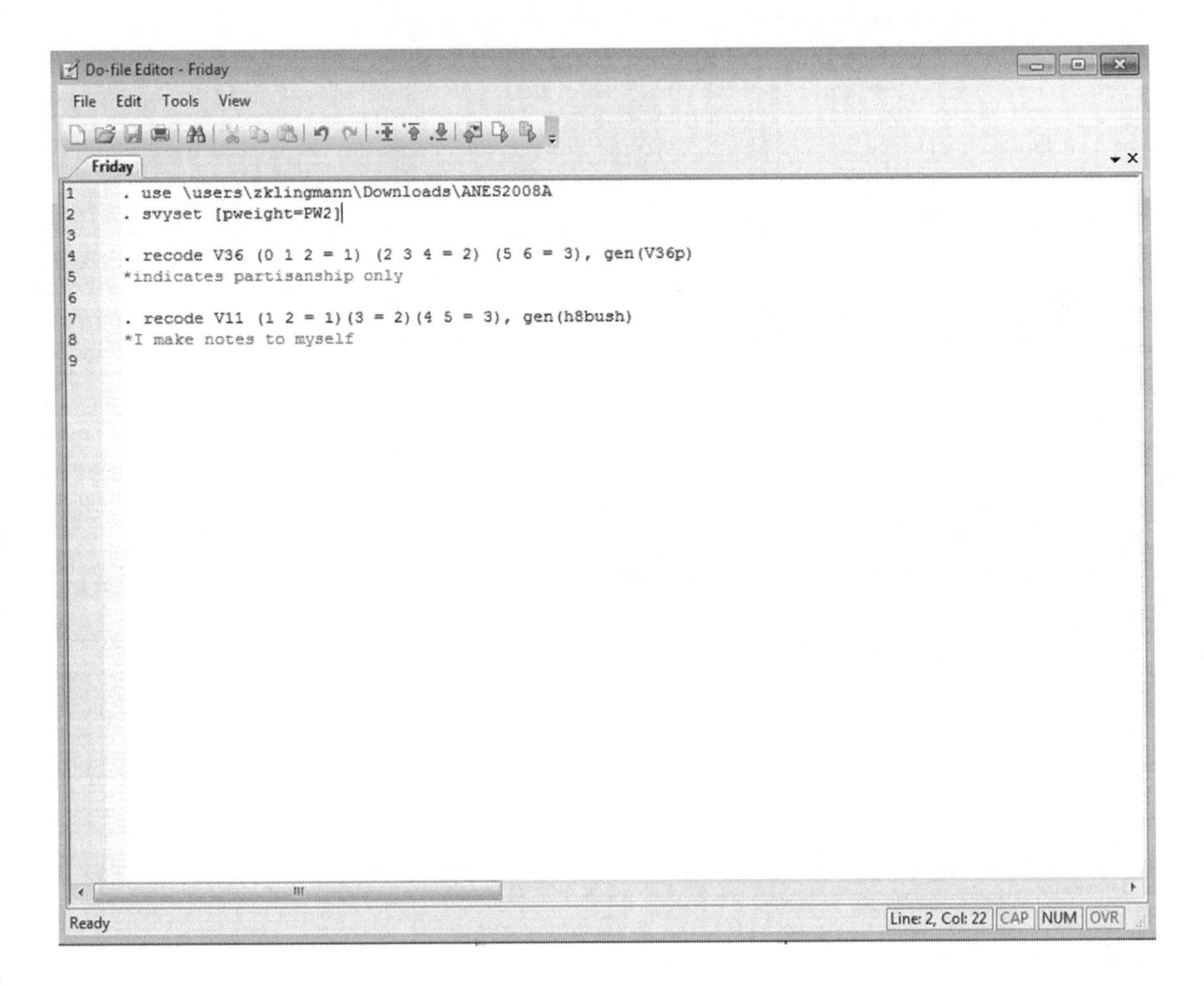

Log Files

Log files also serve as an important record of how you have manipulated and analyzed data. Unlike do-files, log files will contain the entirety of output from your commands in addition to the commands themselves. Everything that appears in your results box will appear in your log file. As such, log files can be a useful way to maintain and share the results of your analyses. To start a log file, click on the "Log" button on the toolbar and select "Begin." Name your file and select the file type "Stata Log" (note: this is not the default). Once you click "save," your log file will be open and all commands and output will be recorded. To close the log, once again click the "Log" button and choose "close."

These actions can also be easily achieved using Stata's **log** command. For example, the command **log using "/Users/eseljan/Documents/testrun.log"** would produce a log file saved in my Documents folder. It is important to specify the .log extension in this command to ensure that your log file is written as a file type that can be opened by any text editor. Omitting the file path in the command is acceptable and would simply result in the file being saved to your computer's current default location. To close the log, simply enter the following command: **log close**.

General Rules for Writing Code in Stata

Understanding the basic syntax of Stata's programming language will allow you to execute a wide variety of statistical procedures. Many, but not all, Stata commands follow the same basic convention.

For illustrative purposes, I will refer to the **list** command, a command that lists the contents of any variable.

1. Commands that are entered without any qualifications will be executed on all variables for all observations in the data set.

Entering the command **list** on its own will prompt Stata to list the contents of every variable for every observation in the data set. This would result in a large amount of output. Push the q key on your keyboard at any time to stop this procedure from running in full.

2. To limit a command to a smaller selection of variables, commands should be followed by what is known as a *varlist*, or a list of variable names. In this manual, I will use the term "*varlist*" when the Stata command is meant to run on multiple variables at once and "*varname*" when only one variable should be specified.

The syntax of a list of variables can be as simple as multiple variable names entered sequentially and separated by a space. The space mark acts as a separator between variables. It is important to note that variable names in Stata preclude space marks for this reason.

For example, the command **list v1 v2 v3** will list the contents of all observations for those three variables.

Shortcuts to Referring to Multiple Variables

A long list of sequential variables can be quickly retrieved by separating the variable list by an en dash. For example, the command **list v1-v3** is an alternate way to produce the same results programmed above. The latter choice may be preferable since you are less likely to make a typographical mistake when you have less to type. The same ends could be accomplished by highlighting multiple variables at once using the Variables box. It is important to note that this grouping will refer to variables as they appear sequentially in your data set, which may or may not be in a standard alphanumeric order.

An asterisk is another way to refer to multiple variables. To reference a set of variables that start with a common prefix, simply enter the common prefix followed by an asterisk. For example, **list var*** would produce output for all variables that start with the prefix var. An asterisk before a common suffix will likewise refer to all variables with the common suffix.

3. To limit the commands to a narrower set of variables and observations in your data set, you can use "if" and "in" qualifying statements. An "in" qualifying statement allows you to precisely choose observations in your data set by referencing their observation number. As previously noted, observations are listed sequentially in the data browser. The sequence depends entirely on how the data are sorted. To list the contents of variables for only the first five observations in the data set, you would use an "in" command. For example, the command **list v1 v2 in 1/5** will produce the following results that show the values of the first five observations.

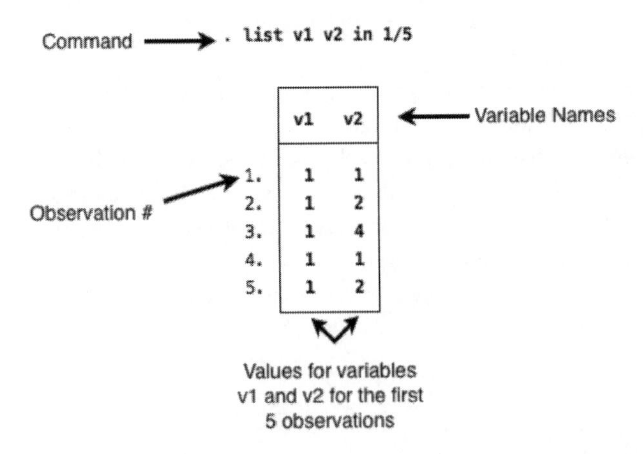

"If" qualifying statements are another way to apply commands to a narrower set of your data's observations. An "if" statement allows you to execute your commands only if observations meet a stated set of criteria. For example, you may want to list values of *V1* only if that variable is non-zero. Alternatively, you may want to list values of *V1* contingent on the value that observation takes on for *V2*.

To achieve these ends, "if" statements must be followed by a variable name and will utilize one or more of the following set of mathematical expressions:

Expression	Meaning
==	Is equal to
!=	Is not equal to
>	Is greater than
<	Is less than
>=	Is greater than or equal to
<=	Is less than or equal to

For example, the command **list v1 if v1!=0** will list the content of *V1* only if that variable is non-zero. Alternatively, the command **list v1 if v2!=0** will list the content of *V1* only if *V2* is non-zero.

More complex "if" statements might add additional contingencies using the following conjunctions:

Expression	Meaning
&	And
|	Or

For example, to produce a list of observations of *V1* only when both *V1* and *V2* are non-zero, you would execute the following command:

list v1 if v1!=0 & v2!=0

It is important to note that both the "if" clause and the conjunction are always followed by a variable name.

4. Many commands allow the **bysort** prefix, which repeats the command for unique observations of a variable. At least one variable name and a colon always follow the **bysort** command. For example, the command **bysort v1: list v2** would execute a list for *V2* by unique values of *V1*. Because the **bysort** prefix will execute your command for every unique value of the indicated variable, it should only be used with discrete variables that take on a low number of unique values. The **bysort** command can be used with multiple variables. In this case, the command would be executed for every unique intersection of the variables in the *varlist.* It should be noted that the **bysort** command automatically sorts the data set by the *varlist* provided. This means that observations in the data set will appear in a different order after executing this command.

5. The final convention of Stata syntax is that a comma always follows a command's "options." For example, the **list** command includes the option to force table format with no divider or separator lines or to omit observations numbers. The command **list v1, noobs clean** would execute these options. The options available for each command are displayed in the help files available for each command.

Putting together these guidelines reveals a general template for Stata syntax. Optional codes appear in brackets.

{bysort *varlist*:} command *varlist* {in/if} , {options}

In summary: Every line of code must include a command. A command can be limited to certain variables by identifying those variables following the command. The observations for which the command applies can be limited using "if" or "in" statements. The command could be repeated automatically for unique variables of a *varlist* with the **bysort** prefix. Finally, options within the command are always included after a comma.

Common syntax errors:

Omitted a variable name following an "if" statement:

- Example: **list v1 if !=0**
- Result: Stata will not be able to execute the procedure because it won't understand to which variable the expression !=0 is supposed to refer.

Comma where it doesn't belong:

- Example: **list v1, v2**
- Result: Stata will not be able to execute the procedure because variables should be separated by spaces, not commas. Only command "options" are allowed following a comma. Because "*V2*" is not an "option" of the list command, it will return the error "option *V2* not allowed."

Case-sensitivity error (all commands and variable names in Stata are case sensitive):

- Example: **List v1**
- Result: Stata will not be able to recognize the procedure and will give you the error message of "unrecognized command." All commands and variable names are case sensitive. Commands will never include capitalized letters.

Accessing Help Files

Stata provides an array of help files to guide users through data management and analysis. If a command is known, simply type the command **help** followed by the command name to access a full help file. For example, the command **help doedit** will pull up the help file on the **doedit** command. Stata help files are extremely detailed and will provide instructions for implementing any command, including all options available. Help files will also provide examples of each command put to use.

If you do not know the name of the command you wish to use, a helpful general command is **help contents**. This will pull up a window to guide you through the contents of Stata help files by category.

CHAPTER 2

CONTENTS

Setting Up Stata Data Files for Analysis

2.1 OPENING DATA FILES

The data files provided with this manual are already saved in Stata's proprietary data format, .dta. Three paths exist to open data files. First, you can simply double click on your file, and, if Stata is installed on the computer, the file will open in Stata automatically.

Second, you can easily open a file through navigating the pull-down menus. Click on the "File" menu and slide your cursor to click on "Open." A new window will pop up that will allow you to browse your computer drives for your file.

Another method to open a file is the **use** command, followed by a correctly specified file path in quotation marks. For example, the command **use "/Users/eseljan/Documents/anes2012.dta"** would open the American National Election Study (ANES) data set that I have filed in my Documents folder. For a Windows computer, the analogous command would be: **use "C:\Users\eseljan\Documents\anes2012.dta"**.

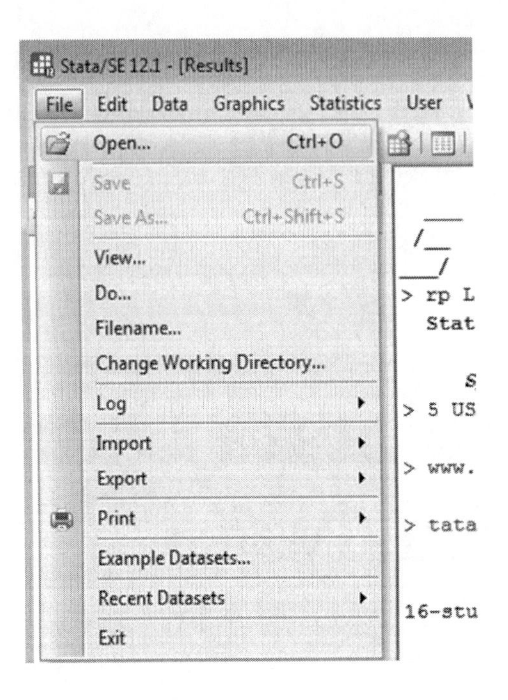
Stata/SE 12.1 - [Results]
File
Edit
Data
Graphics
Statistics
User
Open... Ctrl+O
Save Ctrl+S
Save As... Ctrl+Shift+S
View...
Do...
Filename...
Change Working Directory...
Log
Import
Export
Print
Example Datasets...
Recent Datasets
Exit

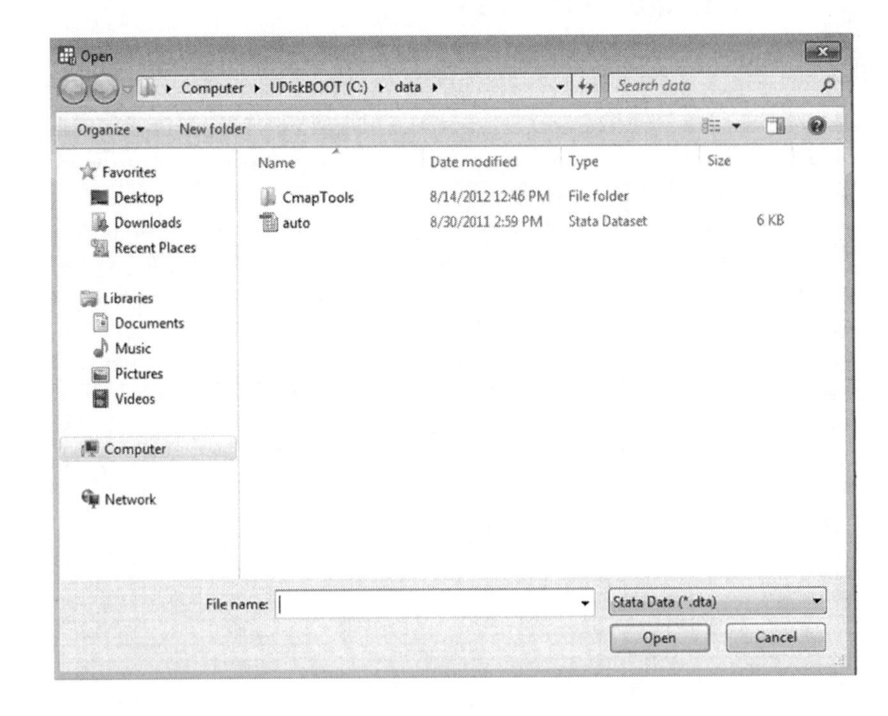
Open
Computer ▸ UDiskBOOT (C:) ▸ data ▸
Search data
Organize
New folder
Favorites
Desktop
Downloads
Recent Places
Libraries
Documents
Music
Pictures
Videos
Computer
Network
Name
Date modified
Type
Size
CmapTools 8/14/2012 12:46 PM File folder
auto 8/30/2011 2:59 PM Stata Dataset 6 KB
File name:
Stata Data (*.dta)
Open
Cancel

2.2 WEIGHTING SAMPLED DATA

Some data sets try but don't achieve a true random sample. Additionally, some groups might be purposely oversampled in order to achieve a large enough sample size for group-specific analysis. For example, in the semi-annual Eurobarometer surveys, approximately 1,000 individuals are sampled in each country in order to guarantee a large enough sample for each. However, if you want to analyze Europe as a whole, you wouldn't want the sample of citizens from the small country of Luxembourg to count as much as the citizens from France. Before doing any further analysis, one needs to readjust the subsample sizes to better approximate what they would look like if the sample was purely random, or equiprobable. This is accomplished using Stata's survey estimation procedures (to view the full help file, use the command **help svy**).

To analyze survey data with weights, you must first declare your data set as survey data and set the weight to be used throughout the analysis. This is accomplished using the **svyset** command. Second, on a command-by-command basis, you will add the **svy** prefix to each command to implement weighting. Weights are discussed further in the *Understanding Political Science Statistics* text (see Chapter 4, section "A Summary Example with Aggregated Data"; Chapter 6, section "Considerations in Sampling"; and elsewhere in the end-of-chapter exercises).

The syntax for the **svyset** command is the following:

svyset [pweight=*varname*]

For example, to use the **ANES2008A.dta** supplied sampling weight, *PW2*, the procedure is as follows:

svyset [pweight= PW2]

This weight adjusts for the unintentional oversampling of women. It will be used on all examples that indicate the need for sampling correction. In recent elections, adjustments were also made to compensate for the intentional oversampling of blacks and Hispanics (a large enough subsample was viewed as important). Both types of adjustments are made by placing each group in line with their proportions in the full U.S. Census.

The survey data employed in this manual use "sampling weights," also known as "probability weights." Please note that other types of weights (e.g., frequency weights) are not compatible with Stata's **svyset** command. If using alternative weights, such as frequency weights, you will need to check for compatibility with Stata commands on a case-by-case basis.

You only need to declare your data as survey data once. After an initial save, Stata will remember the declaration unless directed otherwise. For example, you can revoke your settings with a command (use the command: **svyset, clear**) or by declaring an alternate weight.

To implement a command with the declared weight, you must preface your command with the **svy** prefix. For example, the command **svy: regress V71 V1** would implement a weighted regression to correct for sampling bias. Omitting the **svy** prefix would run the regression on the unweighted sample. Several commands are not compatible with **svy** estimation. In this case, check the help file of the command to see if its options allow for weights.

The graphical user interface (GUI) procedure for declaring a sampling weight is as follows:

Step 1: Start at the "Statistics" pull-down menu.

Step 2: Move your cursor down to "Survey data analysis" and then "Setup and utilities." Choose the option for "Declare survey design for dataset."

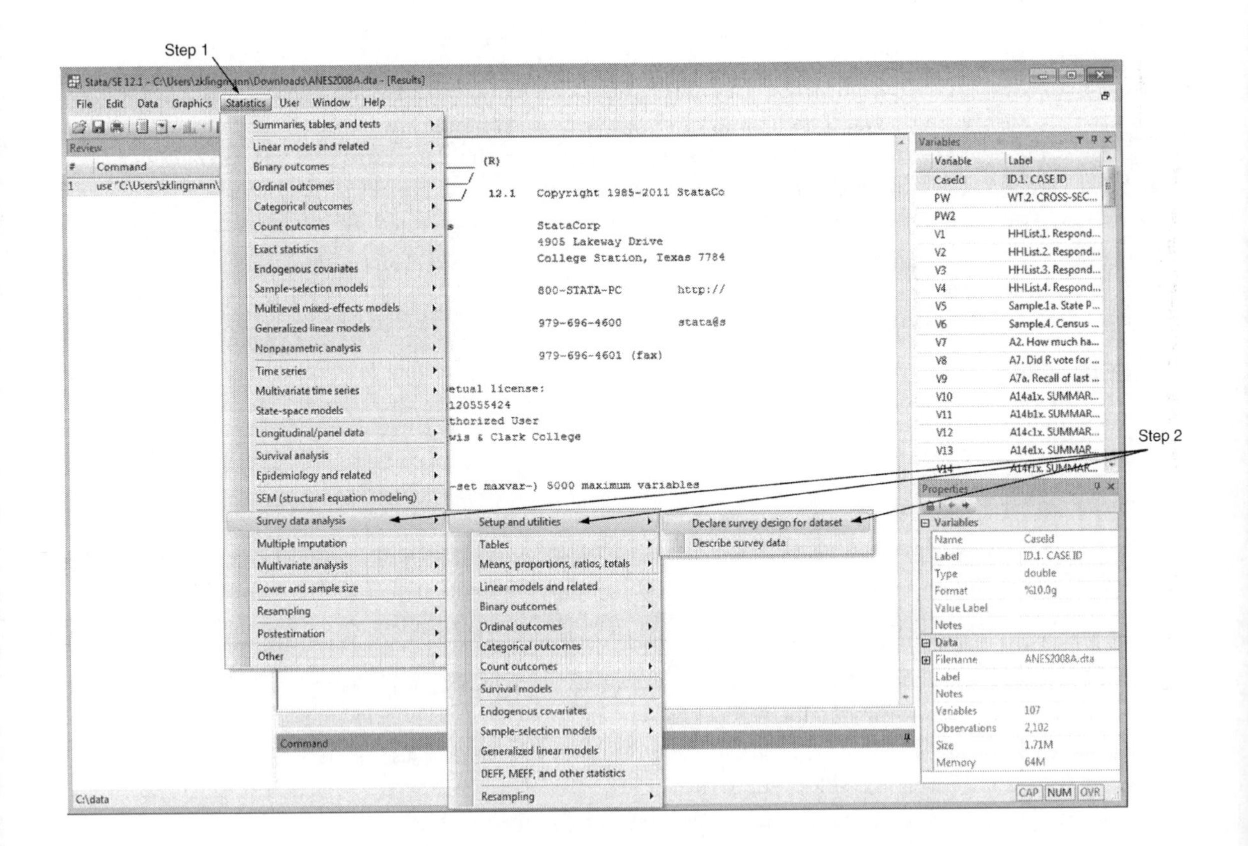

Step 3: Most likely, there will be nothing to change under the "Main" tab. As a default, the "Sampling units" field will be set to _n. This indicates that the unit of your observation for all analyses is a single observation,

which in the **ANES2008A.dta** data set represents a single survey respondent. You will be able to enter your preferred weight under the "Weights" tab. Choose a sampling weight variable (i.e., *PW2*) and click "OK."

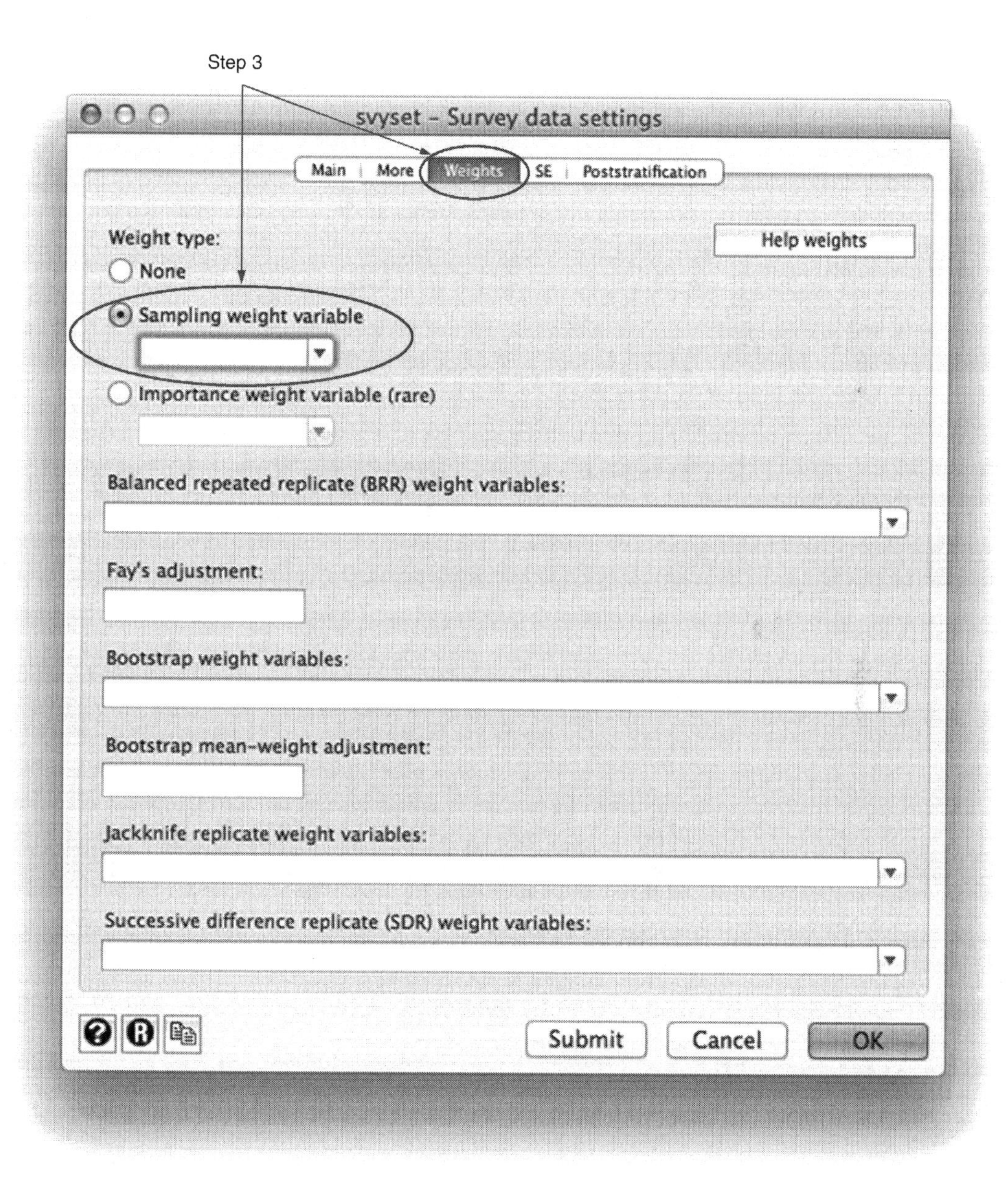

We are now ready to begin some data manipulation and analysis.

CHAPTER 3

CONTENTS

Data Management and Operationalization

The term "operationalization" has to do with going from a concept (say, distrust of a certain group, how one voted, etc.) to a measurement. The first stage in operationalizing a concept is to choose the variable or variables that will constitute your measure. Sometimes that is sufficient. Usually, however, you will either need to manipulate the variable or perhaps combine it with others variables to better match the original concept.

Even though you run one of the following "manipulation" or operationalization commands, no output (other than a generated listing of the syntax equivalent) will be shown until you run an analysis procedure (Chapter 4, this volume). For that reason, you would want to read Section 4.1, "Frequencies" (Chapter 4, this volume), so that you can see the results of your operationalizations.

For demonstration purposes, each of these operationalizations was followed by the **tabulate** command. The **tabulate** procedure will be further discussed in Section 4.1 (Chapter 4).

3.1 VARIABLE RECODING: THE RECODE COMMAND

The function of the **recode** command is to reclassify the values (categories) of a variable in order to reduce the number of categories or better approximate your conceptualization. For more on this topic, see "Measuring Properties and the Importance of Categorization" and Exercise 9 in Chapter 2 of *Understanding Political Science Statistics: Observations and Expectations in Political Analysis.*

The **recode** command can be used to change the contents of any variable. It will also automatically generate a new variable that is specified.

For more complex manipulations of variables, it is best to use the **recode** command. The syntax for the **recode** command is as follows:

recode *varname* (*rule*), generate(*newvar*)

It is helpful to use the generate option (following a comma) in conjunction with the **recode** command when operationalizing new variables. This is preferable to simply modifying the original variable because it allows you to retain the original variable in your data set and can avert recoding errors.

A variety of recoding rules can be used to recode variables. These rules must appear in your command in parentheses. The simplest rule is to recode all instances of an old value to a new value (# = #). It is also possible to direct Stata to recode multiple old values at once by either separating the old values with a space mark or using a slash mark to recode all values within a given range. The following table presents commonly used rules.

Rule	Example	Meaning
# = #	3 = 1	3 recoded to 1
# # = #	2 3 = 9	2 and 3 recoded to 9
#/# = #	1/5 = 4	1 through 5 recoded to 4
else = #	else = 5	all other to 5
nonmissing = #	nonmissing = 8	all other nonmissing to 8
missing = #	missing = 9	all other missing to 9
min/# = #	min/5 = 8	minimum through 5 to 8
#/max = #	6/max = 9	6 through maximum to 9

Example 3.1.1—For the **congress2008.dta** and **ANES2008A.dta** files, I've included a generic missing value code of "." In Stata, periods always represent missing values for numerical data. If, for example, you wish to eliminate from your analysis those districts where an incumbent was not running (open seat), you would need only to recode the unwanted response to a "."

recode inc08 (3 4=.)

Before Recode:

```
. tabulate inc08
```

inc08	Freq.	Percent	Cum.
1	229	52.64	52.64
2	170	39.08	91.72
3	7	1.61	93.33
4	29	6.67	100.00
Total	435	100.00	

After Recode:

```
. tabulate inc08
```

inc08	Freq.	Percent	Cum.
1	229	57.39	57.39
2	170	42.61	100.00
Total	399	100.00	

Notice that the 36 non-incumbents (categories 3 and 4) are now listed as missing and would not be included in any analysis where *inc08* was used.

Caution:

Stata will ignore observations with missing values in most commands, dropping those observations from any analysis. However, Stata will treat missing values as the value of infinity in logical expressions. Keep this in mind if employing a logical expression of "greater than."

Example 3.1.2—What if you wanted a simple two-category analysis where you want to separate those districts in which Obama exceeded his national vote (52.9%) from those where he did not?

recode obama (min/52.9 = 1)(53/max=2)

After Recode:

```
. tabulate obama
```

obama	Freq.	Percent	Cum.
1	225	51.72	51.72
2	210	48.28	100.00
Total	435	100.00	

Caution:

The upper and lower bounds specified in the above codes (min and max) are potentially important. In some data sets, missing values are commonly coded as negative numbers. Without specifying a lower bound, missing values could mistakenly be recoded as districts with low Obama support.

Example 3.1.3—Return to the **ANES2008A.dta** file. Maybe you are not concerned about how "Democratic" or "Republican" individuals are—just whether they are on one side or the other. Recode this variable to fit this operationalization.

recode V36 (0 1 2 = 1)(3 = 2)(4 5 6 = 3)

Categories are separated by spaces. Also note that, in this recode, only "pure Independents" (value = 3) are treated as Independents. If you believe that "Independent leaners" should also be treated as "Independents," the recode becomes the following:

recode V36 (0 1 = 1)(2 3 4 = 2)(5 6 = 3)

If you wished to specify only the intensity of one's partisan preference without regard to partisan *direction* (e.g., to address the hypothesis "the more partisan one is, the more likely one is to vote"), then recode as follows (3 would be the most partisan here).

recode V36 (2 3 4 = 1)(1 5 = 2)(0 6 = 3)

Before Recode:

```
. svy: tabulate V36, count cell
(running tabulate on estimation sample)

Number of strata   =        1          Number of obs      =       2060
Number of PSUs     =     2060          Population size    = 2072.3215
                                       Design df          =       2059

----------------------------------
Party ID   |
Summary    |       count  proportions
-----------+----------------------
         0 |         386       .1863
         1 |       315.7       .1524
         2 |       342.4       .1652
         3 |       237.9       .1148
         4 |       246.8       .1191
         5 |       273.2       .1318
         6 |       270.3       .1304
           |
     Total |        2072           1
----------------------------------
```

After Recodes:

RECODE of V36 (Party ID Summary)	count	proportions
1	**1044**	**.5039**
2	**237.9**	**.1148**
3	**790.3**	**.3813**
Total	**2072**	**1**

Key: count = **weighted counts**
propor~s = **cell proportions**

RECODE of V36 (Party ID Summary)	count	proportions
1	**701.7**	**.3386**
2	**827.1**	**.3991**
3	**543.5**	**.2623**
Total	**2072**	**1**

Key: count = **weighted counts**
propor~s = **cell proportions**

RECODE of V36 (Party ID Summary)	count	proportions
1	**827.1**	**.3991**
2	**588.9**	**.2842**
3	**656.3**	**.3167**
Total	**2072**	**1**

Key: count = **weighted counts**
propor~s = **cell proportions**

Example 3.1.4—The previous example demonstrates that the **recode** command not only simplifies some analysis, but also allows us to use the same variable (*V36*) to measure multiple concepts (partisan *direction* and partisan *intensity*). If you are doing both in the same run, I recommend using the generate option to create new variables for each operationalization.

The following two lines would create a separate variable (*V36p*, *V36s*) for "direction of partisanship" and "strength of partisanship" separate from the original variable (which would maintain its original coding):

recode V36 (0 1 2 = 1)(3 = 2)(4 5 6 = 3), gen(V36p)

recode V36 (2 3 4 = 1)(1 5 = 2)(0 6 = 3), gen(V36s)

Example 3.1.5—The **recode** command can also be used to create an entirely new variable not related to what already exists in the file. For example, what if we wanted to attach to each respondent's listing the type of electoral system under which they are governed (see the **EURO69.dta** codebook in Appendix B). The International Institute for Democracy and Electoral Assistance (IDEA) classifies countries into three general election rule types: (1) Single Member District, (2) Mixed, and (3) Proportional (additional variations are listed for each—see codebook). One could then create a new variable (e.g., etype) from the existing variable (country) by recoding each set of countries into their respective election system.

recode country (8 9 16 17 24 = 1)(3 4 21 23 = 2)(nonmissing = 3), gen(etype)

Before the recode, 29 country codes would be presented. After the recode, these three values would appear as follows:

RECODE of COUNTRY (NATION (SAMPLE))	count	proportions
1	6691	.2512
2	5033	.1889
3	1.5e+04	.5599
Total	2.7e+04	1

```
Key:  count    =  weighted counts
      propor~s =  cell proportions
```

Note: You will be shown how to add category names (SMD, MIXED, PR) to the table in Section 3.4 of this chapter.

Example 3.1.6—When deciding how to reclassify or recode information, two common methods are used. The first is preferable; the second might be necessary. This will be discussed more in your course. Conceptually, and based on sound theoretical judgment, how would you like to reclassify categories? Return to the **ANES2008A.dta** file. Conceptually, you may wish to collapse the categories of those variables indicating approval or disapproval of the former president Bush's handling of the economy into three possibilities (Approve/Neutral/Disapprove).

recode V11 (1 2 = 1)(3 = 2)(4 5 = 3)

However, you might find that you will have few individuals in the recoded "Approve" category (1). Sometimes, in order to have enough cases in any grouping, we must fall back onto an alternate reclassification. Here are the original percentages (weighted by *PW*):

1. Approve strongly	7.6%
2. Approve not strongly	10.6%
3. Neither/don't know (DK)	3.3%
4. Disapprove not strongly	16.9%
5. Disapprove strongly	61.5%

Given how few survey respondents approved of the president's handling of the economy, you might decide to split individuals into two groups, "Disapprove strongly" or "Not." The recode would then be as follows:

recode V11 (1 2 3 4 = 1)(5 = 2)

Note:

Recoding a value into itself (0 1 2 = 1), as was demonstrated in Example 3.1.3, isn't really necessary, but listing it would cause no harm, and it might help you to guarantee that all of your categories have been covered. It must be done when creating a new variable via the generate option, otherwise those non-listed categories will be eliminated.

Example 3.1.7—Recode several variables simultaneously. If multiple variables are to be recoded the same way, there is no need to repeat the value alteration instructions. For example, the following will recode the entire list of feeling thermometer (*V15* to *V19*) scores into just three categories—cold, neutral, and warm (the following is only one type of breakdown).

recode V15-V19 (0/40=1)(41/59=2)(60/100=3)

Question:

What if, as in the "partisan intensity" example, one wanted to separate those individuals with extreme (low or high) feelings from those who are more neutral?

Note:

You will not see the results of any recode or new variable in your spreadsheet until you run an analytic procedure (tab, sum, etc.).

It is also possible to recode and create variables through Stata's pull-down menus, or graphical user interface (GUI). The GUI procedure for the recoding and creation of a new variable for Example 3.1.3 is as follows. From the "Data" pull-down menu, move your cursor to "Create or change data" > "Other variable-transformation commands" > "Recode categorical variable."

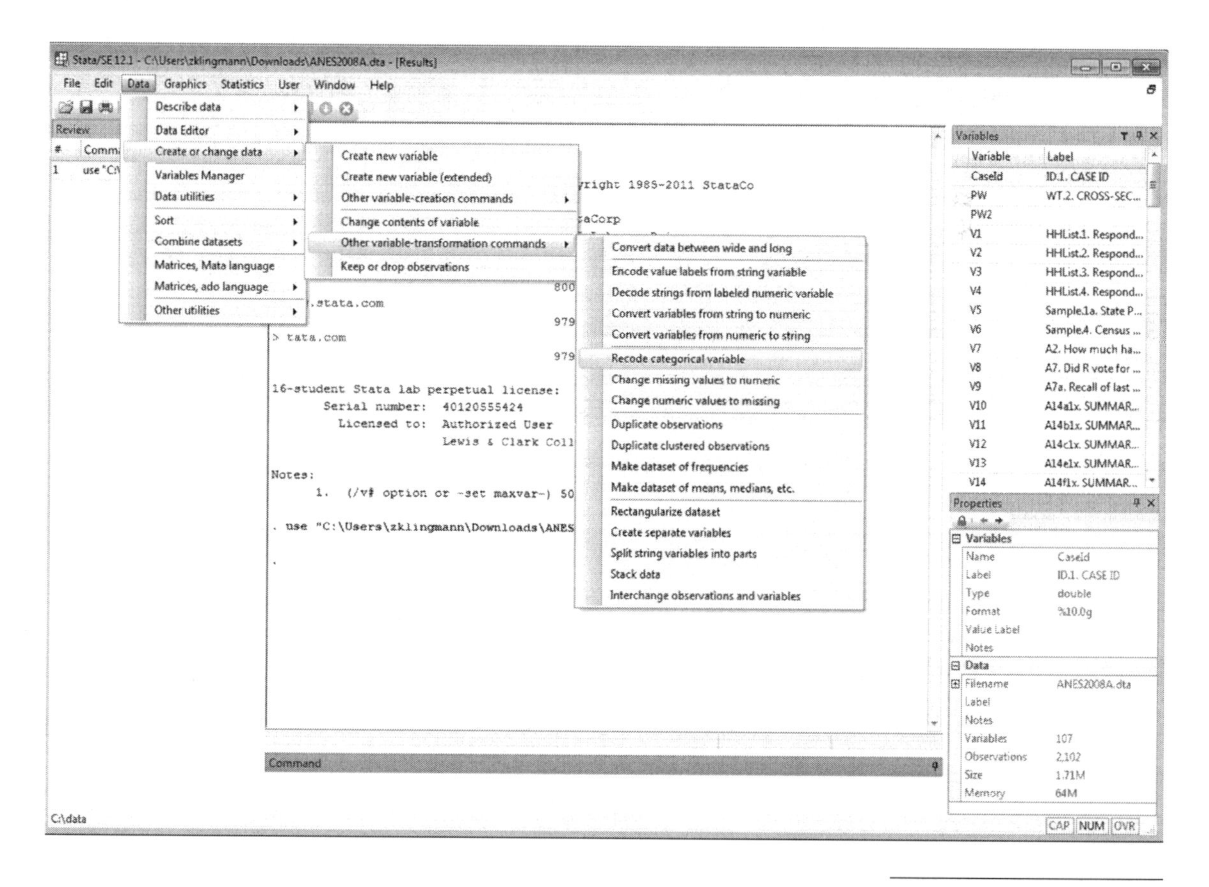

In the pop-up window, select or type the name of the variable that you want to recode in the "Variables" field. You are required to recode at least one value of this variable in first field provided ("Required"), though you can optionally recode several other values at once ("Optional").

When you click on the "Required" or "Optional" fields in this window, Stata will provide you with a template for the various recoding rules. Select the applicable rule and replace the stand-in "#" symbols with your values of interest.

To recreate Example 3.1.3, select variable *V36* in the variables field. We will be recoding this variable to take on the value of 1 for those who express some form of Democratic partisanship (*V36* is 0, 1, or 2), 2 for those who identify as pure Independents (*V36* is 3), and 3 for those who express Republican partisanship (*V36* is 4, 5, or 6). The correct rules for these recodes is "(# # = #)" for partisans and "(# = #)" for Independent. After entering in the appropriate old and new values, the GUI would look as follows:

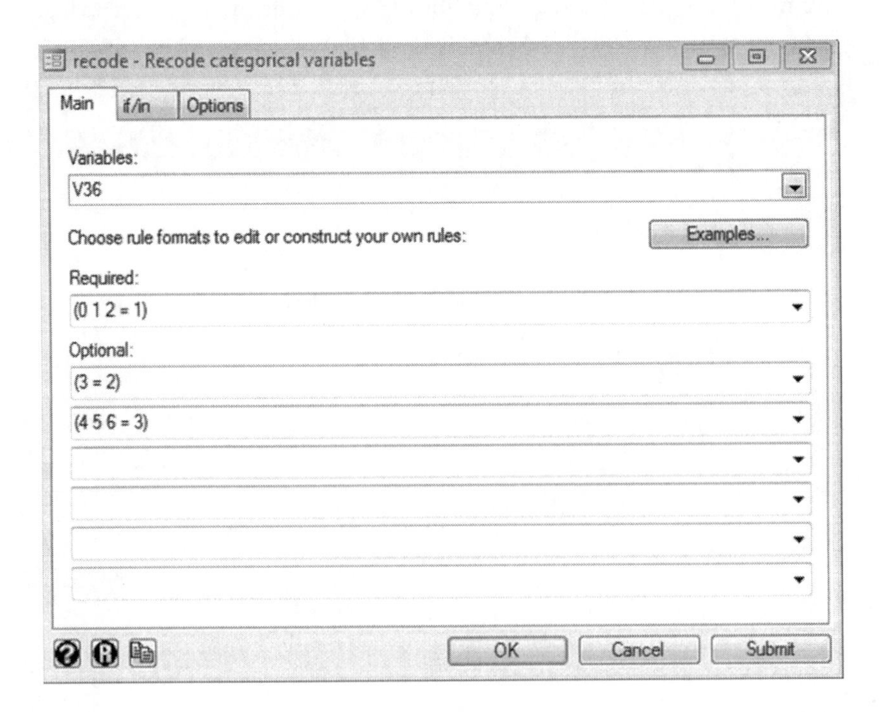

After you click OK, Stata will complete the appropriate recodings. Alternatively, to recode this variable into a new variable, named *V36p*, click on the options tab before pressing "OK." Click the radio button labeled "Generate new variables:" and enter your new variable name.

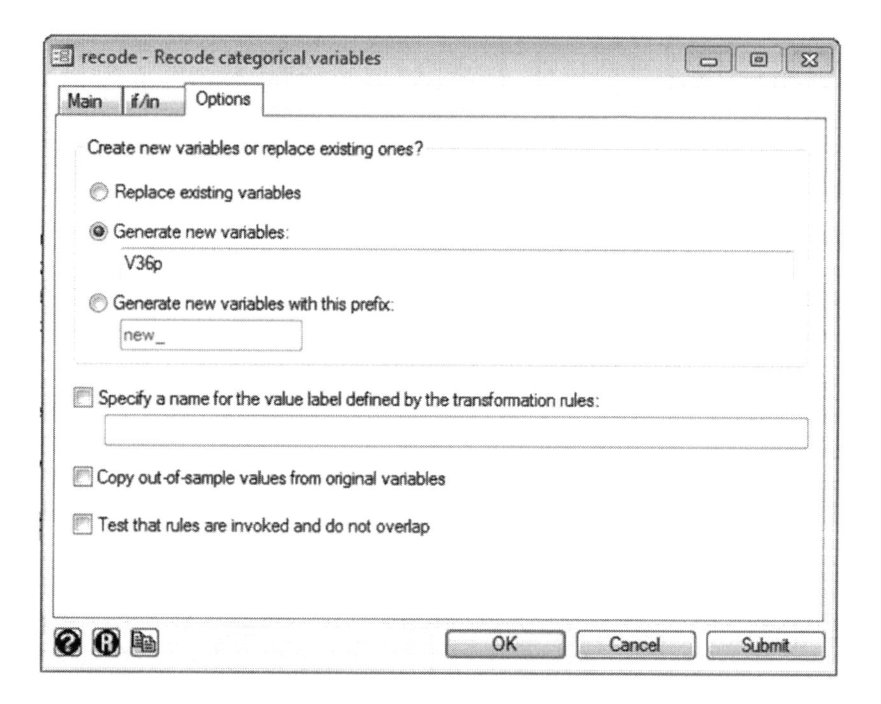

Click "OK" on either tab to execute the command. If you performed these steps properly, you will notice that a new variable has been added to your data spreadsheet and variable list (*V36p*).

Sample Exercises 3.1

Note: I believe that programs like Stata are only useful if they help us to answer logically derived and developed questions. Consequently, certain exercises will be cumulative. The coding and procedures in a later section will often rely on results obtained in a previous section. I recommend keeping your work from each of these sections as you proceed through your course. For faculty wishing to have exercises that use just one of the data sets, the exercises here will be reformatted and placed on the book's website by data set.

In order to see your results, proceed and follow any recode with the **list** command to display the variable's values for the first five observations. The syntax for viewing the first five observations in your data set using the **list** command is as follows:

list *varlist* in 1/5

ANES2012A

1. Recode Age (*V4*) into four categories. List the values of *V4* for the first five observations before and after your recode. Use the following categories:

   1: 18–30
   2: 31–50
   3: 51–64
   4: 65–90

2. Recode Marital Status (*V60*) into a new variable, *V60A*, with those who are married or widowed into a new category 1 and all others listed into category 2. List the values for each of these variables for the first five observations in your data set.
3. Recode *V13* (Approve/disapprove president's handling of health care) into three categories: those who have strong feelings of approval or disapproval (1,5), those with more moderate feelings (2,4), and those who have no opinion (3). List the values of *V13* for the first five observations in your data set both before and after your recode.

Congress 2008–2012

No weight is required as these represent entire populations.

1. Recode Incumbency Status (INC) for any or all (separately) of the three years to separate Incumbent (1,2) from Non-Incumbent (open = 3,4) races. List the values of INC for the first five observations in your data set before and after your recode.
2. Recode any Per Capita Income (PCI) into two categories, those under the national mean and those above. List the values of PCI for the first five observations in your data set before and after your recode. The national means are as follows (not adjusted for inflation):

   2008 $27,466
   2010 $26,952
   2012 $27,385

3. Recode any Winning Percentage (WV) into a new variable, SAFE, with three categories:

   Those who won with less than 55% of the vote
   Those who won with 55.1% to 60% of the vote
   Those who won with more than 60% of the vote

List the values of WV for the first five observations in your data set before and after your recode. In 2008, 68.7% won by more than 60%. What does this tell you about the level of competition in congressional elections?

EURO69

1. Recode *V20* (Globalization-Threat to National Culture) into a new variable, *V20A*, with three new categories: Strongly or Somewhat Agree (1), Don't Know (2), and Somewhat or Strongly Disagree (3). List the values of *V20* and *V20A* for the first five observations in your data set.
2. Recode *V25* (Ideological placement) into two categories: all Left, 1–5 (1), all Right, 6–10 (2). Eliminate categories 11 and 12 by recoding those values as missing. List the values of *V25* for the first five observations in your data set before and after your recode. Category one contains 62.3% of all valid cases. What does this tell you about the ideological placement of Europeans in 2008?
3. Recode all three EU Proposal questions (*V16*, *V17*, *V18*) to remove the DK categories (recode to missing), and change support to the value of 1 and opposition to the value of 0. List the values of *V16*, *V17*, and *V18* for the first five observations in your data set before and after your recode.
4. Recode all three EU Voice questions (*V11*, *V12*, *V13*) to remove the DK categories (recode to missing), and change agreement to the value of 1 and disagreement to the value of 0. List the values of *V11*, *V12*, and *V13* for the first five observations in your data set before and after your recode.

CCES2012

1. Recode Education (*V2*) into three categories:

   1: ≤HS
   2: Some or 2-year college
   3: 4-year or post grad

List the values of *V2* for the first five observations in your data set before and after your recode.

2. The variable coding Party ID (*V8*) can be used to create several different conceptualizations of partisanship.

   Recode Party ID (*V8*) into three new variables:

PID1	All Democrats (1–3)
	Pure Independents (4)
	All Republicans (5–7)
PID2	All Democrats except non-leaners (1,2)
	Leaners and Independents (3,4,5)
	All Republicans except non-leaners (6,7)

PID3	All strong partisans (1,7)
	Not very strong partisans (2,6)
	All leaners and independents (3,4,5)

List the values of *PID1*, *PID2*, and *PID3* for the first five observations in your data set.

3. Recode *V29* and *V30* each into two categories: approve and disapprove. In the first 10 observations of your data set, are there individuals who approve of Congress as an institution but not their own individual congresspeople?

Crossnational

1. Recode *idea_esp* into a new variable, named *presidential*, so that you separate countries that have a presidential system from those that do not. List the values of the variables *country*, *idea_esp*, and *presidential* for the first five observations in your data set.
2. Recode Percentage Turnout VAP-President (*idea_vtr_pa*) into a new variable, named turnout, with two categories: those with turnout below the mean of all countries with listed data and those above. List the values of the variables *country*, *idea_vtr_pa*, and *turnout* for the first five observations in your data set for the variables.

3.2 CREATING NEW VARIABLES: THE GENERATE COMMAND

The function of the **generate** command is to create a new variable from some combination of two or more other variables. This command is useful when creating multivariable scales or difference measures that better approximate the concepts we are trying to measure.

Text: For more on this topic, see Chapter 2 in *Understanding Political Science Statistics: Observations and Expectations in Political Analysis*. The section "From Nominal to Interval Data" gives a brief discussion of creating a scale from several variables.

The **generate** command (abbreviated to **gen** as shown in the examples below) can be used to create a new variable. Using Stata's **generate** command, the syntax for generating a variable is as follows:

gen *varname= value, variable, or expression*

Immediately following the **generate** command, you will create a name for your new variable (here, "varname"). Variable names must be unique in your data set and are case sensitive. Symbols and space marks are not allowed in variable names, with the sole exception of an underscore. Variable names cannot begin with numbers.

A single equal sign ("=") will always follow the variable name in the **generate** command syntax. In Stata, a single equal sign is used to assign a variable to a new value or set of values. For example, the command **gen newvar=2** would create a new variable, called newvar, and would set that variable equal to the number 2 for all observations.

In addition to setting a variable equal to a single value, it is possible to generate new variables that are replicas or manipulations of old variables. For example, the command **gen newvar=oldvar** would create a new variable, newvar, identical to the old variable, *oldvar*. Likewise, the command **gen newvar=oldvar/1000** would create a new variable that recodes the old variable in thousands.

All standard arithmetic expressions can be used in Stata commands, in addition to more advanced mathematical functions. The following table lists some of the most common functions and basic descriptions. In these examples, "x" can be either a specific number or a variable name.

Arithmetic Expression	Meaning
+	Addition
–	Subtraction
*	Multiplication
/	Division
^x	Signifies x is an exponent
abs(x)	Returns the absolute value of x
ln(x)	Returns the natural logarithm of x
max(x1,x2, . . .,xn)	Returns the maximum value of x1 . . . xn. Missing values ignored.
min(x1,x2, . . .,xn)	Returns the minimum value of x1 . . . xn. Missing values ignored.
sqrt(x)	Returns the square root of x

Example 3.2.1—To create a new variable (*ideo_difference*) assessing the difference between feelings toward Liberals and Conservatives (**ANES2008A.dta** file):

gen ideo_difference=V75-V76

The variable *ideo_difference* would range from -100 (pro-Conservative) to 100 (pro-Liberal). Note that a 0 indicates equal warmth (at any level), not necessarily chilliness toward both. Unless you are doing a means, correlation, or regression analysis, you may want to recode this variable into fewer categories (pro-Conservative/no preference/pro-Liberal).

Example 3.2.2—To create a scale (variable named *dem_affect*) that indicates how many of the four variables (*V23*, *V24*, *V25*, and *V26*) one answered for had a positive affect toward the Democratic Party candidate (in 2008, Obama):

gen dem_affect=V23+V24+V25+V26

This will produce a new variable (*dem_affect*) that will range from "0" (no positive affect) to "4" (positive on all four aspects). It is important to note that any respondent with a missing value for any of the four original variables will be counted as missing on the new variable *dem_affect*. Note also that, according to the codebook, the categories "yes" and "no" are in different numerical order depending on whether or not they represent a positive or negative "affect." This ensures that the created variable matches its intended operationalization.

Try this:

Create a scale indicating whether one was more positively inclined (affect) toward the Democratic or the Republican presidential candidate.

Your values should range from –4 to +4

What would a "0" mean?

Example 3.2.3—Using the **congress2008.dta** file, create a variable that indicates the difference in spending between the Republican and Democratic candidates.

gen exdiff=rh_spend08-dh_spend08

The new variable (*exdiff*) will be negative if the Democratic candidate spent more than the Republican, positive if he or she spent less, "0" if spending was equal.

Caution:

One might wish to consider creating a ratio: Democratic Spending divided by Republican Spending. The concept makes sense, but, as is often the case, if no Republican candidate ran, *rh_spend08* would equal $0, and the division could not be calculated (any number divided by 0 = ∞).

The GUI menu procedure for generating a new variable is rather straightforward and allows you to use a calculator-like approach to creating your compute statement. Let's use the last example. Remember to first open the congress2008.dta data set:

Step 1: From the "Data" pull-down menu, move your cursor to "Create or change data" and select "Create new variable."

Step 2: In the pop-up window, type the name for your new variable in the "Variable name" (*exdiff*) field.

Step 3: Click the option to "Specify a value or an expression" and enter in the applicable expression, in this case "*rh_spend08-dh_spend08*." Clicking the "Create . . ." button next to this field would guide you through the creation of more advanced expression.

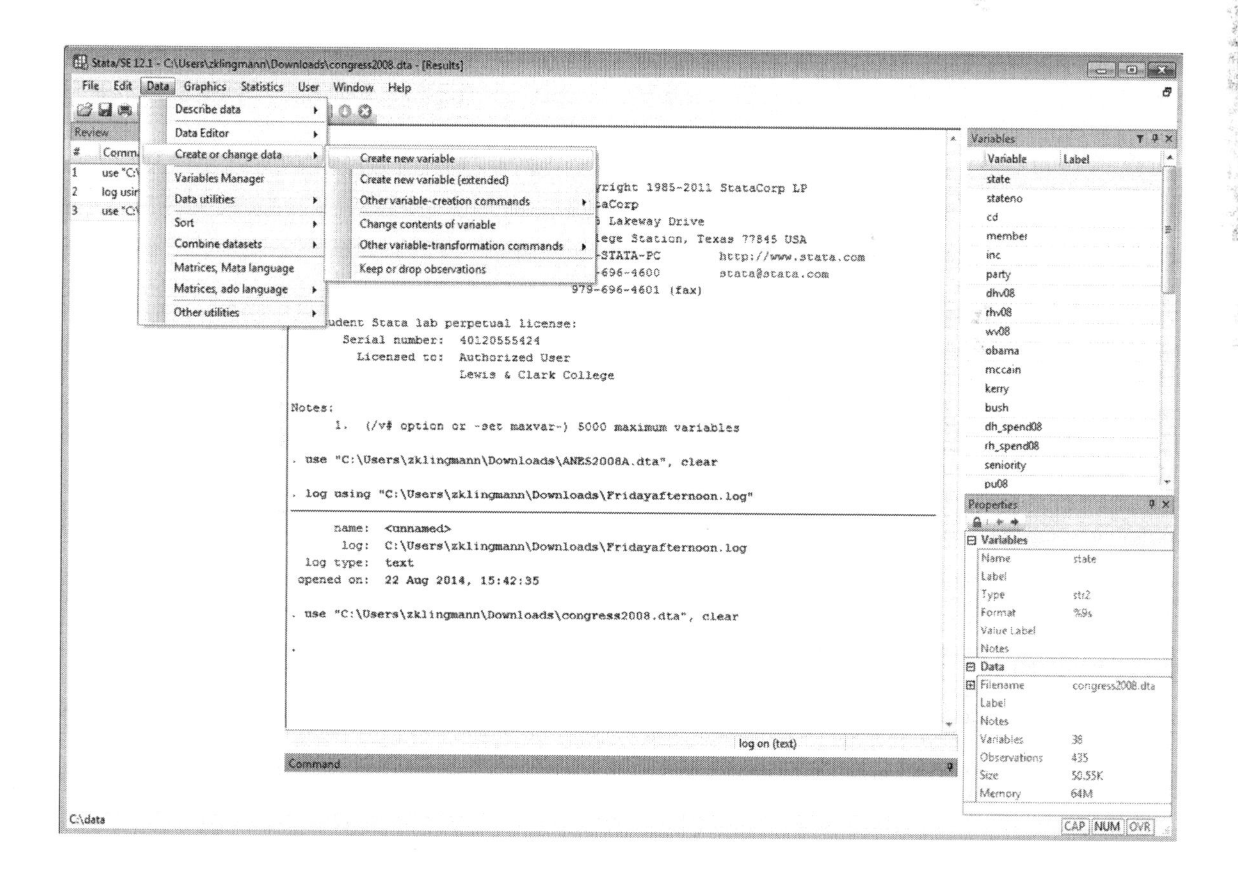

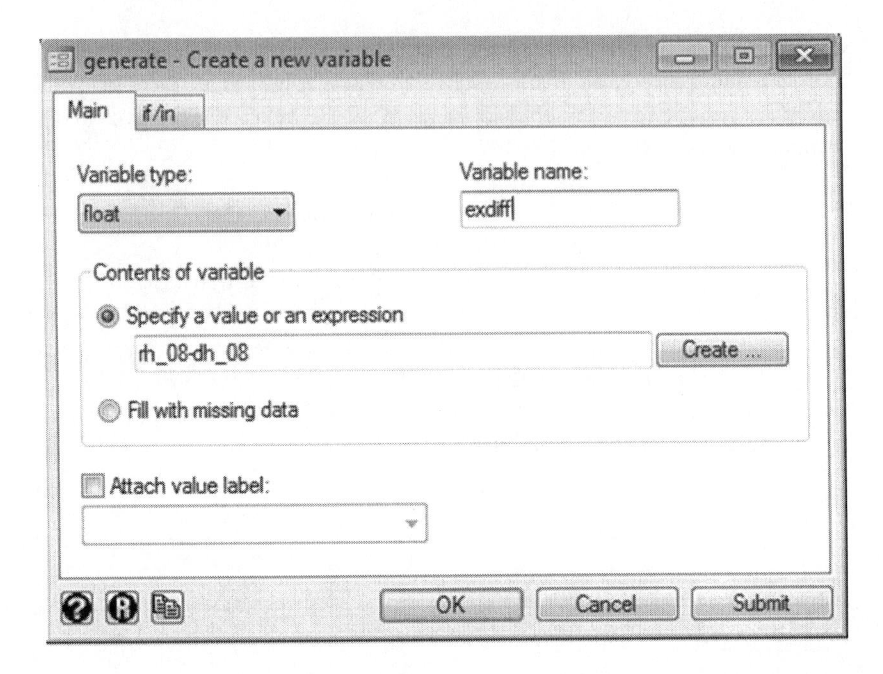

Note: If you have already created this variable using command line instructions, you will get an error message saying that the "variable name you specified already exists." You will need to either delete the variable (**drop exdiff**) or change its variable name to something unique.

Sample Exercises 3.2

In order to see your results, proceed and follow any recode with the **list** command to display the variable's values for the first five observations. The syntax for viewing the first five observations in your data set using the **list** command is as follows:

list *varlist* in 1/5

ANES2012A

1. Create a new variable (*ideodiff*) that measures the difference in feeling thermometer ratings toward liberals (*V75*) and conservatives (*V76*). List the values of all three variables for the first five observations in your data set. What do high or low values of *ideodiff* signify?
2. Create a new variable (*presapprove*) creating a scale of presidential approval by adding the following: *V10*, *V11*, *V12*, *V13*, *V14*. Your lowest value

should be 5 (approve on all counts), and your highest 25 (disapprove on all counts). List the values of your new variable for the first five observations in your data set.

Congress 2008–2012

1. Create a new variable (*spenddiff*) that, for any year, measures the difference Democratic and Republican candidate expenditures (e.g., *dh_spend08-rh_spend08*). List the values of your new variable for the first five observations in your data set. What do those values tell you?
2. Create a new variable (*windiff*) that, for any year, measures the difference between the Democratic House vote and the Republican House vote (e.g., *dhv08-rhv08*). List the values of your new variable for the first five observations in your data set. What do those values tell you?
3. Create a new variable (*demdiff*) that measures the difference between the Democratic House vote in 2010 and 2008). List the values of your new variable for the first five observations in your data set. What do those values tell you?
4. Repeat problem 3 for 2012 versus 2008.

EURO69

1. Create a new variable (*EUpolicy*) that creates a scale measuring support toward common EU policies. Use the three recoded variables (*V16*, *V17*, *V18*) from problem 3 in "EURO69" in "Sample Exercises 3.1." Your scale should range from supportive on all three counts (3) to not supportive on all three (0), with numbers in between corresponding to categories of support for at least one policy but not all. List the values of the *EUpolicy* variable for the first five observations in your data set.
2. Create a new variable (*EUvoice*) that creates a scale measuring political efficacy when assessing the EU using variables *V11* and *V13* (recoded in Sample Exercises 3.1, problem 4). Your scale should range from fully efficacious (2) to fully non-efficacious (0) with a 1 implying efficacy only for oneself or one's country, but not both. List the values of *EUvoice* for the first five observations in your data set.

CCES2012

1. Create a new variable (*odiff*) that measures the absolute value of the difference between a respondent's self-placement (*V48*) and his or her placement of President Obama (*V49*) ideologically. Create a similar variable (*rdiff*) that measures the absolute value of the difference between self-placement

and placement of Governor Romney. List the values of both variables for the first five observations in your data set.

2. Create a new variable (*proximity*) that measures the difference between your two new variables (*odiff-rdiff*). List the values of your new variable for the first five observations in your data set. What does a negative number mean? Zero? A positive number?

Crossnational

1. Create a new variable (*imdiff*) that codes the difference between the infant mortality rates of males (*wdi_imm*) and females (*wdi_imf*). List the values of your new variable for the first five observations in your data set. What do those values tell you?
2. Generate a new variable (*healthgdp*) that calculates health expenditures per capita (*wdi_he*) as a proportion of GDP per capita (*wdi_gdp*). The values should range from .03 to .24. List the values of your new variable for the first five observations in your data set.

3.3 GENERATING NEW VARIABLES USING LOGICAL EXPRESSIONS: "IF" STATEMENTS

The **generate** command can also be used to create a new variable based on some logical condition. This can be accomplished by employing an "if" statement. As previously noted, the mathematical operations of logical statements include the following:

Expression	Meaning
==	Is equal to
!=	Is not equal to
>	Is greater than
<	Is less than
>=	Is greater than or equal to
<=	Is less than or equal to

Generating a new variable using a logical expression is often executed in conjunction with the **replace** command. The **generate** command allows you to create a new variable, whereas the **replace** command allows you to modify the coding of that variable.

The syntax for generating or replacing variables in accordance with logical statements is identical. The thing to remember is that you will always use the **generate** command if a variable does not yet exist in your data set, and the **replace** command if it does. Below I employ the "==" expression to denote a logical statement based on equality (recall that a double equal sign ["=="] is always used in logical statements). It is also possible to employ other mathematical operators, such as less than (<) or not equal to (!=).

gen *newvar= value, variable, or expression* if *oldvar== value, variable, or expression*

replace *newvar= value, variable, or expression* if *oldvar==value, variable, or expression*

Example 3.3.1—To create a new variable (*minority*) to determine whether blacks or Hispanics constitute the larger minority in a district (**congress2008.dta** file).

generate minority=1 if black>hispanic

replace minority=2 if black==hispanic

replace minority=3 if black<hispanic

The new values would be coded as 1 if blacks were the predominant minority, 2 if blacks and Hispanics were equal in size, and 3 if Hispanics outnumbered blacks. If you stopped only after the first line of code, you would have created a variable coded as 1 if blacks were the predominant minority, but missing otherwise.

minority	Freq.	Percent	Cum.
1	203	46.67	46.67
2	2	0.46	47.13
3	230	52.87	100.00
Total	435	100.00	

Caution:

As presented in this data file, black and Hispanic are not mutually exclusive categories.

Note:

Any cases not given a classification will be treated as missing. In this case, we have exhausted all possibilities.

The **replace** command can be accessed via the GUI from the "Data" pull-down menu by moving your cursor to "Create or change data" and selecting "Create new variable." As before, enter the name of the new variable in the "Variable name" field and specify the value or expression that you wish to assign for this variable. For the last example, for instance, we wanted to create the variable called "minority" and assign it a value of 1, though only under certain circumstances.

To enter a logical statement that explains when you want this variable to take on the value of 1, click on the "if/in" tab. The window will appear as follows:

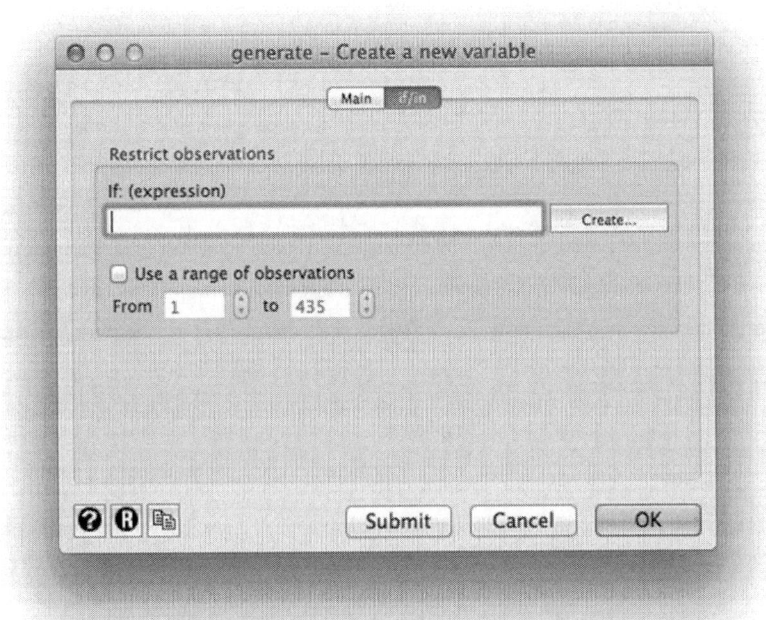

As you only want this variable to take on the value of 1 when blacks outnumber hispanics, the correct logical expression is "*black>hispanic*." When you hit "OK," this variable would be created according to this logical statement, again with missing values created for all other circumstances.

To replace the resulting missing values using the GUI, again use the "Data" pull-down menu, move your cursor to "Create or change data," and this time select "Change contents of variable." The window that will appear will allow you to select or type the variable you want to change, in this case minority, and assign a different value to this variable based on a second logical statement. As before, this will require entering information into both the "main" and "if/in" tabs of this pop-up window.

Note: "If" statements can also be inserted into any analysis command to limit an analysis to a specific subset of cases. The syntax for this usage of an "if" statement is identical to that used for variable creation

Sample Exercises 3.3

In order to see your results, proceed and follow any recode with the **list** command to display the variable's values for the first five observations. The syntax for viewing the first five observations in your data set using the **list** command is as follows:

list *varlist* in 1/5

ANES2012A

1. Create a new variable (*ideodiff2*) that contains the following three categories about ideological placement:

   Liberals > Conservatives (*V75* > *V76*)
   Liberals = Conservatives (*V75* = *V76*)
   Liberals < Conservatives (*V75* < *V76*)

List the values of your new variable for the first five observations in your data set.

Congress 2008–2012

1. In the previous exercise, the **generate** command produced a measure of the mean difference between Democrat and Republican House candidate spending. We will now use an if statement to measure the number of districts where Democrats outspent Republicans or were outspent by Republicans (we have no ties, but we'll enter in that possibility). Name that variable partyspend08 or partyspend10 or partyspend12 depending on the year of the data. Have this variable take on the following values:

   1. if DH$ > RH$ (e.g., *dh_spend08* > *rh_spend08*)
   2. if DH$ = RH$
   3. if DH$ > RH$

List the values of your new variable for the first five observations in your data set.

EURO69

1. Create a new variable (*voicediff*) that contains the following three categories about voice in one's *country* versus the *EU*. Make sure to use the recoded versions of the variables that eliminated Don't Know (DK) responses (see problem 4 in "EURO69" in "Sample Exercises 3.2")

   1 if country > EU (V12 > V11)
   2 if country = EU (V12 = V11)
   3 if country < EU (V12 < V11)

   List the values of your new variable for the first five observations in your data set.

CCES2012

1. Create a new variable (*proximity2*) that contains the following three categories about ideological placement:

   odiff > rdiff
   odiff = rdiff
   odiff < rdiff

   List the values of your new variable for the first five observations in your data set. How does *proximity2* compare to *proximity* (created in problem 2 in "CCES2012" in "Sample Exercises 3.2")?

Crossnational

1. Return to our infant mortality example. Create a new variable (*imdiff2*) with three possible categories:

   wdi_imm > wdi_imf
   wdi_imm = wdi_imf
   wdi_imm < wdi_imf

   List the values of your new variable for the first five observations in your data set. Notice anything unusual?

2. Create a new variable (named *votediff*) that compares presidential with parliamentary turnout with three possible categories:

   idea_vtvap_pa > idea_vtr_pr
   idea_vtvap_pa = idea_vtr_pr
   idea_vtvap_pa < idea_vtr_pr

List the values of your new variable for the first five observations in your data set. Voter turnout in parliamentary elections will exceed turnout in presidential elections in an overwhelming majority of countries. Question: Why are there so many missing cases?

3.4 USEFUL COMMANDS FOR DATA MANAGEMENT

Rename

To rename a variable, you can use the **rename** command. The syntax for this command is as follows:

rename *oldvarname newvarname*

As previously noted, variable names must be unique in your data set and are case sensitive. Symbols and space marks are not allowed in variable names, with the sole exception of an underscore. Variable names cannot begin with numbers.

Variables can also be renamed using the Variables Manager. To access the Variables Manager, use the Data pull-down menu and select "Variables Manager."

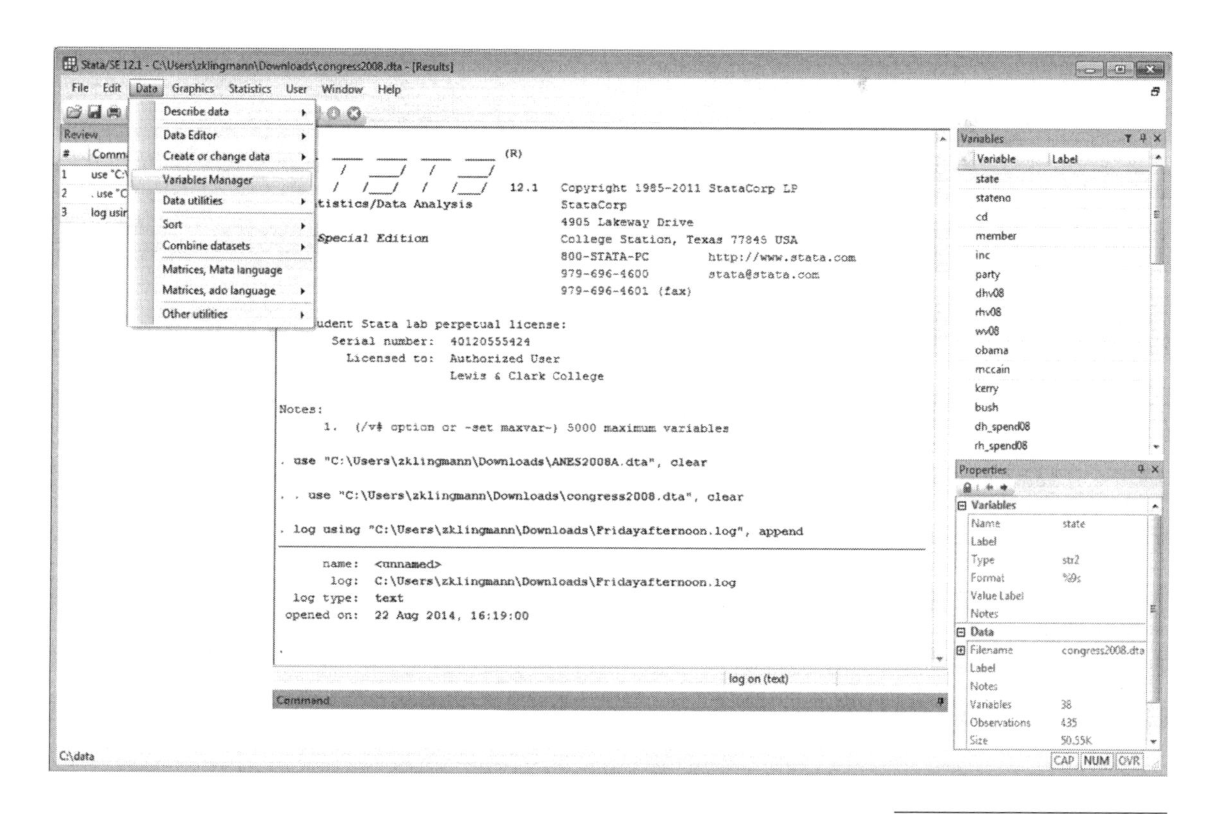

When the Variables Manager window pops up, you can select any variable and change the name manually by editing the text in the "Name" field.

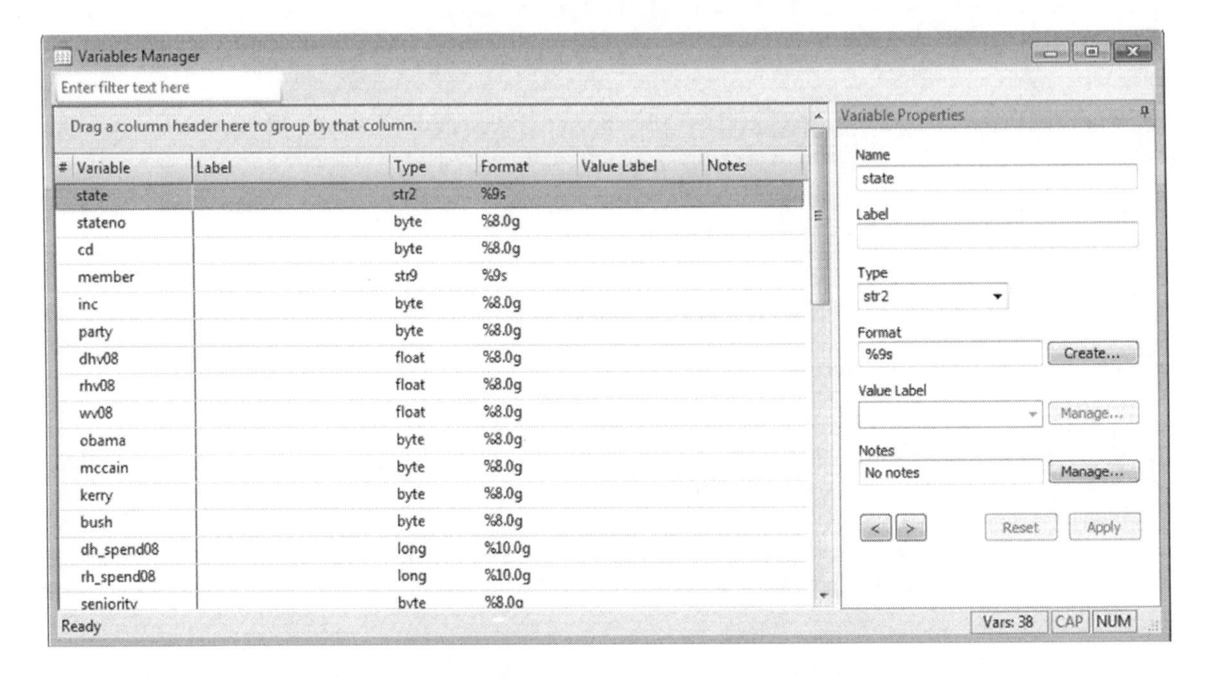

Variable Label

It is often helpful to have variable descriptions attached to variable names to more thoroughly describe a variable. In Stata, this can be achieved by entering a "variable label." The syntax for entering a variable label through the command line is as follows:

label variable *varname "variable description"*

The variable description must be placed in quotes and is limited to 80 characters. For example, in the **ANES2008A.dta** data set, the command label variable *V36*, "Party ID," would add the label Party ID to the variable. Note that all variables in the data sets provided with this manual already include variable labels.

Variable labels can also be easily added through the Variables Manager by selecting a variable and entering the description in the "Label" field.

Value Labels

It can also be useful to add value labels to your data. Value labels provide descriptions for each unique value, or category, of your variable. Adding value labels to a variable using Stata's command line is a two-part process. First, you must define a label, then you must add that label to a variable. Use the following syntax:

label define *lblname # "label"*

label values *varname lblname*

For example, the following code would apply value labels for the variable for gender, *V1*, in the **ANES2008A.dta** data set.

label define gender 1 Male 2 Female

label values V1 gender

Note that quotation marks around the label should be used if the label is more than one word. If you enter Stata's data editor mode, you will note that the variable *V1* has now changed from the color black to blue, and the values read as text instead of numbers.

It is easy to add value labels to a variable using the Variables Manager. Once you have entered the Variables Manager, select a variable and click the "Manage . . ." button next to the variable labels field. In the pop-up window, select "Create Label." From there, choose a label name and enter each value and corresponding label one by one, clicking "Add" between each unique value. After you have completed all value labels, return to the main Variables Manager window and change the field for value labels to the new label name you have just created.

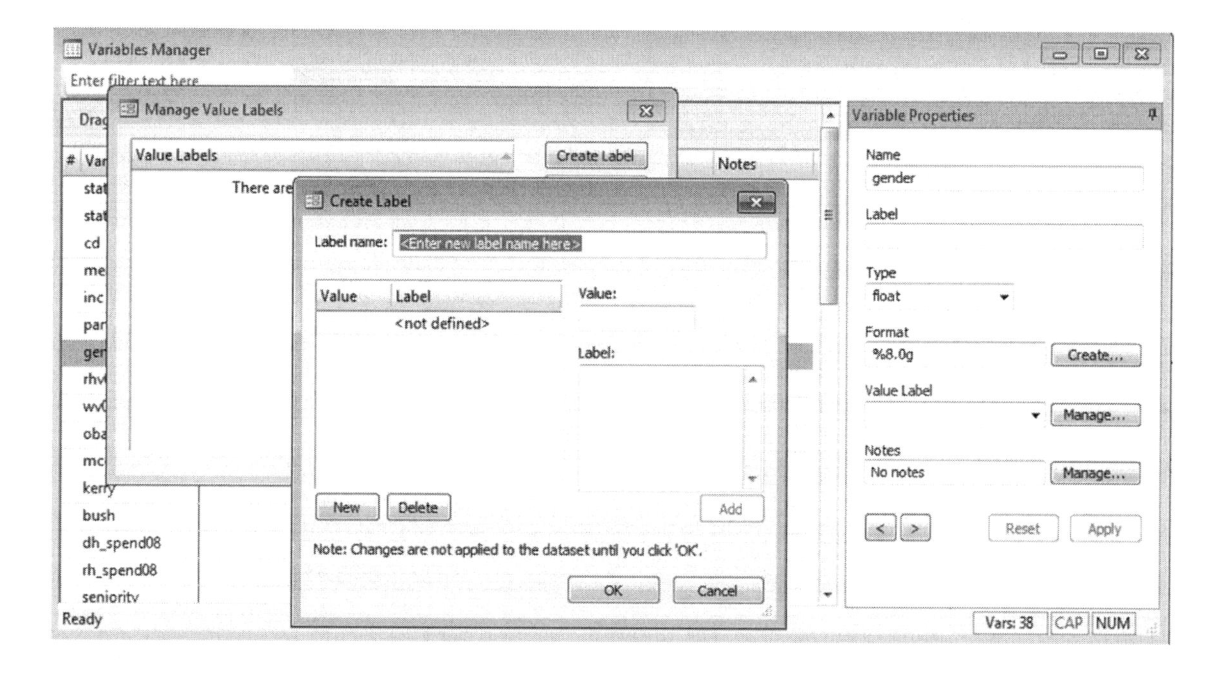

Dropping Variables

If you have created a variable that you no longer need in your data set, or have made an error while recoding, you will want to use the **drop** command. Use the following syntax:

drop *varname*

You can eliminate multiple variables at once by listing multiple variables after the **drop** command.

You can also drop variables from you data set from the Variables box (or Variables Manager). Simply right click on the variable and select the field that indicates it will drop the variable.

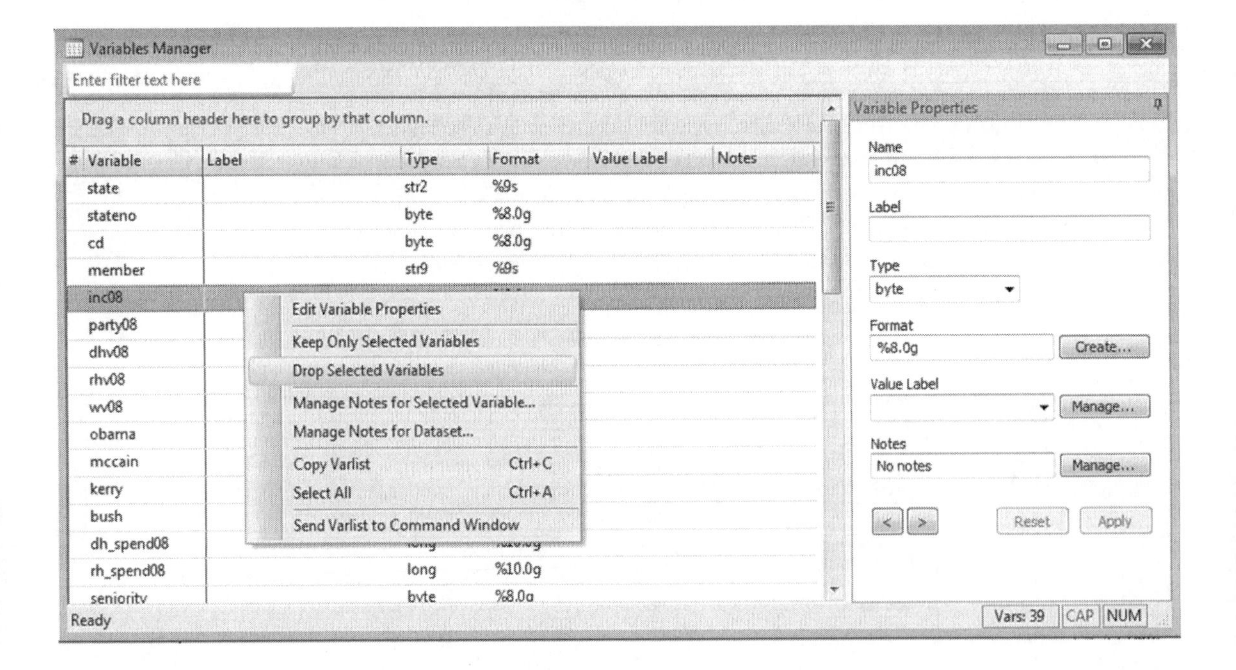

> **Caution:**
>
> When you use the **drop** command in conjunction with an "if" or "in" statement, Stata will eliminate observations within your data set, not the entire variable.

CHAPTER 4

CONTENTS

Commonly Used Stata Commands for Data Analysis

Once all appropriate transformations have been done, you will then proceed to analyzing the data in order to confirm or disconfirm your hypotheses. Several types of statistical analysis are possible. Examples will be given for each, along with an explanation of the output that Stata will produce. For each of these sets of analysis, the graphical user interface (GUI) always starts with clicking on the "Statistics" pull-down menu, though it may otherwise vary based on whether or not survey weights are appropriate in the analysis.

4.1 FREQUENCIES

A frequency distribution is a simple way to learn how often a variable takes on each of its possible values. This is best employed for discrete or categorical data. For more information on frequency distributions and graphs, refer to Chapter 2 in *Understanding Political Science Statistics: Observations and Expectations in Political Analysis.*

Frequency Distribution Tables

The **tabulate** command creates frequency distribution tables for single variables (one-way tables) or combinations of variables (two-way tables). It is recommended that frequencies be produced for all categorical variables for which you wish to recode, especially in the **ANES2008A.dta** file. That will allow you to view how the data are coded and distributed. Once recoded, you should again use the **tabulate** command to make sure that the recode was done correctly.

The syntax for the **tabulate** command to obtain a frequency distribution for a single variable is as follows:

tabulate *varname*, {options}

Example 4.1.1—Using the **congress2008.dta** file, produce a frequency table of the political parties of U.S. congressional House representatives.

tabulate party

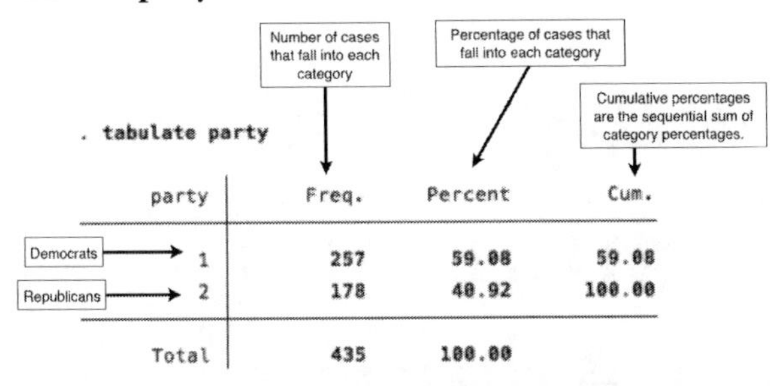


```
. tabulate party

      party |      Freq.     Percent        Cum.
------------+-----------------------------------
          1 |        257       59.08       59.08
          2 |        178       40.92      100.00
------------+-----------------------------------
      Total |        435      100.00
```

Alternatively, this table could be produced using the pull-down menus by navigating from "Statistics > "Summaries, tables, and tests" > "Tables" > "One-way tables" and entering the variable *party08* in the "Categorical variable" field.

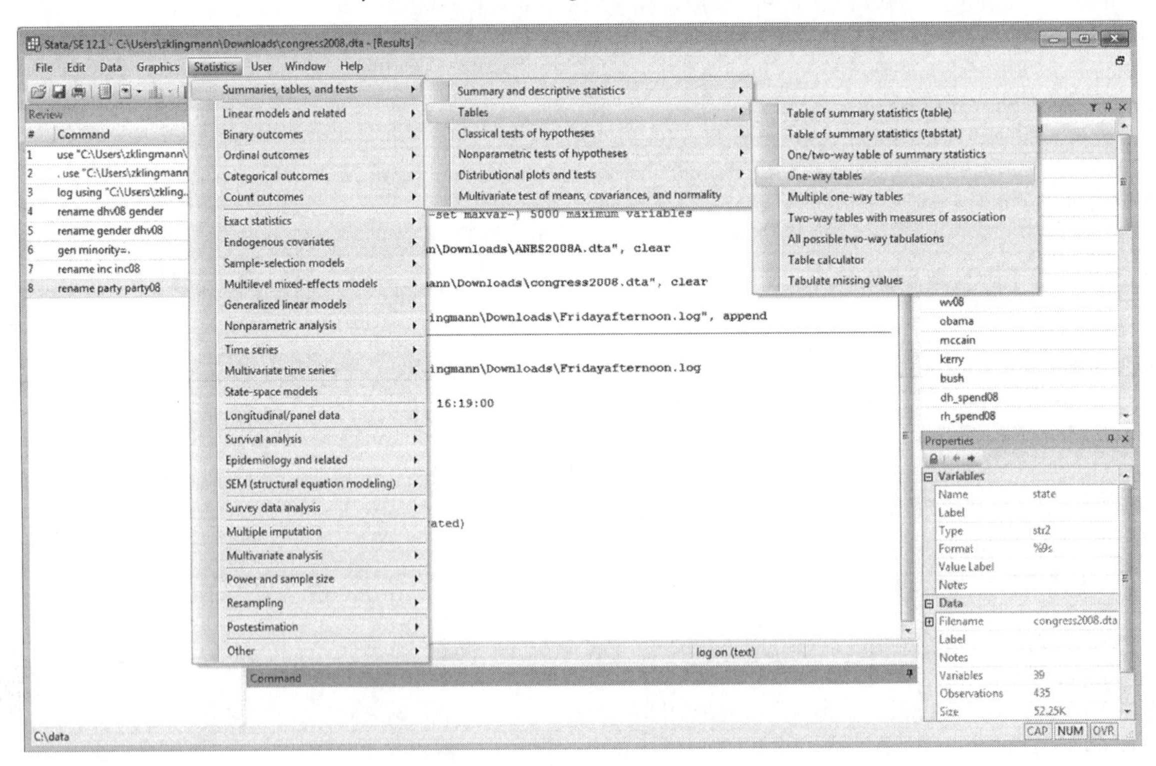

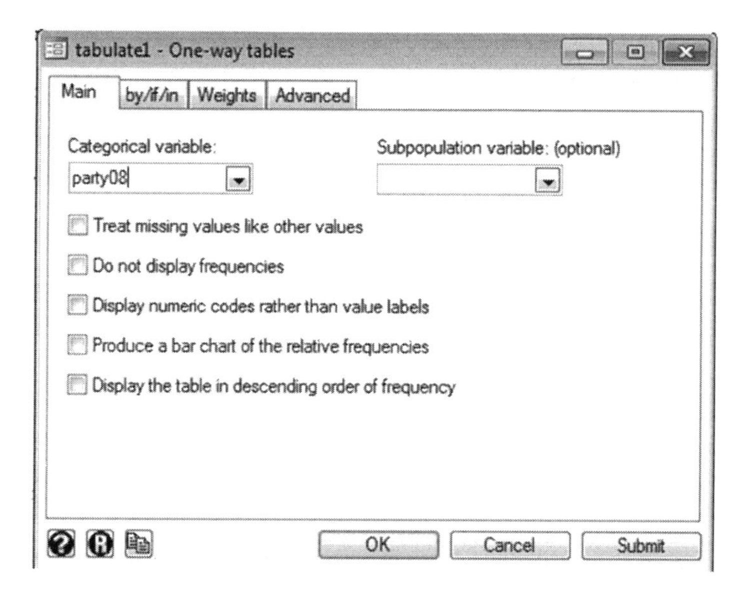

If the data are survey data and require weighting, you will begin the command with the **svy** prefix. To obtain expected frequencies, you will need to add the option "count," as the default will be to produce only expected cell proportions, not frequencies. To view both, add the options "count" and "cell."

Example 4.1.2—Produce an expected frequency distribution of the party identification measure (*V36*) in the **ANES2008A.dta** file with sampling bias correction.

svy: tabulate V36, count cell

In this example, a frequency table of *V36* is produced, weighted by the variable *PW2*, the weight chosen when this data set was declared to be survey data (see Chapter 2, Section 2.2 (in this volume) for instructions on how to declare a data set to be survey data). I've indicated for both counts and proportions to be displayed.

Question:

What is the modal response to the party ID question?

Answer:

The modal response is 0, or "Strong Democrats." More respondents claimed to be strong Democrats than any other category, as indicated by the fact that this value reports the largest proportion of respondents.

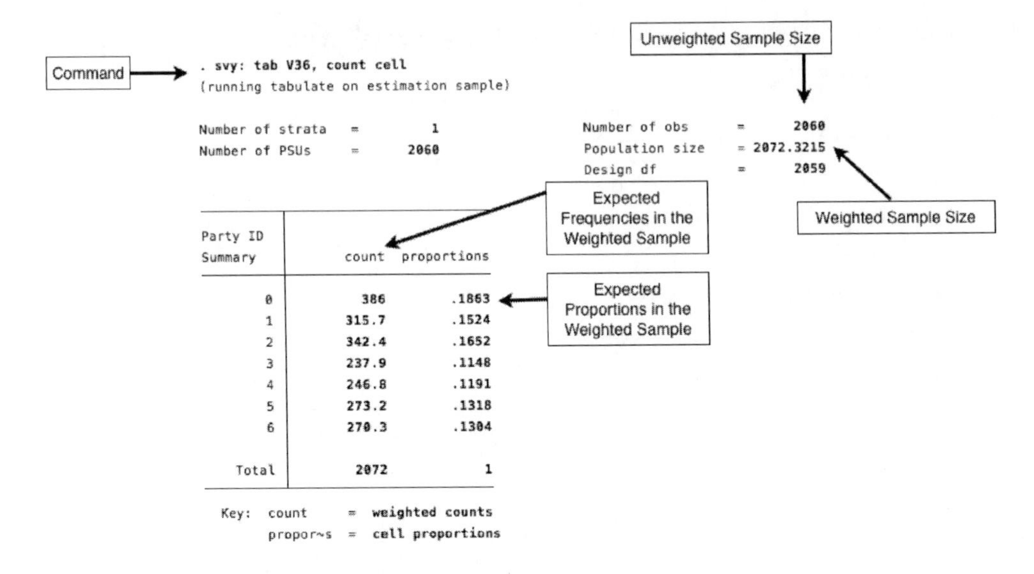

To use the GUI interface to produce this output, start with the "Statistics" pull-down menu and move your cursor to "Survey data analysis" and then "Tables." Choose the option for "One-way tables" as shown below.

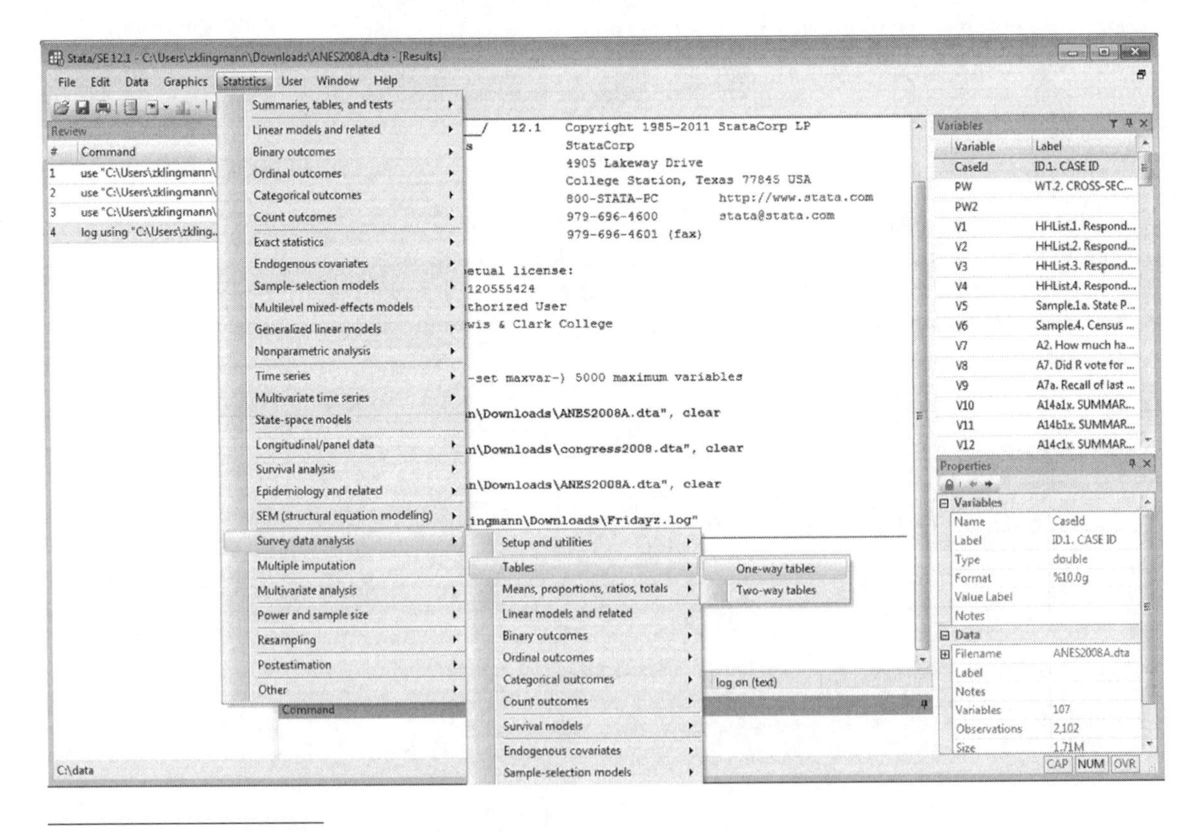

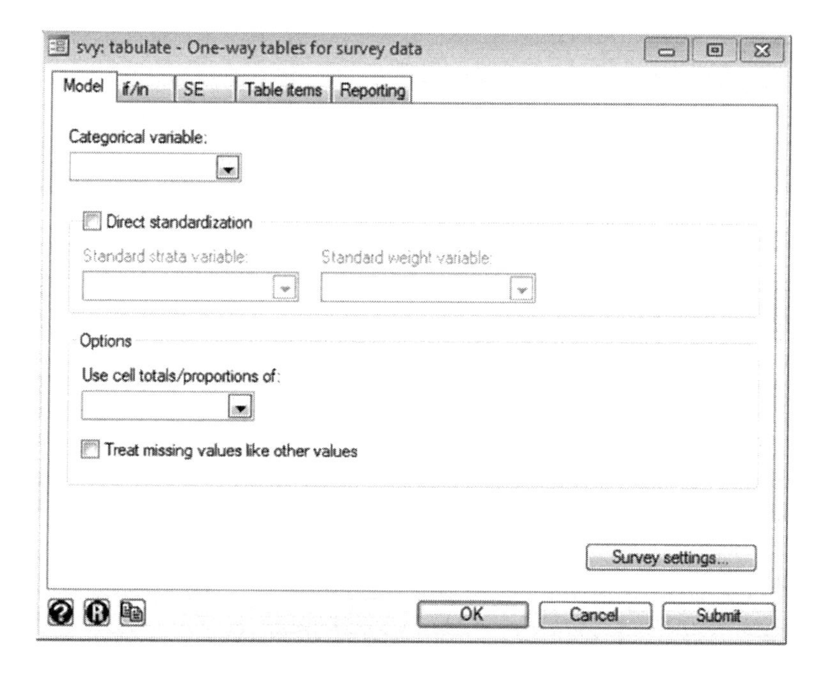

In the pop-up window, you will enter or select the variable *V36* in the "Categorical variable" field. Note that a variety of options are available. To add expected frequencies, navigate to the "Table items" tab and check the boxes for "Weighted cell counts" and "Cell proportions."

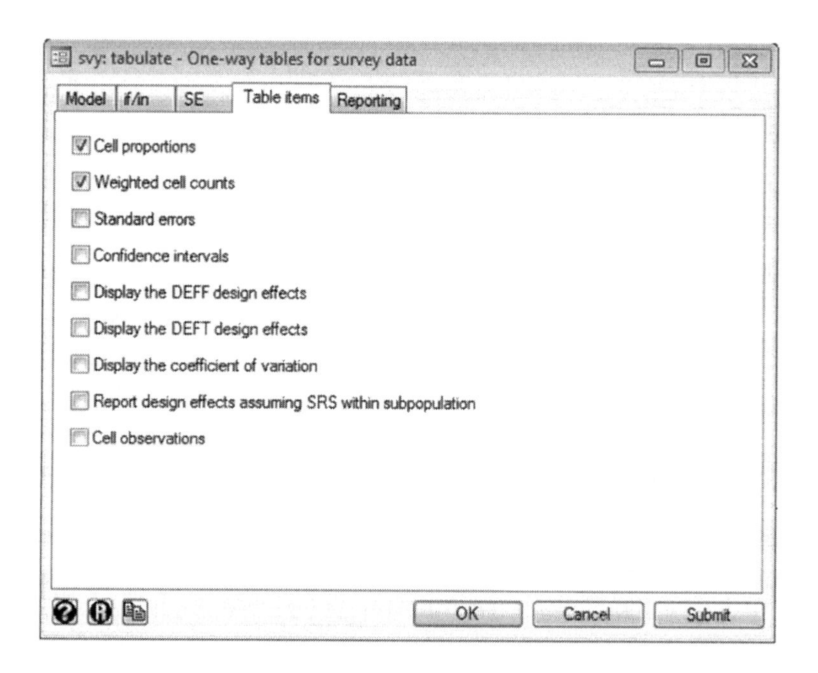

Bar Graphs

Bar graphs are an excellent way to visualize data distributions. Stata has two commands useful for producing these graphs, **graph bar** and **histogram.** Your choice of command will depend on the coding of your data and whether or not you wish to employ sampling weights.

The **histogram** command is often the easiest way to produce a bar chart of a variable's distribution. The syntax for the **histogram** command is the following:

histogram *varname*, {options}

Options allow you to specify how the distribution is displayed on the y-axis. For example, if you want to display a frequency distribution (counts), you would request the option "frequency." Other relevant options include density, percent, and fraction.

Example 4.1.3—Produce a bar chart of the seven identification categories of partisan identification (*V36*) in the **ANES2008A.dta** file.

histogram V36, frequency

If the frequency option is not included, Stata will produce a density plot by default.

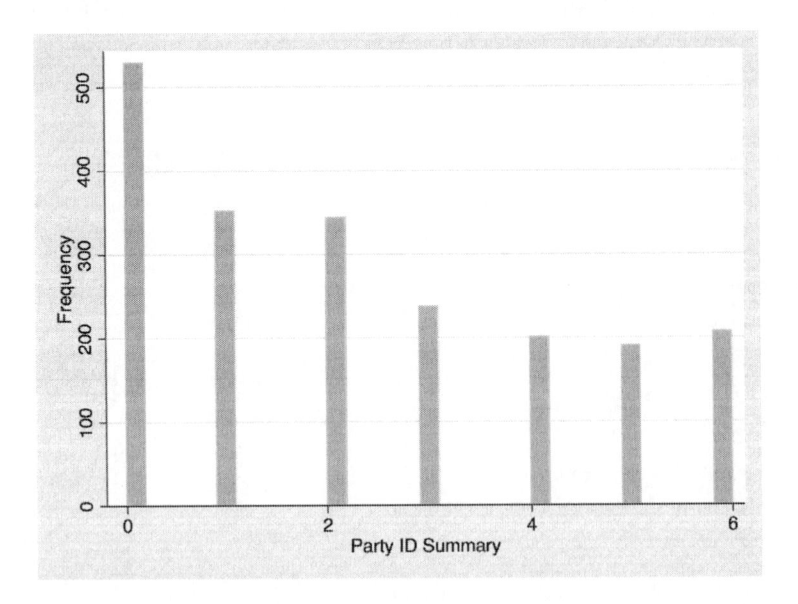

You can also access the **histogram** command using the GUI interface. This is an excellent way to explore Stata's plentiful graphing options. Simply go to the "Graphics" pull-down menu and choose "Histogram." Your variable of interest can be selected in the "Variable" field. You can select whether or not your data are continuous or discrete, or alter the number or width of bins. You can also choose whether your histogram displays densities, frequencies, fractions, or percentages. Take time to explore the other tabs in this window. For example, you can also add graph titles quite easily.

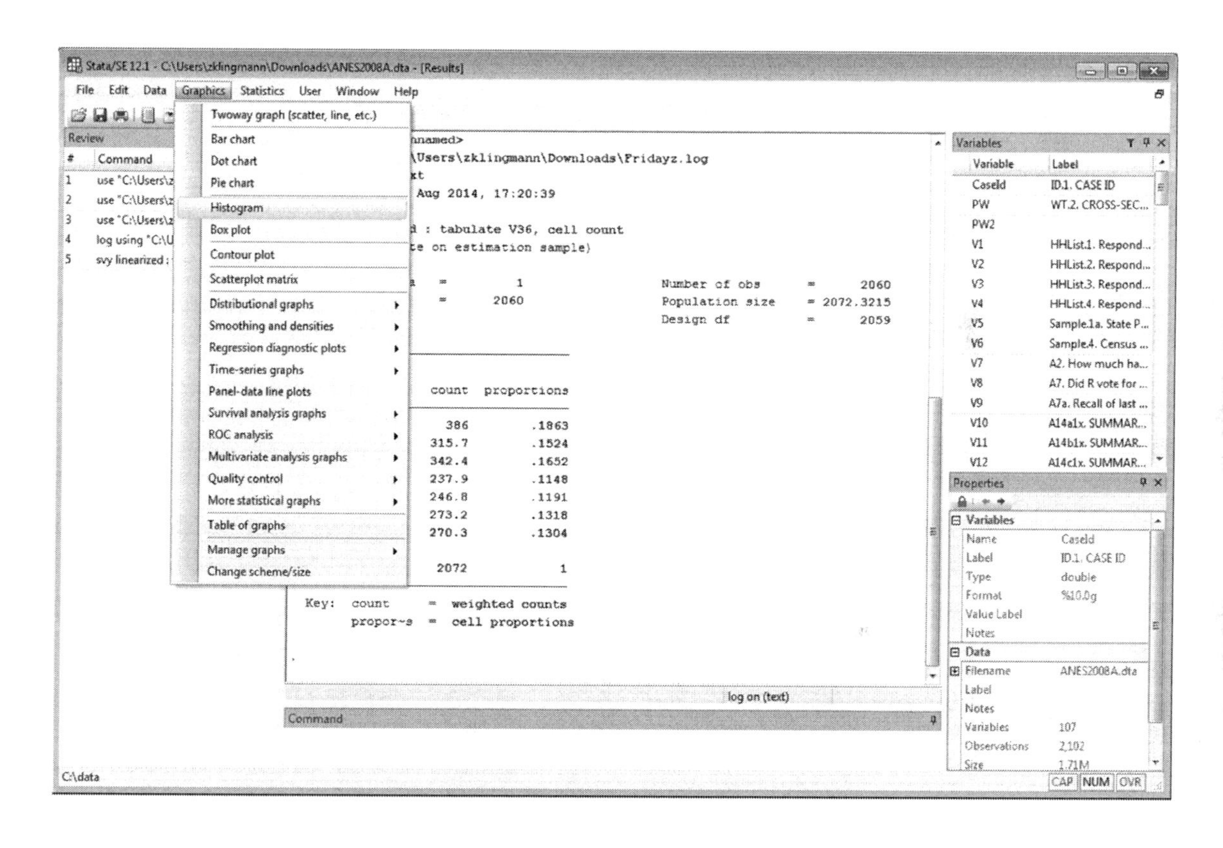

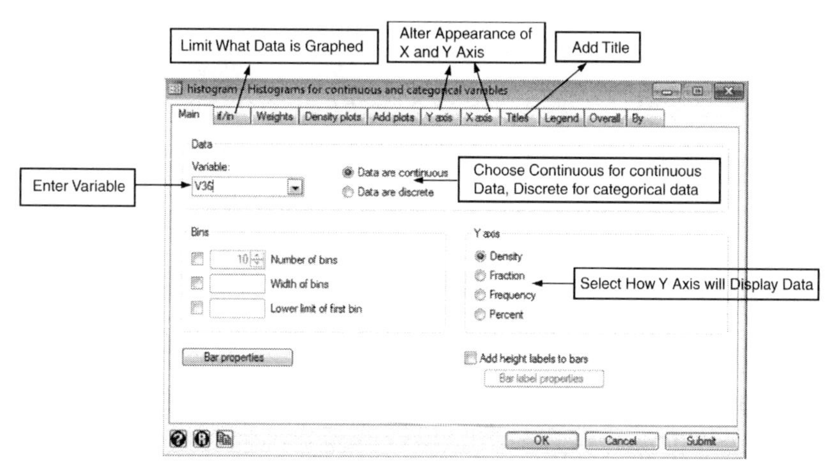

The **histogram** command is not compatible with sampling weights. However, the **graph bar** command can be used as a workaround solution. In addition to our variable of interest, *V36*, you will also need to employ the variable *all_respondents*, a variable that takes on the value of 1 for all respondents in the data.

The following syntax will produce a frequency count of *all_respondents* with respect to the unique categories of *V36*. By manually specifying pweights, or probability weights, the graph will account for the necessary sampling correction. This manual specification is not possible with all Stata commands.

graph bar (count) all_respondents [pweight = PW2], over(V36)

You will produce the following graph:

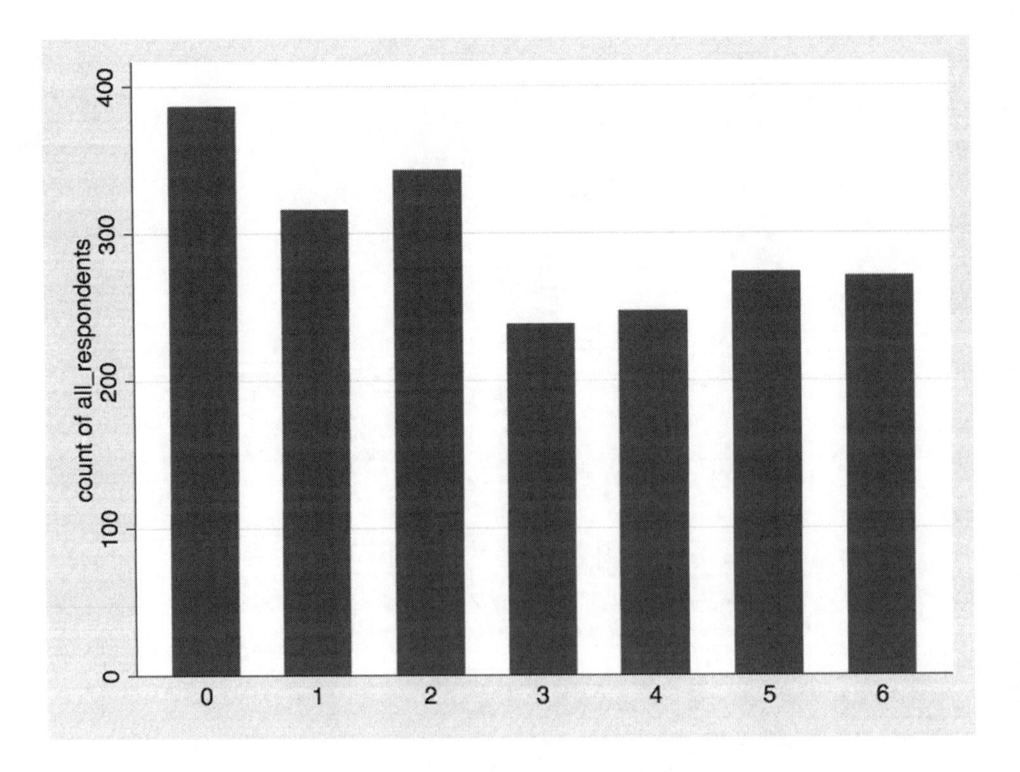

To create this graph using the pull-down menus, start at the "Graphics" drop-down menu and select "Bar chart."

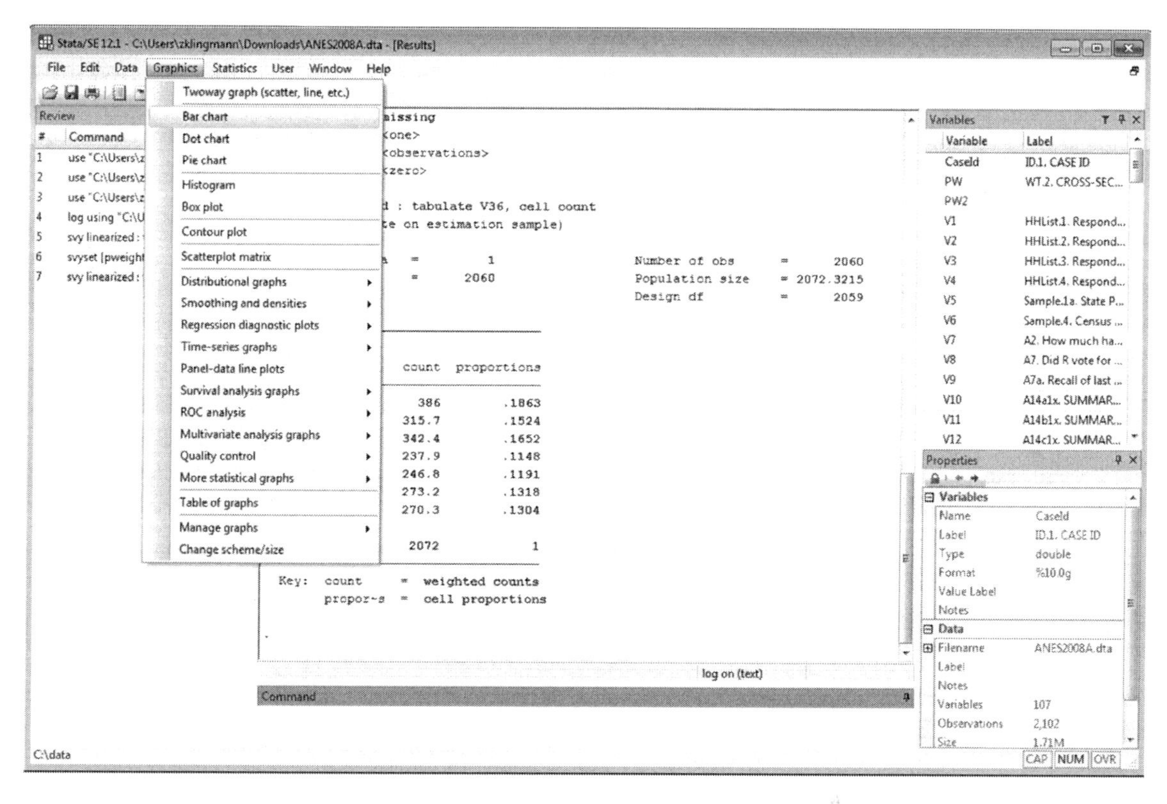

The following window will appear:

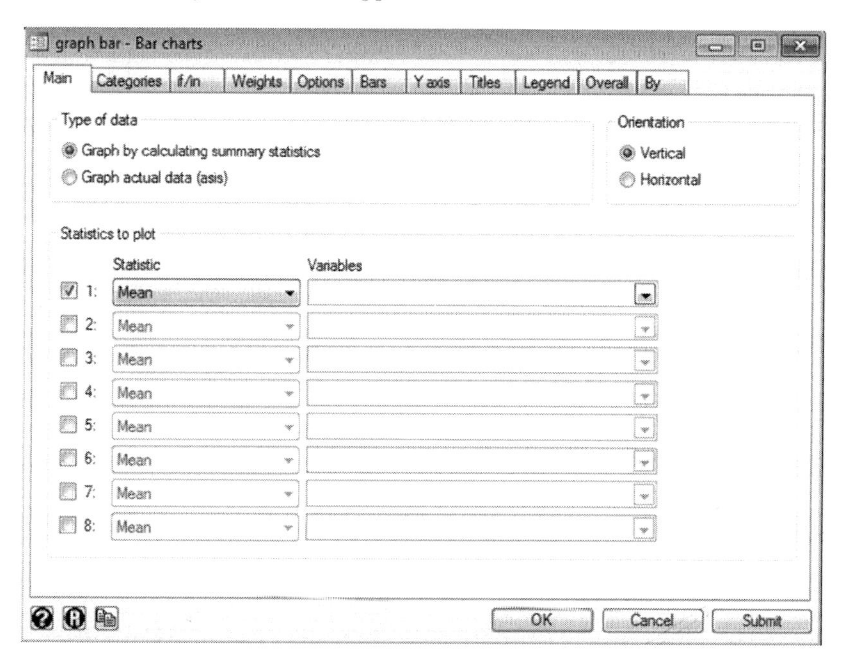

Using the **graph bar** command, with or without the inclusion of sampling weights, in lieu of the **histogram** command, may be preferable for plotting ordinal or dichotomous variables. Conventionally, histograms are used to display continuous-level data distributions. Although this command will produce the appropriate graphs for ordinal variables (see Example 4.1.3), in some instances you may have to edit the labels to omit values that could not possibly exist for your variable, such as decimals or empty categories. In particular, the **graph bar** command is preferable to the **histogram** command if there is a gap in the data distribution that you do not want displayed. For example, if you have a variable coded exclusively as 1 or 5, the **histogram** command will still display empty bars for 2, 3, and 4. In contrast, the **graph bar** command will only display bars for the values that exist in your data, 1 and 5.

Pie Charts

Pie charts are another way to graphically display the distribution of categorical data, particularly when your variable takes on a small number of values. Pie charts can be created using the **graph pie** command with the following syntax:

graph pie, over(*varname*)

Alternatively, the GUI interface is often an excellent way to make charts. To make a pie chart, simply use the "Graphics" pull-down menu and choose "Pie

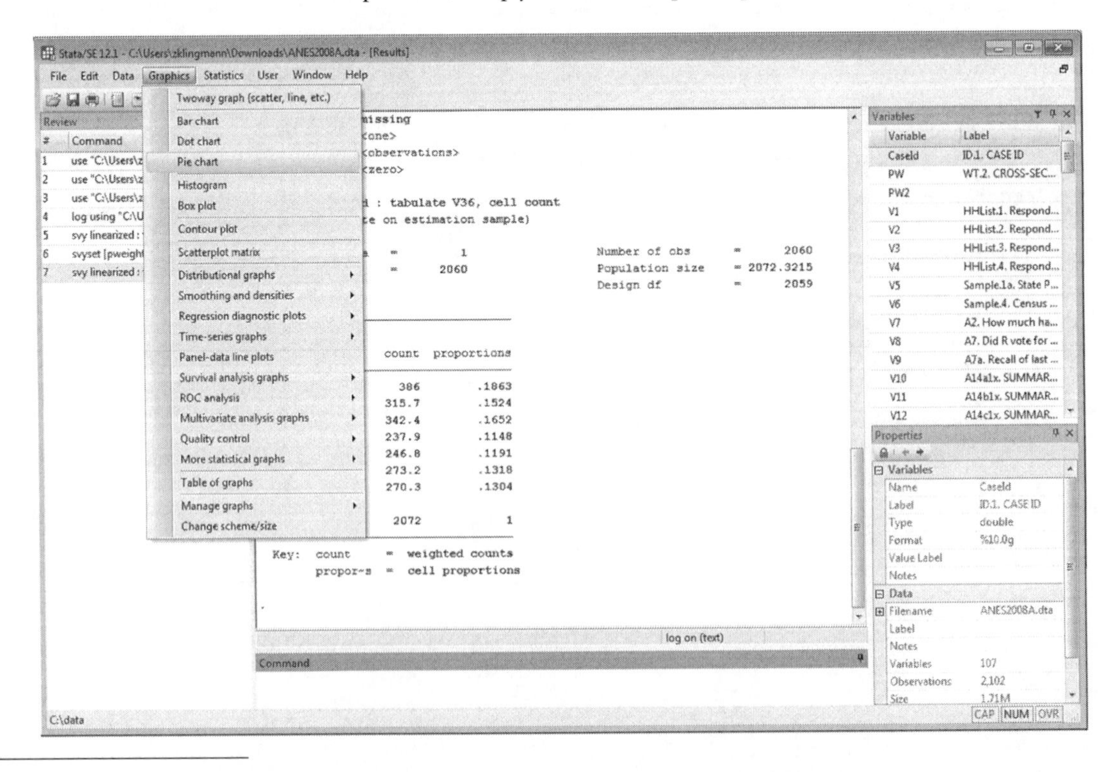

chart." Choose the option to "Graph by categories" and choose your variable of interest in the "Category variable" field. Again, you may want to explore the other graphing options available in this pop-up window. For example, the "Slices" tab will allow you to choose coloring options for your pie chart. Such changes can also be made manually using the graph editor, which is discussed in Appendix A.

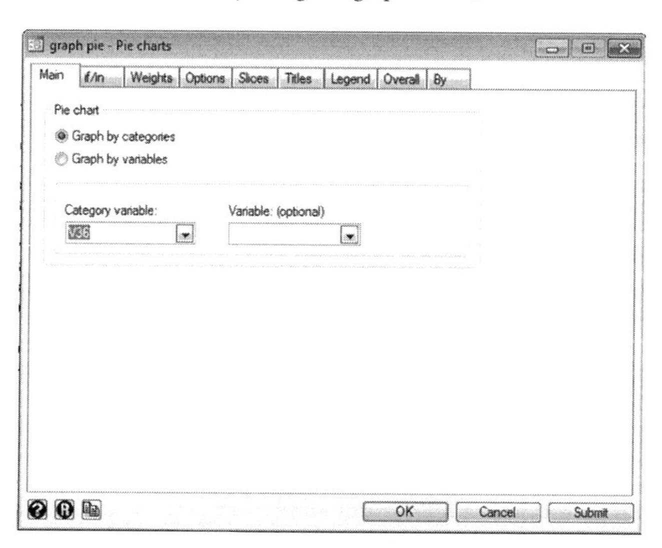

As with the **graph bar** command, the **graph pie** command is compatible with sampling weights. To employ sampling weights, include the pweight option as follows:

graph pie [pweight = *varname*], over(*varname*)

You can add sampling weights through the GUI interface by clicking on the "Weights" tab, choosing the option "Sampling weights," and entering in the weight variable.

graph pie - Pie charts
Main | if/in | Weights | Options | Slices | Titles | Legend | Overall | By
Weight type:
None
Frequency weights
Sampling weights
Analytic weights
Help weights
Sampling weight:
PW2
OK | Cancel | Submit

Example 4.1.4—Produce a pie chart to show the distribution of Party ID (*V36*) using sampling weights (*PW2*):

graph pie [pweight = PW2], over(V36)

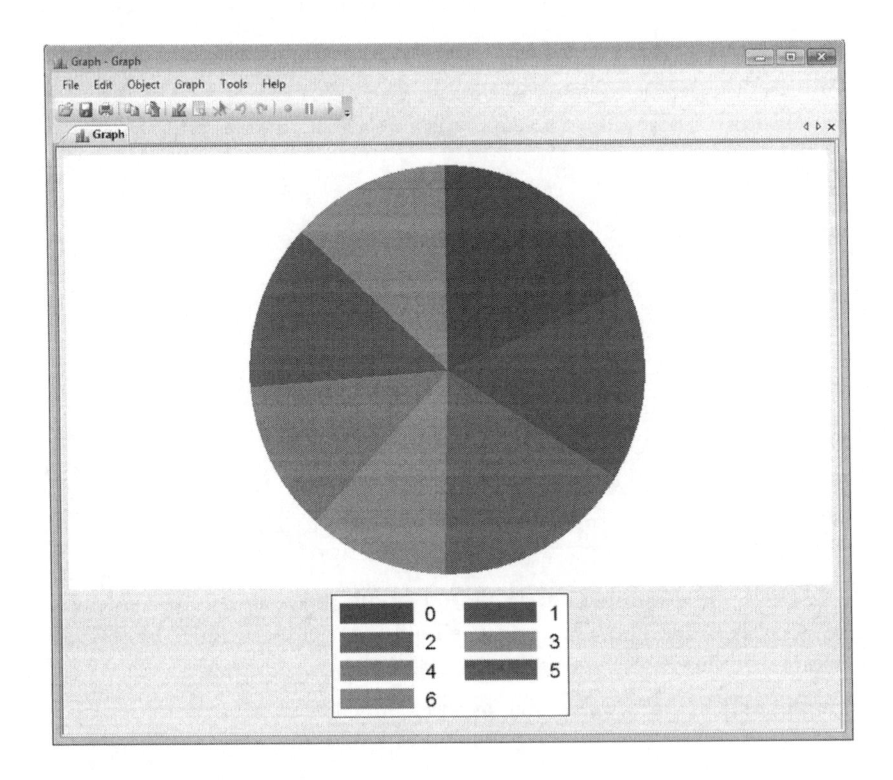

Sample Exercises 4.1

ANES2012A

For each exercise, weight the sample by *PW2012*.

1. Produce a frequency distribution table and frequency bar chart for *presapprove*, a variable created in problem 2 in "ANES2012A" in "Sample Exercises 3.2" (Chapter 3, this volume). What can you say about President Obama's job approval?
2. Produce a frequency distribution table and pie chart of *ideodiff*. What can you say about Americans' ideological preferences?
3. Repeat problem 2, but only for voters by attaching an "if" statement. Is there any difference?

Congress 2008–2012

1. Produce a histogram for each of the winning party variables (*party08, party10, partyY12*). What has changed over time?
2. Produce a frequency distribution table and pie chart for the original Incumbency Status Variables (*inc08, inc10, inc12*).

EURO69

For each exercise, weight the sample by *W27*. If analyzing only one country or comparing just two countries against each other, use *W1*.

1. Produce a frequency distribution table and bar chart for EUvoice (computed in problem 2 in "EURO69" in "Sample Exercises 3.2" [Chapter 3, this volume]). What can you say about one's perception of one's voice counting in the EU and one's country?
2. Produce a bar chart and pie chart of *V20A*.
3. Repeat problem 2, but only for men, using an "if" statement. Is there any difference?

CCES2012

For each exercise, weight the sample by *weight*.

1. Produce a bar chart for *proximity*, computed in problem 2 in "CCES2012" in "Sample Exercises 3.2" (Chapter 3, this volume). What can you say about one's ideological proximity to the two major party candidates?
2. Produce a frequency distribution table and pie chart for your three previously recoded Party ID variables (recoded in problem 2 in "CCES2012" in "Sample Exercises 3.1" [Chapter 3, this volume]). What can you say about Americans' partisan preferences in 2012?
3. Using frequency distributions, compare adult Americans' views toward tax cuts and deficits (*V43, V43, V45*).

Crossnational

1. To demonstrate the extreme difference in infant mortality rates for males and females, produce a frequency distribution table and pie chart for *imdiff2* (created in problem 1 in "Crossnational" in "Sample Exercises 3.3" [Chapter 3, this volume]).

2. Produce bar charts for every variable dealing with funding and subsidies for elections: *idea_dpfp* to *idea_lcs*. Where does the difference seem greatest? The bar heights seem to reverse. Does this signify a change in electoral policy direction or a difference in the variable coding?
3. Produce a bar chart for your previously computed *healthgdp* (created in problem 2 in "Crossnational" in "Sample Exercises 3.2" [Chapter 3, this volume]). Describe the shape and skew of the distribution.

4.2 SUMMARY STATISTICS

The **summary** (which can be abbreviated to **sum** as shown in all examples) command is a useful way to produce many summary statistics. In its basic form, the **summary** command will produce information on the number of observations, mean, standard deviation, minimum value, and maximum value. For more information on summary statistics, see Chapters 3–5 in *Understanding Political Science Statistics: Observations and Expectations in Political Analysis*. The syntax for the **summary** command is as follows:

sum *varlist*

Example 4.2.1—To produce basic summary statistics of expenditures for Republican House candidates (*rh_spend08*) in the **congress2008.dta** file.

sum rh_spend08

```
. sum rh_spend08
```

Variable	Obs	Mean	Std. Dev.	Min	Max
rh_spend08	435	853719.7	1052039	0	7038552

For additional descriptive statistics, such as the median and skewness, it is useful to apply the "detail" option.

Example 4.2.2—To produce detailed summary statistics of expenditures for Republican House candidates using the **congress2008.dta** file.

sum rh_spend08, detail

The following output will be produced. Some of the statistics are interpreted for you.

The **sum** command can be accessed via the following series of pull-down menus: "Statistics" > "Summaries, tables, and tests" > "Summary and descriptive statistics" > "Summary statistics."

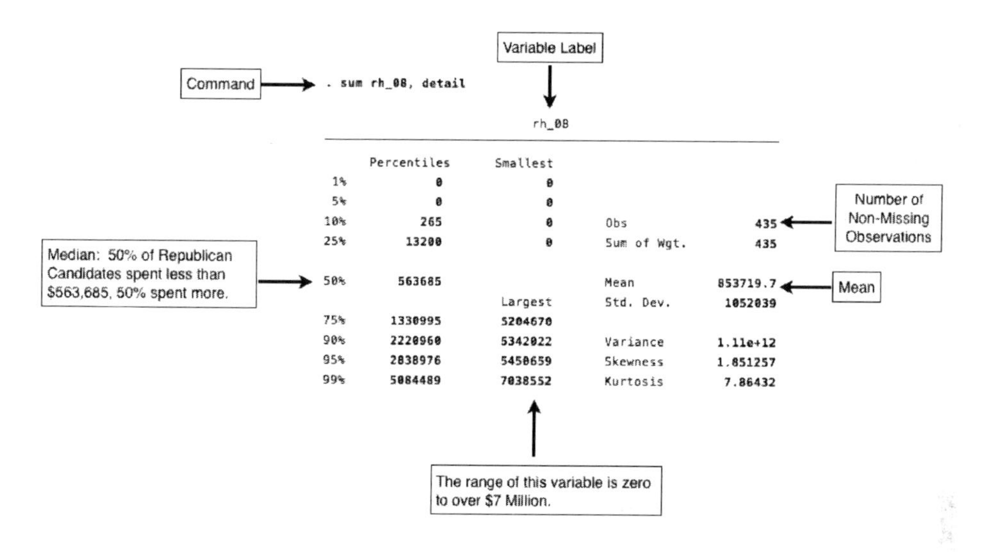

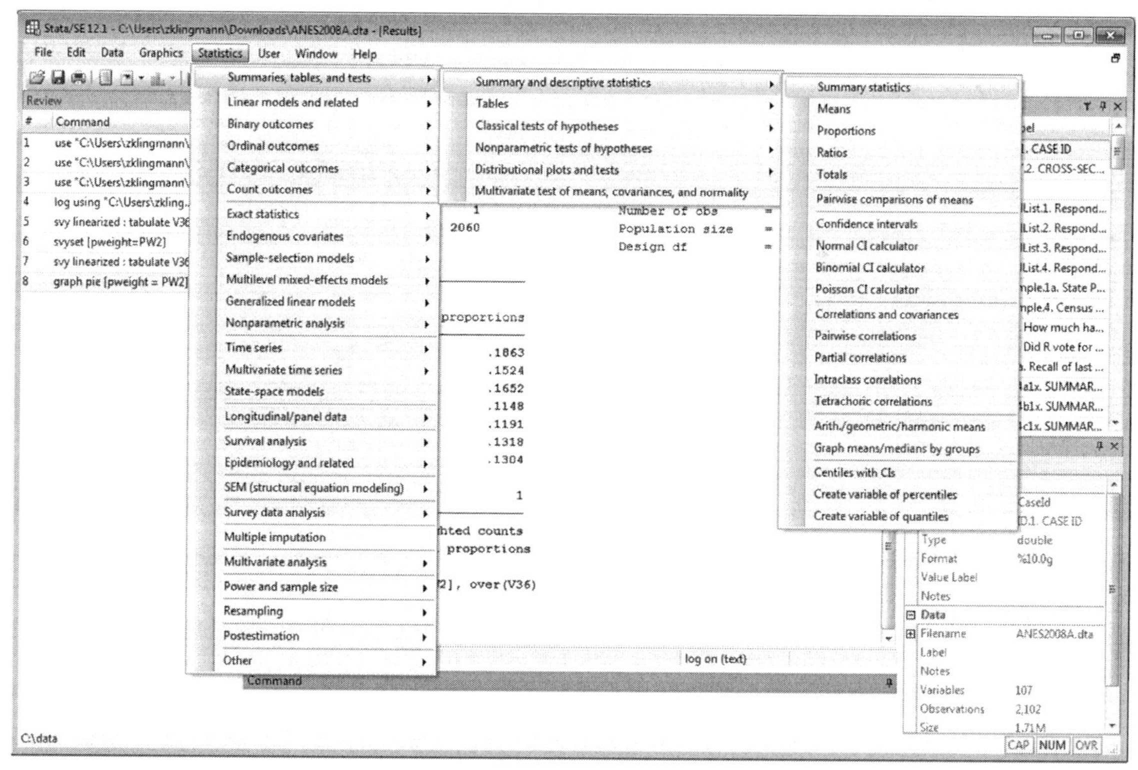

You will see the following pop-up window appear, at which point you can enter your variable(s) of interest and preference for detailed statistics (select the radio button "Display additional statistics."

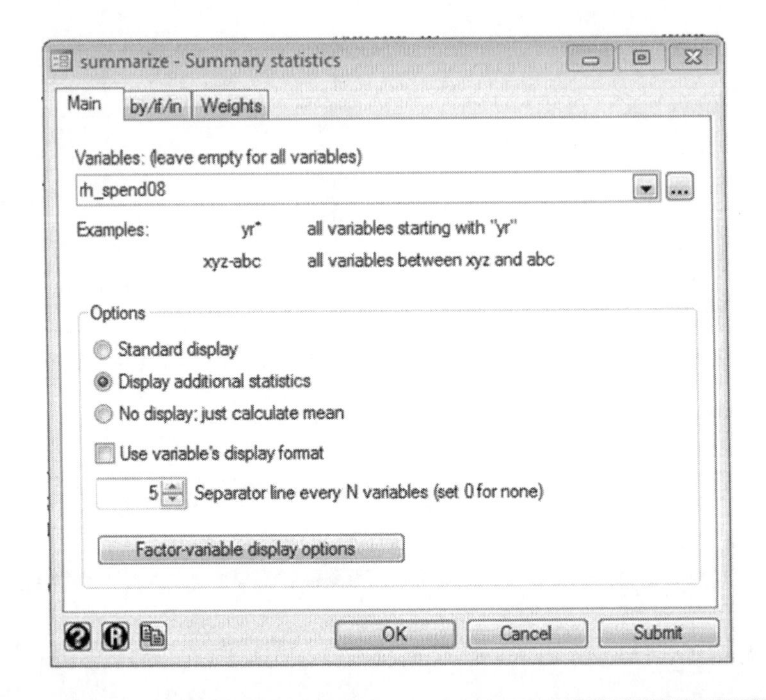

Caution:

Stata will not deny you the opportunity to choose statistics that are not appropriate for your level of measurement. It will calculate a mean of numerically coded nominal variables, such as the four census categories, even though a mean is, well, meaningless.

You may also be interested in computing descriptive statistics for weighted survey data. The **summary** command will not work using a **svy** prefix. Instead, you can use the **mean** command to estimate the mean and standard deviation of your weighted sample. Percentile information, including the median, is not readily calculable. The syntax for the **mean** command is the following:

svy: mean *varname*

To obtain the standard deviation of the weighted, you would then enter Stata's post-estimation command **estat sd**. Note that this command does not specify any variable name. Post-estimation commands must follow an analysis command and refer to the last variable analyzed.

svy: mean *varname*

estat sd

Example 4.2.3—Produce descriptive statistics of a feeling thermometer of George W. Bush with sampling correction (**ANES2008A.dta** file).

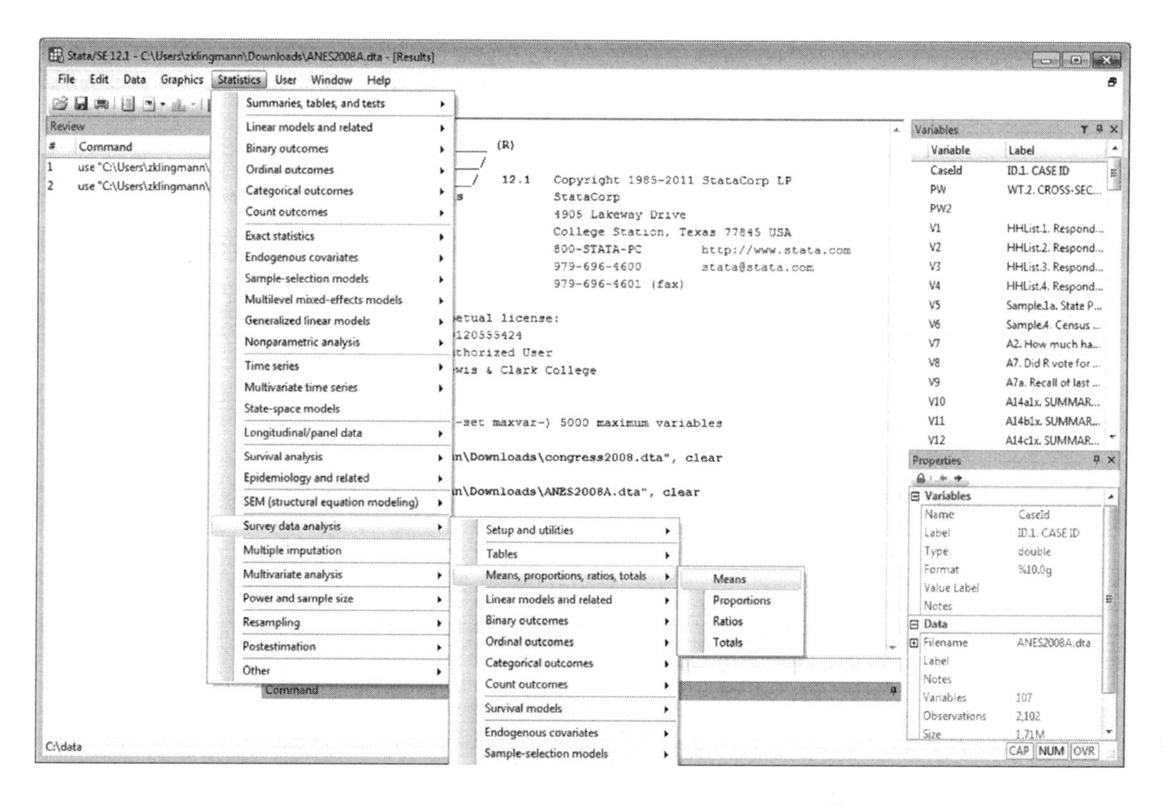

To use the GUI interface to produce tables of means of survey data, click on the "Statistics" menu and move your cursor to "Survey data analysis." Choose "Means, proportions, ratios, totals" and then finally "Means."

svy: mean - Estimate means for survey data
Model | if/in/over | Weights | SE/Cluster | Reporting
Variables:
V15
Direct standardization
Standard strata variable: Standard weight variable:
Do not rescale the standard weight variable
OK Cancel Submit

```
. svy: mean V15
(running mean on estimation sample)

Survey: Mean estimation

Number of strata =         1          Number of obs     =     2091
Number of PSUs   =      2091          Population size   =  2096.41
                                      Design df         =     2090

--------------------------------------------------------------
             |             Linearized
             |       Mean   Std. Err.     [95% Conf. Interval]
-------------+------------------------------------------------
         V15 |   40.61255    .827935      38.98888    42.23621
--------------------------------------------------------------

. estat sd

-------------------------------------
             |       Mean   Std. Dev.
-------------+-----------------------
         V15 |   40.61255    30.1633
-------------------------------------
```

It is often useful to compute means and other statistics of one variable for each category of a second variable. Make sure that you do not have too many categories in the second variable. The **table** command will produce such a display table of summary statistics. You will again use the following general syntax:

table *byvariable*, contents(*stat varname*)

Here, *byvariable* denotes the variable for which you will produce summary statistics for each of its unique categories. In parentheses following the option "contents," you can enter any of the following statistics options, followed by your variable of interest. You can select up to five statistics, separating your request by space marks within the parentheses. Note that standard deviation is only calculable by this command in an unweighted sample.

Stat Option	Description
mean	Mean
count	Count of non-missing observations
sum	Sum
freq	Frequency
max	Maximum
min	Minimum
Iqr	Interquartile range
sd*	Standard deviation
p1	1st percentile
p5	5th percentile
p10	10th percentile
p25	25th percentile
median	Median (same as p50)
p50	50th percentile (same as median)
p75	75th percentile
p90	90th percentile
p95	95th percentile
p99	99th percentile

*The standard deviation is not allowed when sampling weights are specified.

Example 4.2.4—Produce the mean, median, standard deviation, and range for the ACU scores given to Democratic (*party08* = 1) and Republican (*party08* = 2) members of the U.S. House who ran for reelection in 2008 (*acu08*) and for all elected members in 2009 (*acu09*). Use the **congress2008.dta** file.

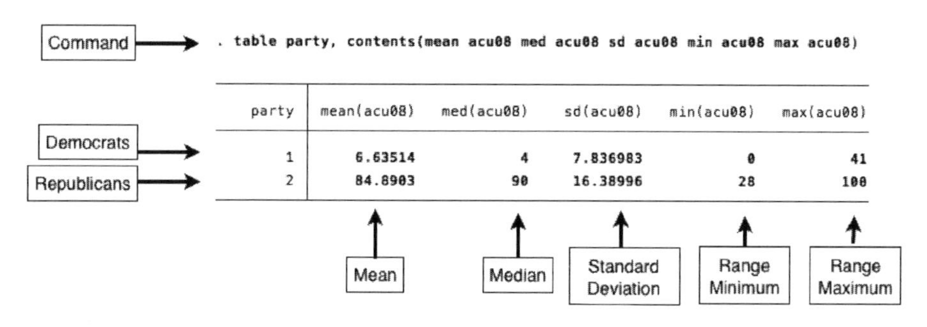

table party, contents(mean acu08 med acu08 sd acu08 min acu08 max acu08)

Repeat this command for the 2009 elected members:

table party, contents(mean acu09 med acu09 sd acu09 min acu09 max acu09)

To use the GUI interface to produce tables of summary statistics, click on the "Statistics" pull-down menu; then move your cursor to "Summaries, tables, and tests," "Tables," and, finally, "Table of summary statistics (table)."

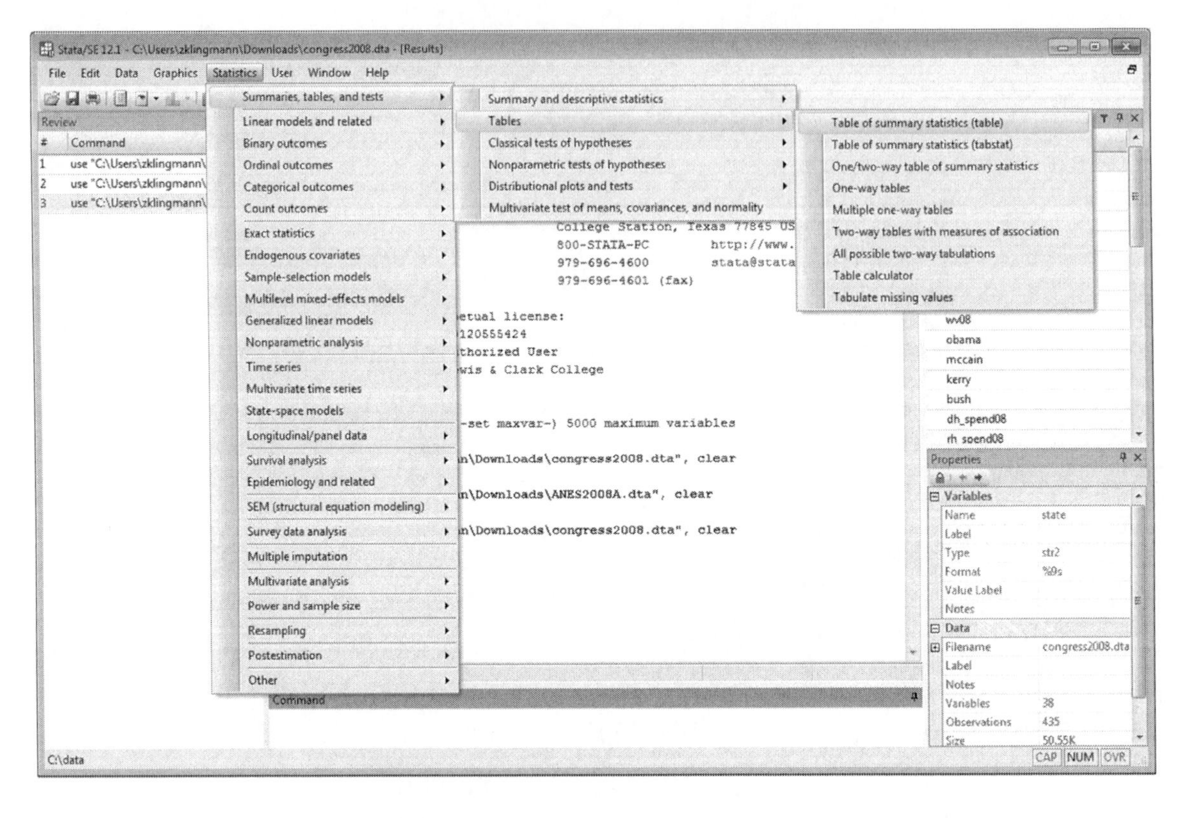

The following will appear:

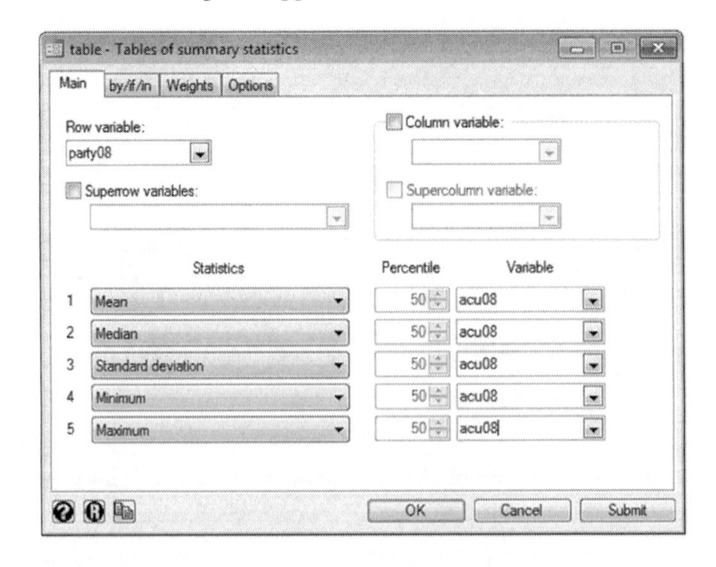

In the "Row variable" field, enter the variable for which you want to produce summary statistics by its unique categories. Under "Statistics," use the pull-down menus to select your statistics of interest. Enter the variable for which these statistics will be produced in the corresponding "Variable" field.

> **Exercise:**
>
> Compare the statistics for Democrats and Republicans and all members for either 2008 or 2009. Compare the statistics between 2008 and 2009. Remember, however, that *acu08* scores only exist for those who ran for reelection, so the number of cases is different. What might that tell you about the new members of Congress?

Note that the same information could have been produced by using the **summary** command in conjunction with the **bysort** prefix (e.g., **bysort V1: sum acu08 acu09, detail**). The **table** command, however, has the advantage of letting you precisely specify what statistics you are interested in and then displaying them neatly in a single table.

Example 4.2.5—Compute means of feeling thermometer scores for Sarah Palin (**ANES2008A.dta** variable *V72*) by gender (*V1*) with sampling weights. The **table** command is incompatible with the **svy** prefix but allows for sampling weights to be entered manually. The following syntax illustrates how to enter your weights:

table *byvariable* [pweight=*weight*], contents(*stat varname*)

For this example, employ the variable *PW2* as your weight variable:

table V1 [pweight=PW2], contents(mean V72)

```
. table V1 [pweight=PW2], contents(mean V72)
```

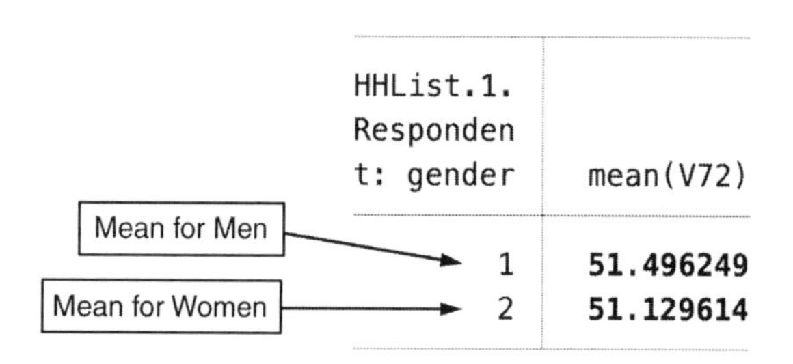

HHList.1. Responden t: gender	mean(V72)
1	51.496249
2	51.129614

Weights can be manually entered using the GUI by clicking on the "Weights" tab of the table pop-up window. Select the marker to indicate "Sampling weights" and enter the variable *PW2* as shown:

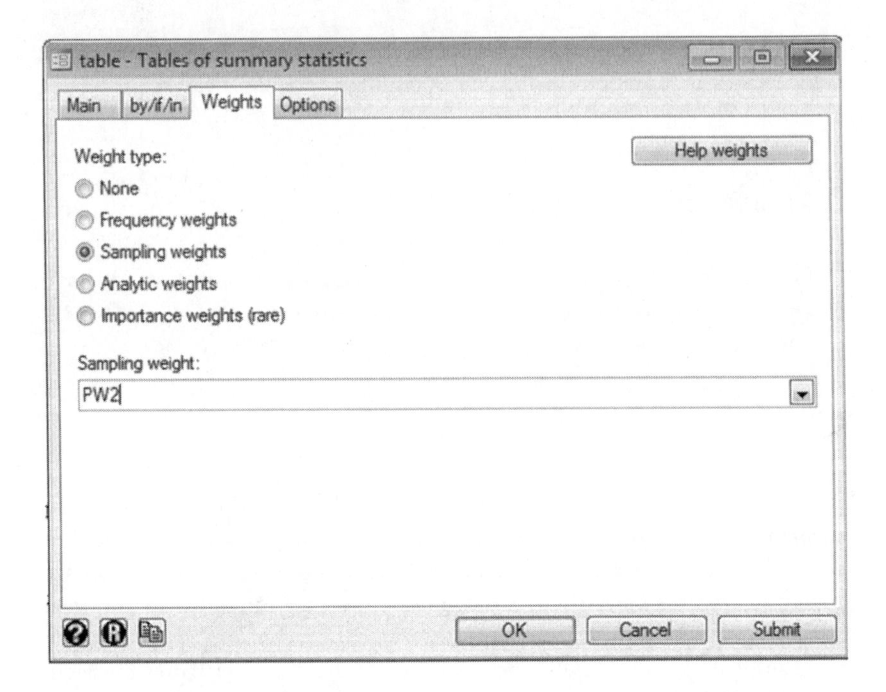

Sample Exercises 4.2

ANES2012A

For each exercise, weight the sample by *PW2012*.

1. Compute and interpret the means and standard deviations of the feeling thermometer rating for former president George W. Bush (*V15*).
2. Do the same for feeling thermometer ratings of President Obama (*V16*) and former governor W. Mitt Romney (*V17*). Discuss the differences and similarities among the three.
3. Compute and interpret the means and standard deviations of the feeling thermometer rating for former president George W. Bush (*V15*) for men and women separately (*V1*).
4. Do the same for feeling thermometer ratings of President Obama (*V16*) and former governor W. Mitt Romney (*V17*). Discuss the differences and similarities among the three.

Congress 2008–2012

1. Provide detailed summary statistics for the percentage of black residents in a district for any year (*black08* or *black10* or *black12*).

2. Using the percentage of black residents in a district for any year (*black08* or *black10* or *black12*), compute and interpret the means and standard deviations for districts won by Democrats and districts won by Republicans (use the matching *party08* or *party10* or *party12*).
3. Provide detailed summary statistics for district per capita income (*pci08* or *pci10* or *pci12*).
4. Compute and interpret the difference between means and standard deviations of per capita income for districts won by Democrats and districts won by Republicans (use the matching *party08* or *party10* or *party12*).

EURO69

For each exercise, weight the sample by *W27*. If analyzing only one country or comparing just two countries against each other, use *W1*.

1. Compute and interpret the mean and standard deviation of the intention to vote scale (*V22*).
2. Compute and interpret the means and standard deviations of the intention to vote scale (*V22*) for men and women (*V27*).
3. Do the same for each of the three categories of your computed variable EUvoice (first created in problem 2 in "EURO69" in "Sample Exercises 3.2" [Chapter 3, this volume]). On mean average, which EUvoice group is most/least likely to intend to vote?

CCES2012

For each exercise, weight the sample by WEIGHT.

1. Produce means and standard deviations for the percentage allocation for budget deficits (*V60*). Reproduce these statistics for those who voted for Obama, Romney, and any other candidate. Discuss the differences.
2. Do the same for (*V60*) the three unique values of *proximity2* (created in problem 1 in "CCES2012" in "Sample Exercises 3.3" [Chapter 3, this volume]). Discuss the differences and compare your findings to the previous problem.

Note that in both, we are comparing *profiles* of Obama and Romney supporters/proximates. The *causal order* (are you more likely to vote for a candidate based on how you feel about budget deficits or for the candidate you are more ideologically proximate to?) is ambiguous.

Crossnational

1. Using the **summary** command, does compulsory voting seem to increase voting turnout for parliament and, separately, for president? Use the voting age population figures for each.
2. We know that voting turnout in the United States is higher during presidential election years than non-presidential years, leading to the conclusion that presidential elections are viewed as more salient and exciting. As an indirect follow-up test to this hypothesis, is turnout for parliamentary elections, on mean average, higher in countries with a president than those without? Use your previously recoded variable *presidential* (created in problem 1 in "Crossnational" in "Sample Exercises 3.1" [Chapter 3, this volume]).

4.3 COMPARISON OF MEANS TESTS

To perform a comparison of means test, use Stata's **ttest** command. This will allow you to (1) determine if the mean of a certain variable is significantly different from a hypothesized population mean; (2) compare the mean values on two different variables within a data set in order to determine if they are significantly different from each other; or (3) compare and test for significance the difference on one variable for two different groups within a sample. For more information on comparison of means testing, see Chapters 5–7 in in *Understanding Political Science Statistics: Observations and Expectations in Political Analysis.*

Form 1: One Sample, One Variable Tested against a Hypothesized Population Value

ttest *varname=test value*

Example 4.3.1—To test whether the mean support for House Democrats (*dhv08*) was significantly different from 50% in 2008 (use **Congress2008.dta**).

ttest dhv08 = 50

Note: The output will likely show both significant and insignificant hypotheses tests. If the hypothesis Ha: mean(diff) > 0 is significant, it will necessarily mean that the hypothesis Ha: mean(diff) < 0 is insignificant. Be sure to interpret the p-value that correctly corresponds to your alternative hypothesis.

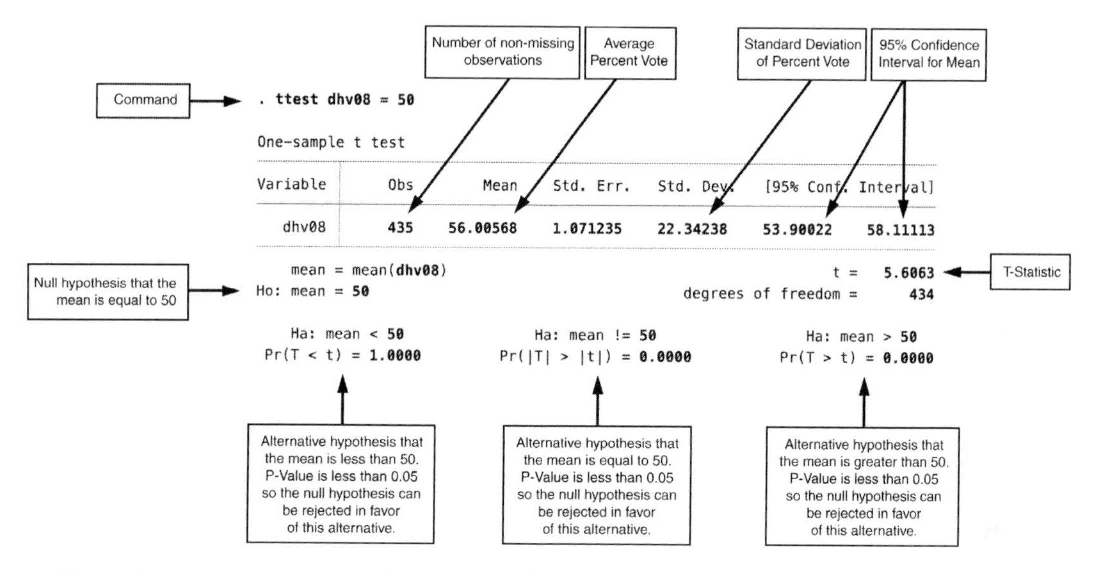

To produce this output using the GUI interface, click on "Statistics" and move your cursor to "Summaries, tables, and tests" and then "Classical tests of hypotheses." From there, you will select "One-sample mean-comparison test."

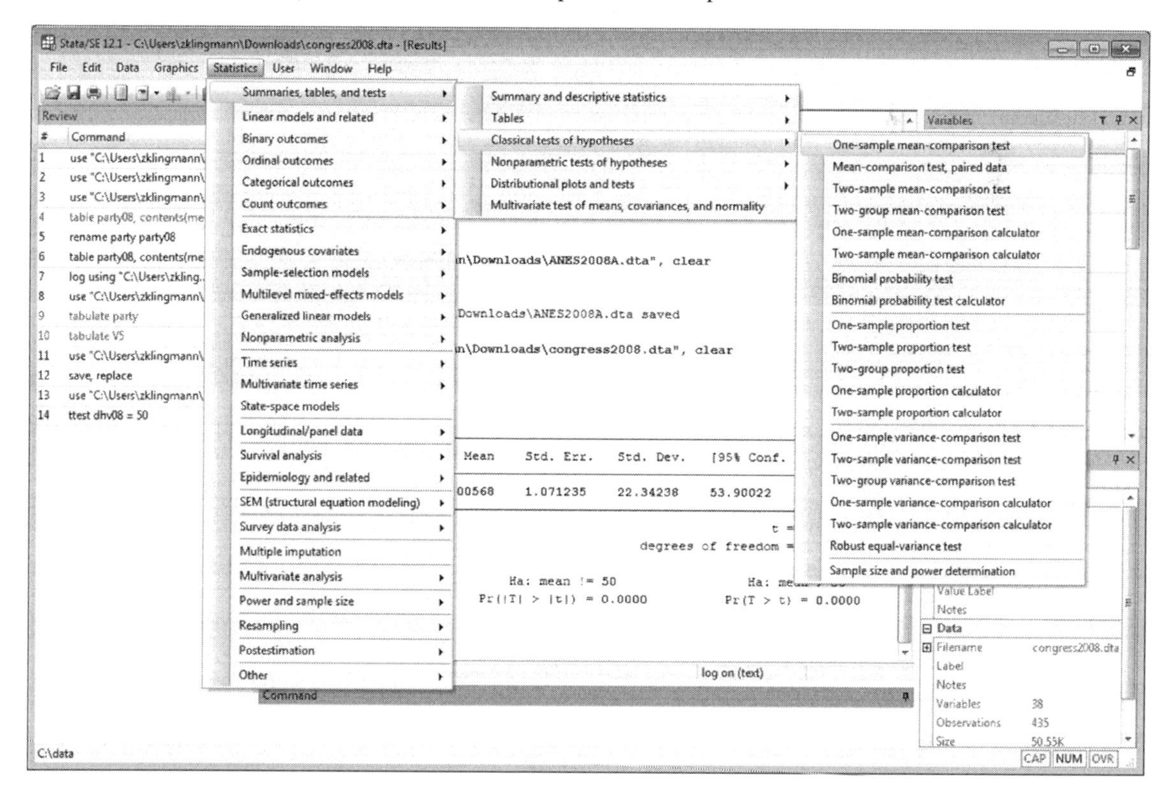

The following dialogue box will appear:

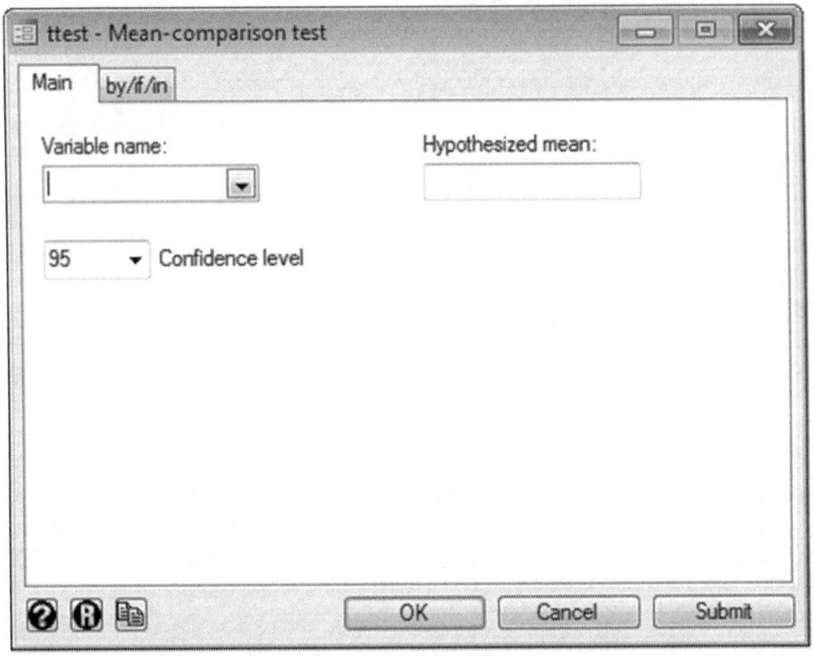

Enter the variable name and the hypothesized mean for which you will conduct the t-test. Once you click "OK," the above output should be produced.

Conducting a t-test with weighted survey data is a two-step process because the **ttest** command is not compatible with the **svy** prefix. To conduct a t-test, first calculate your variables weighted mean.

svy: mean *varlist*

After that command has been executed successfully, follow it with the **test** command. Note that you can test whether or not the mean of the variable is equal to any value (a two-sided test) or whether the mean of the variable is greater than any value (a one-sided test). The following syntax is for the two-sided test:

test *varname=value*

Example 4.3.2—To test whether the mean support for Sarah Palin is significantly different from 50 (neutral) with sampling bias correction (**ANES2008A.dta** file).

svy: mean V72

test V72=50

This second command will produce the necessary statistics by which to judge whether or not variable *V72* is significantly different than the value of 50 in the weighted sample. The annotated output of these two commands appears below.

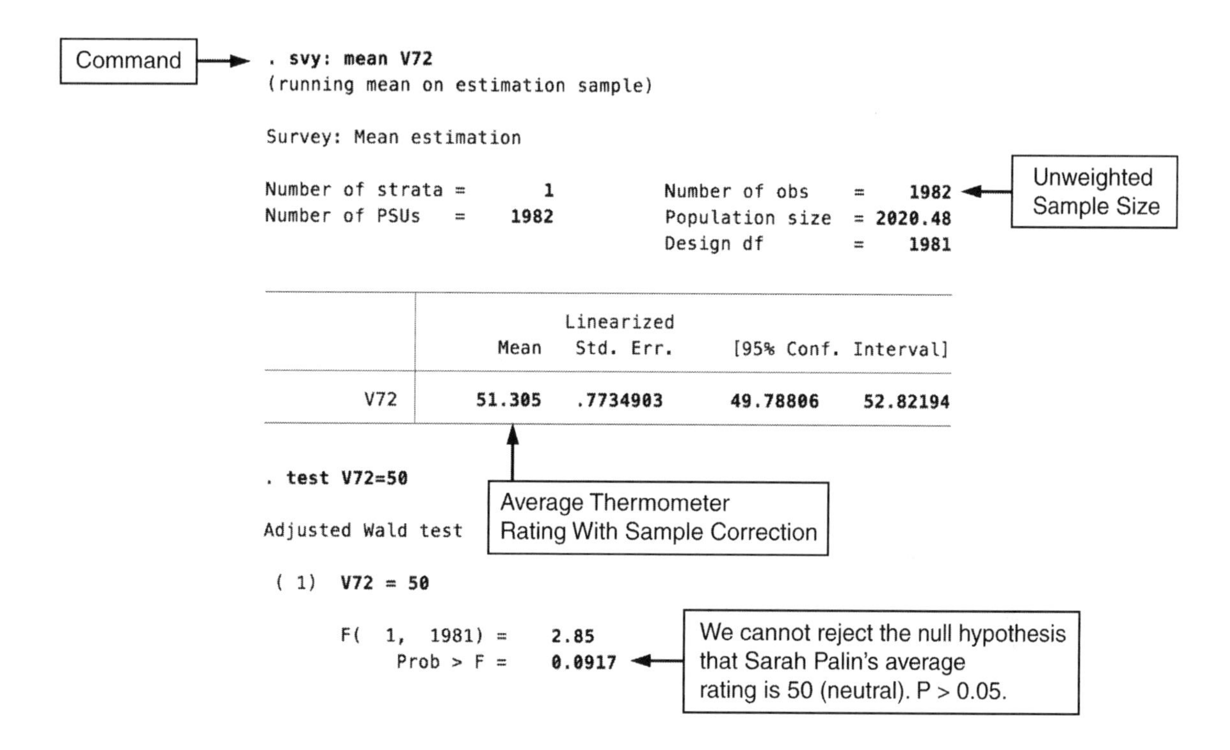
Command
Unweighted Sample Size
Average Thermometer Rating With Sample Correction
We cannot reject the null hypothesis that Sarah Palin's average rating is 50 (neutral). P > 0.05.

```
. svy: mean V72
(running mean on estimation sample)

Survey: Mean estimation

Number of strata =         1          Number of obs     =      1982
Number of PSUs   =      1982          Population size   =   2020.48
                                      Design df         =      1981

--------------------------------------------------------------
             |             Linearized
             |       Mean   Std. Err.     [95% Conf. Interval]
-------------+------------------------------------------------
         V72 |     51.305   .7734903      49.78806    52.82194
--------------------------------------------------------------

. test V72=50

Adjusted Wald test

 ( 1)  V72 = 50

       F(  1,  1981) =    2.85
            Prob > F =    0.0917
```

In the weight-corrected sample, the null hypothesis cannot be rejected. Sarah Palin's average thermometer rating cannot be statistically distinguished from the proposed population value of 50 in the corrected sample.

Note:

This test uses the unweighted sample size for its degrees of freedom. Other statistical programs may use the weighted sample size. This may produce different statistical results, though the difference should be minimal if the sample size is sufficiently large.

The **mean** command can be accessed via the pull-down menus by going to "Statistics" > "Survey data analysis" > "Means, proportions, ratios, totals" > "Means."

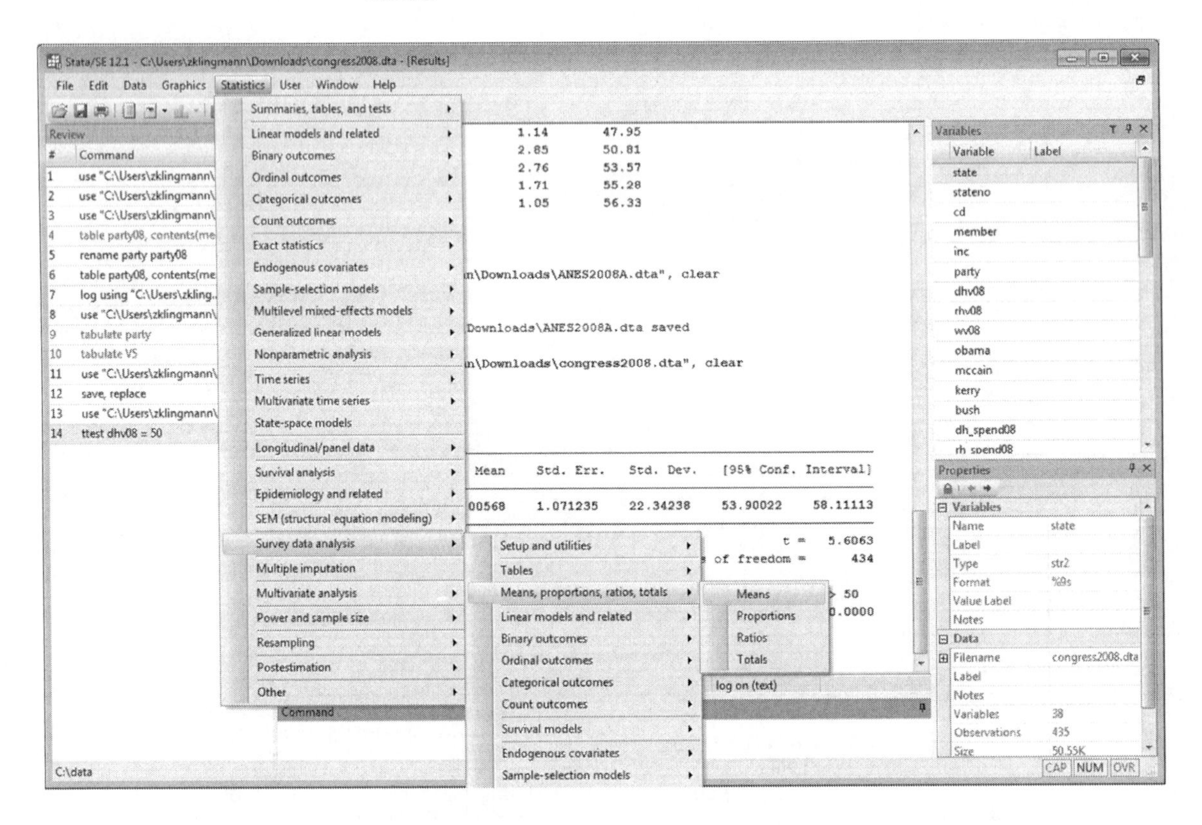

Form 2: One Sample, Two Variables (Paired Samples—"Dependent" Test)

The following syntax produces a t-test for two variables within the same sample:

ttest *varname1* = *varname2*

Example 4.3.3—To test whether the mean expenditure for Democratic House candidates (*dh_spend08*) is significantly different from the mean support for Republican House candidates (*rh_spend08*).

ttest dh_spend08=rh_spend08

It is important to note that the number of observations listed for each variable is equal. This will always be the case in a paired samples test. Observations that are missing for one variable, but not the other, are automatically dropped from the analysis.

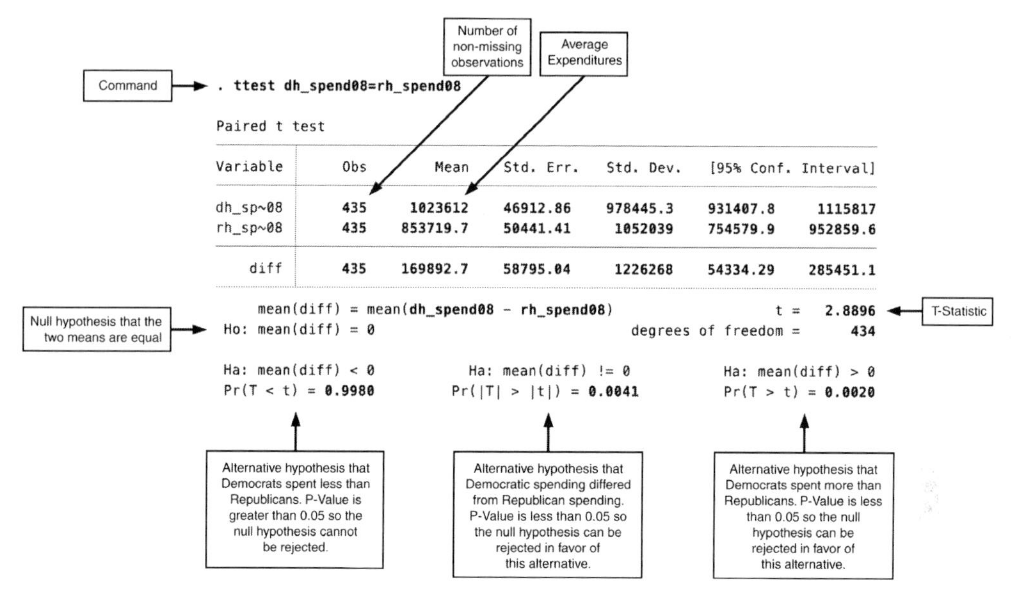

To produce this output using the GUI interface, click on "Statistics" and move your cursor to "Summaries, tables, and tests" and then "Classical tests of hypotheses." From there, you will select "Mean-comparison test, paired data."

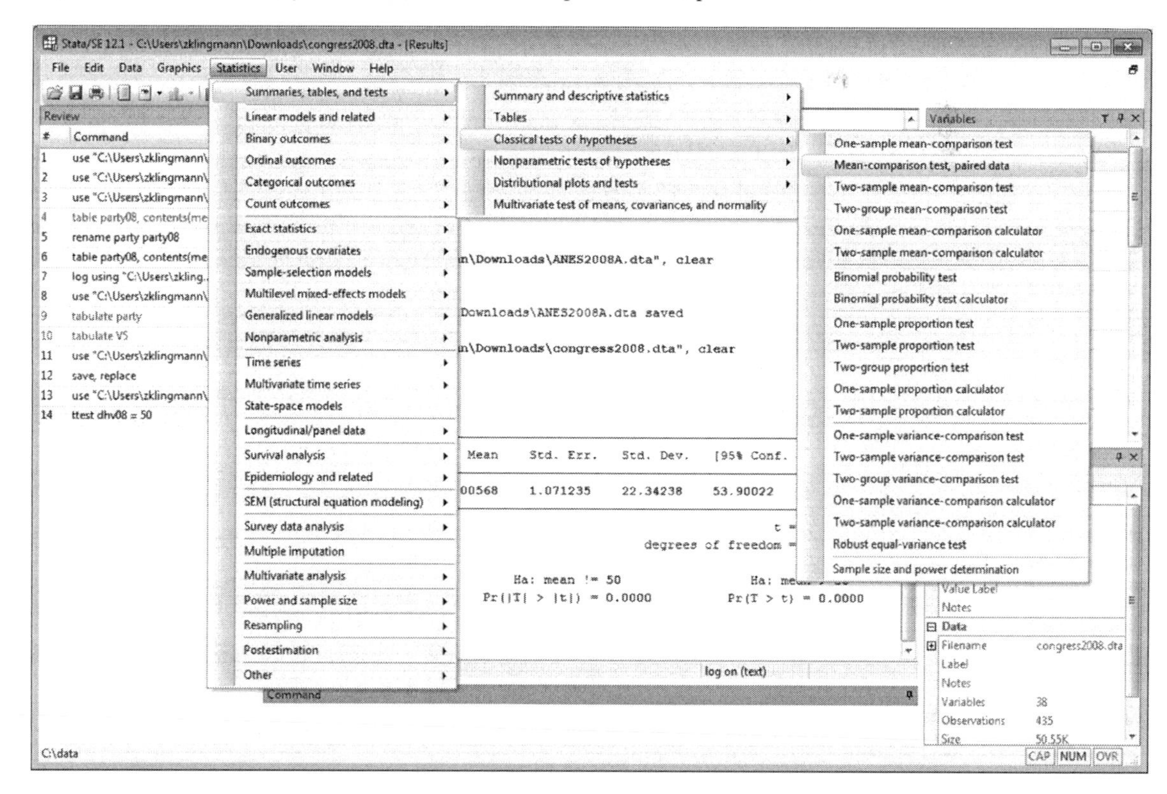

The following dialogue box will appear:

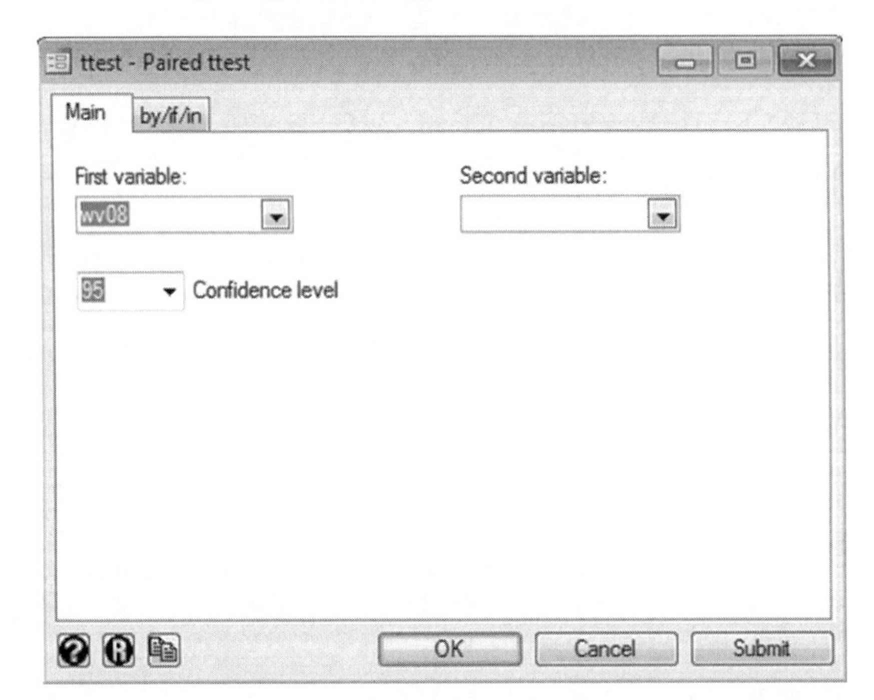

Entering the two variables (order doesn't matter) and selecting "OK" will produce the output that appears above. From this tab in the dialogue box, you can also easily modify the confidence interval (default is 95%).

Example 4.3.4—To test whether the mean support for Sarah Palin (*V72*) is significantly different from the mean support for Joe Biden (*V71*), correcting for sampling bias (**ANES2008A.dta** file). As before, this test requires two commands in order to be conducted with sampling bias correction. The following commands complete the test:

svy: mean V71 V72

test V71=V72

Caution:

A "significant difference" doesn't necessarily mean that your hypothesis is correct. What if you hypothesized that the mean thermometer rating for Palin was greater than Biden's? Or, for the first example, what if you hypothesized that, for the entire sample, it was less than 50? The differences are significant, but in our examples they are in the wrong direction. The same "directional" rule for hypotheses will apply in our last statistic to be used—regression.

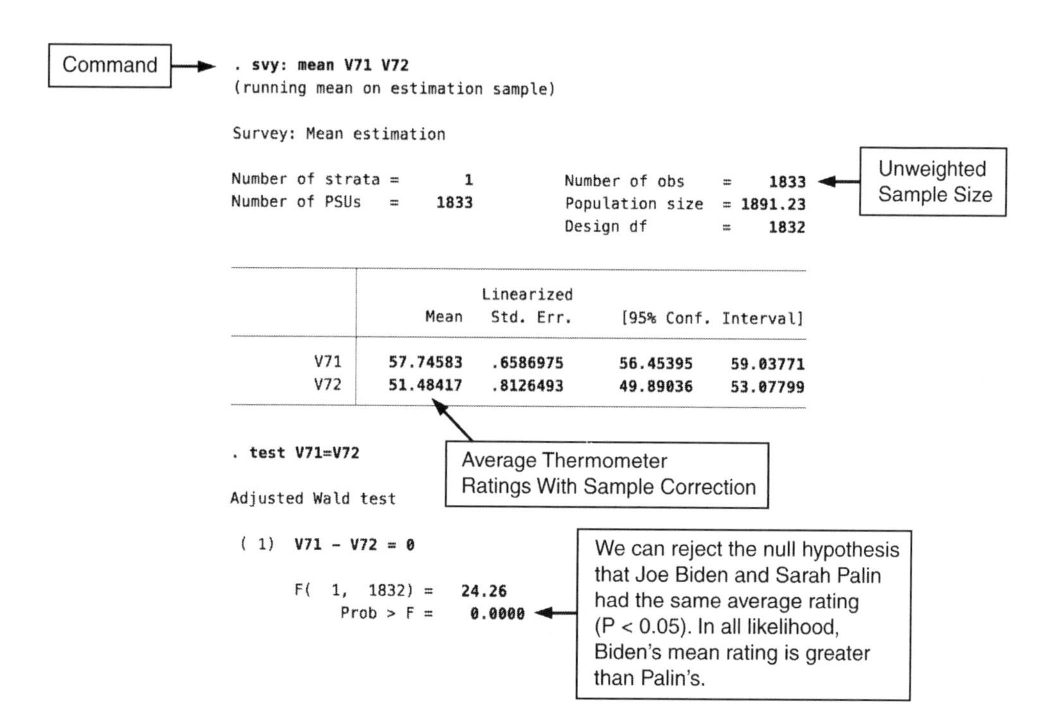

Form 3: One Variable, Two Different Subsamples ("Independent Samples Test")

There may be cause for you to test whether one variable has different means contingent on the value of a second variable. Such a test is also possible with the **ttest** command with the following syntax:

ttest *varname1*, by(*varname2*)

Example 4.3.5—To test whether the mean support for the winning candidate (*wv08*) is significantly different for Democrats and Republicans (categories 1 and 2 on *party*, respectively) correcting for sampling bias (**congress2008.dta** file).

ttest wv08, by(party)

Note: The second variable must only take on two unique values. In this case, the variable *party08* only takes on two values, so no additional manipulations are necessary. However, suppose the variable party took on three values, 1 through 3, with 3 representing a third-party winning candidate. Here, you would need to do one of two things to execute a t-test for mean differences between only Republicans and Democrats. First, you could add an "if" statement to your command, explicitly limiting what values of the variable you are or are not interested in (e.g., **ttest wv08 if**

party08!=3, by(party08)). Alternatively, you could recode the party variable to be missing if it took on the value of 3.

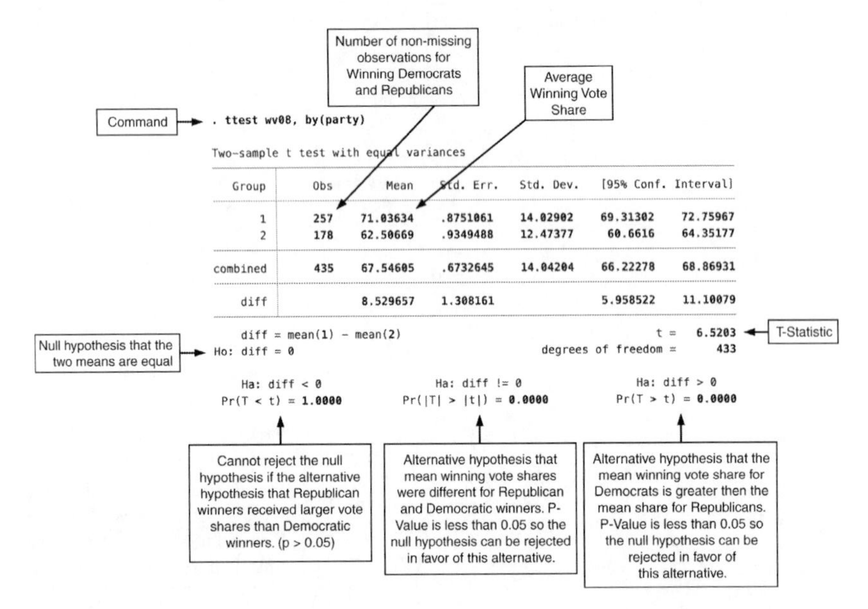

To produce this output using the GUI interface, once again click on "Statistics" and move your cursor to "Summaries, tables, and tests" and then "Classical tests of hypotheses." From there, you will select "Mean-comparison test, paired data." After filling in your variables in the "Main" tab, switch to the "by/if/in" tab. Check the box that allows you to "Repeat command by groups" and enter the variable of interest in the "Variables that define groups" field.

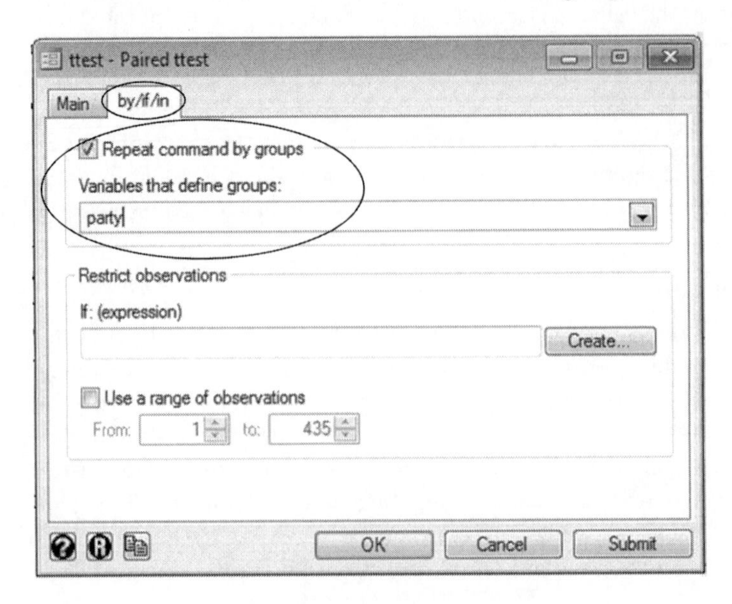

Example 4.3.6—To test whether the mean support for Joe Biden (*V71*) is significantly different between men and women (categories 1 and 2 on *V1*, respectively) correcting for sampling bias (**ANES2008A.dta** file). To achieve this test with sample correction, again employ the **mean** command followed by the **test** command:

svy: mean V71, over(V1)

test [V71]1=[V71]2

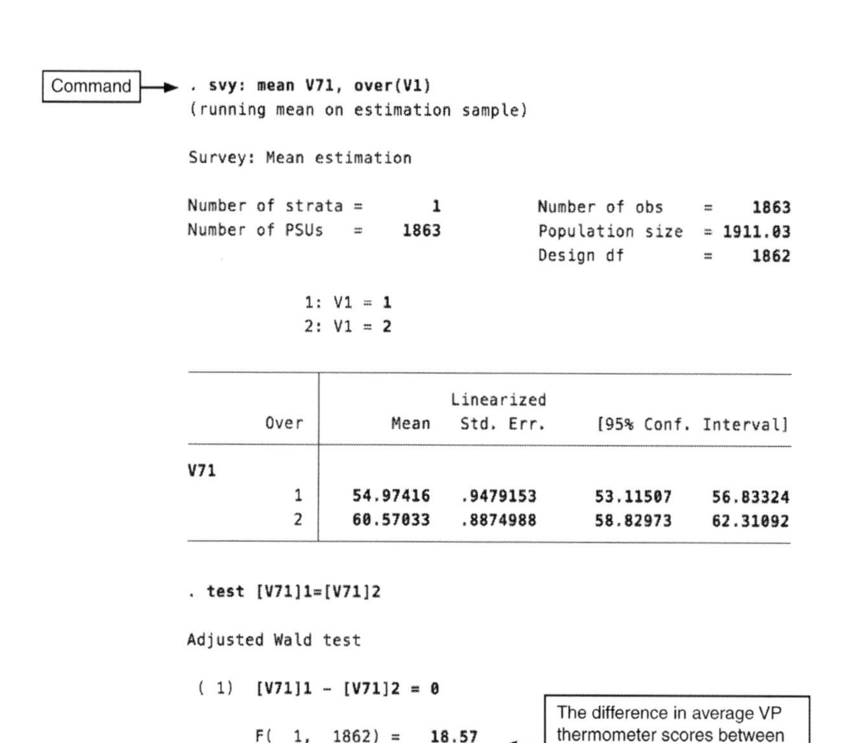

```
. svy: mean V71, over(V1)
(running mean on estimation sample)

Survey: Mean estimation

Number of strata =       1          Number of obs    =     1863
Number of PSUs   =    1863          Population size  =  1911.03
                                    Design df        =     1862

            1: V1 = 1
            2: V1 = 2

--------------------------------------------------------------
             |             Linearized
        Over |       Mean   Std. Err.     [95% Conf. Interval]
-------------+------------------------------------------------
V71          |
           1 |   54.97416    .9479153      53.11507    56.83324
           2 |   60.57033    .8874988      58.82973    62.31092
--------------------------------------------------------------

. test [V71]1=[V71]2

Adjusted Wald test

 ( 1)  [V71]1 - [V71]2 = 0

       F(  1,  1862) =   18.57
            Prob > F =    0.0000
```


Sample Exercises 4.3

ANES2012A

For each exercise weight the sample by *PW2012*.

1. Using the feeling thermometer rating for former President George W. Bush (*V15*), can you confidently reject ($p < .05$) the possibility that this

sample, with a mean of 46 degrees, could have been randomly drawn from a population with a mean of 50 degrees or higher? Use Form 1 of the t-test procedure. Your answer should be "yes." Using 95% confidence interval testing procedures, what would you estimate the range of mean thermometer values to be in the population from which this sample was drawn?

2. Can you confidently reject that it is no lower than 45 degrees? Your answer should be "no." Use Form 1 of the t-test procedure to confirm this.
3. Using Form 3 of the t-test procedure, is the difference between Latinos and non-Latinos (*V3*) on *V15* significant? That is, is the difference observed in the sample large enough to confidently reject the null hypothesis of no difference in the population? Your answer should be "yes." Which group feels warmer towards George W. Bush on mean average?
4. Using Form 2 of the t-test procedure, is there a significant difference between the mean feeling thermometer rating of former President Bush (*V15*) and 2012 GOP candidate W. Mitt Romney (*V17*)? Your answer should be "yes."

EURO69

For each exercise weight the sample by *W27*. If analyzing only one country or comparing just two countries against each other, use *W1*.

1. Using the 10-point perception of global warming scale (*V24*), can you confidently reject ($p < .05$) the possibility that this sample, with a mean of 8.21, could have been randomly drawn from a population with a mean of 5.5 degrees (middle of the scale) or lower? Use Form 1 of the t-test procedure. Your answer should be "yes." Using 95% confidence interval testing procedures, what would you estimate the range of mean perceptions to be in the population from which this sample was drawn?
2. Can you confidently reject that it is no lower than 8.1? Your answer should be "yes." Use Form 1 of the t-test procedure to confirm this. Why is such a small difference statistically significant?
3. For the following, you will compare only those who felt both their countries and their own voice counted in the eu (euvoice=2) with those who felt it counted in neither (EU=4). Using Form 3 of the t-test procedure, is the difference between those two groups' mean intention to vote (*V22*) significantly different? That is, is the difference observed in the sample large enough to confidently reject the null hypothesis of no difference in the population?
4. Using Form 3 of the t-test procedure, is the difference between males and females (*V27*) on *V22* significant? That is, is the difference observed in the sample large enough to confidently reject the null hypothesis of no difference in the population?

CCES2012

For each exercise weight the sample by WEIGHT.

1. Using the percentage allocation for budget deficits (*V60*), can you confidently reject ($p < .05$) the possibility that this sample could have been randomly drawn from a population with a mean value equal to a 50/50 allocation split between tax increases and cuts? Use Form 1 of the t-test procedure. Your answer should be "yes." Using 95% confidence interval testing procedures, what would you estimate the range of mean allocation values to be in the population from which this sample was drawn?
2. Repeat step 1, but this time change your population estimate to 58% cuts. Can you still reject this null hypothesis? Your answer should still be "yes." Explain your findings. Why can such a small difference between what we observe in the sample and our population expectation be statistically significant?

4.4 CROSSTABULATIONS

Crosstabulations, also known as contingency tables or crosstabs, display the cross-classification frequencies of two or more variables. For more information on crosstabulations, see Chapters 9 and 10 in *Understanding Political Science Statistics: Observations and Expectations in Political Analysis*. Stata will allow you to produce crosstabulations that also provide multiple measures of association and significance. The **tabulate** command will produce crosstabulations when multiple variables are listed.

The basic syntax for the **tabulate** command to produce a two-way table is as follows:

tabulate *varname1 varname2*, {options}

Following convention, we will list the dependent variable as the first variable in all examples.

Example 4.4.1—Crosstabulate gender with the party of one's House vote without correcting for sampling bias in the **ANES2008A.dta** data set (sampling weights will be employed in a later example).

tabulate V68 V1

By default, the table produced will contain frequencies that count the number of respondents who fall into each cross-classification. The "Total" figures are often referred to as "marginals." In this instance, those in the right-most column reflect the total number of those who voted Democratic (category 1) = 755 and Republican (category 2) = 467. Those in the bottom row are the total number of males (1 = 500) and females (2 = 722). The bottom right corner marginal reflects the total number of respondents represented in the table: 1,222.

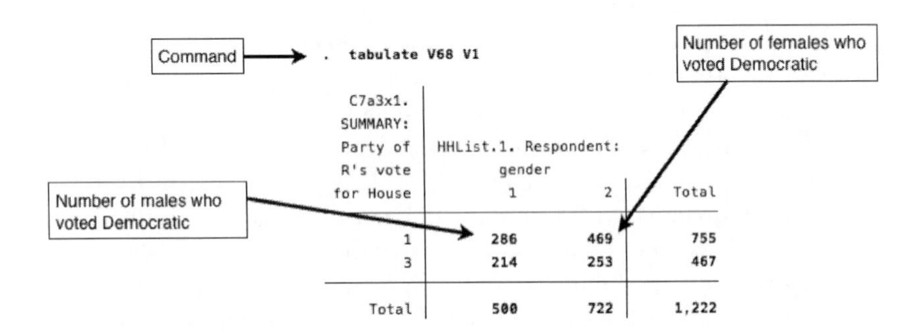

To use the GUI interface to produce frequency crosstabulations, click on the "Statistics" pull-down menu and move your cursor to "Summaries, tables, and tests" and then "Tables." Choose the option for "Two-way tables with measures of association." Enter the row and column variables, leaving all other boxes unchecked if no measures of association are desired.

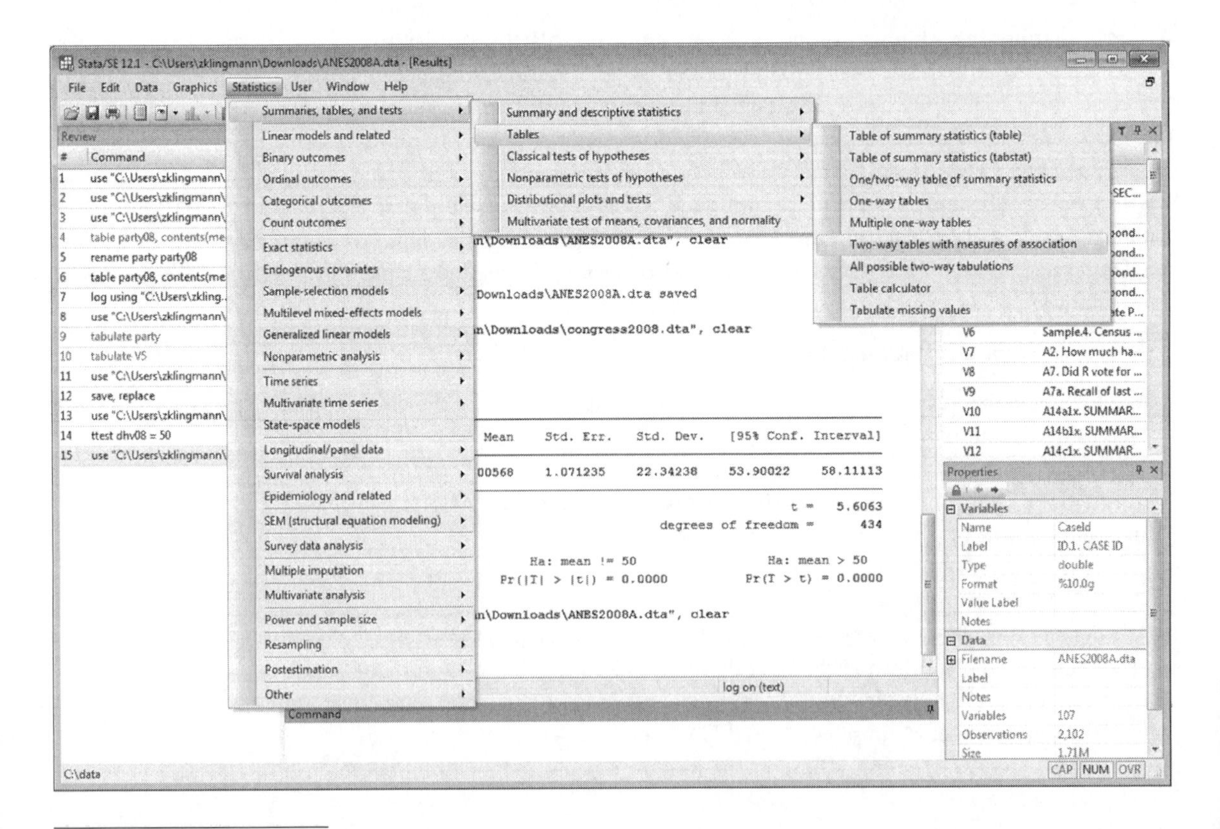

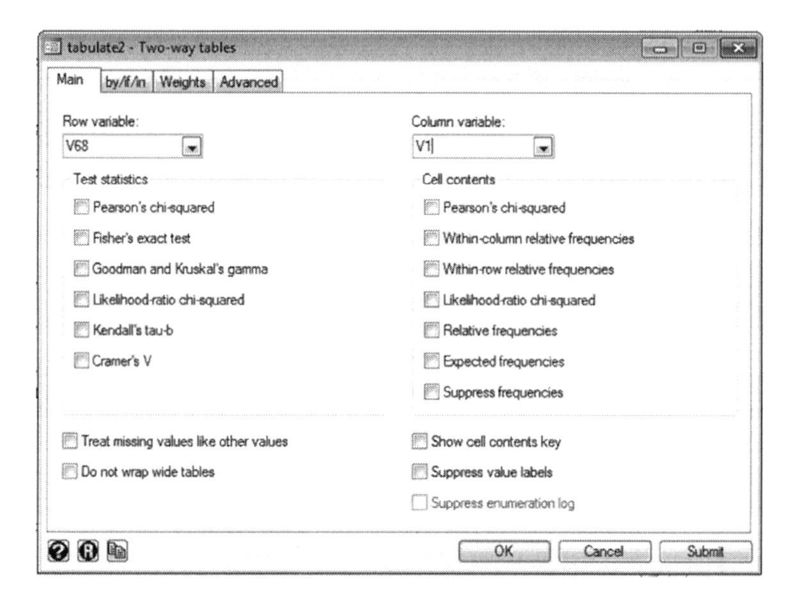

Example 4.4.2—Because the proportion of females in the sample exceeds the proportion of males (unequal or imbalanced marginals), a comparison between gender must be based not on raw counts or absolute frequencies, but on proportions or percentages. To add standardized percentages, use the **row** or **column** options in the **tabulate** command. For this example, with the independent variable on the top, defining the columns, we would specify column. That will give us the percentage of who voted Democratic both for males and for females. For example:

tabulate V68 V1, column

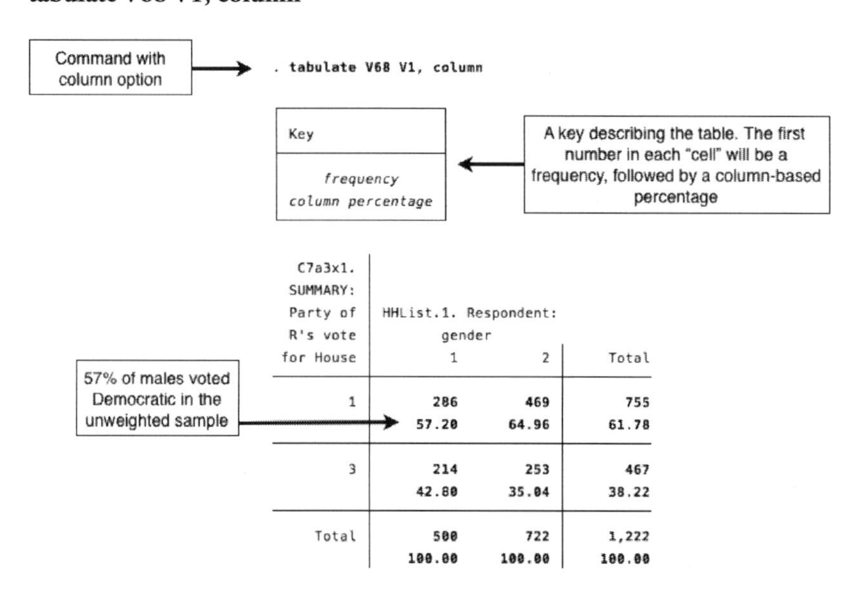


```
. tabulate V68 V1, column
```

Key
frequency *column percentage*

C7a3x1. SUMMARY: Party of R's vote for House	HHList.1. Respondent: gender 1	2	Total
1	286 57.20	469 64.96	755 61.78
3	214 42.80	253 35.04	467 38.22
Total	500 100.00	722 100.00	1,222 100.00

To use the GUI interface to produce frequency crosstabulations, click on the "Statistics" pull-down menu and move your cursor to "Summaries, tables, and tests" and then "Tables." Choose the option for "Two-way tables with measures of association." Again, enter the row and column variables, but this time, also check the box for "Within-column relative frequencies."

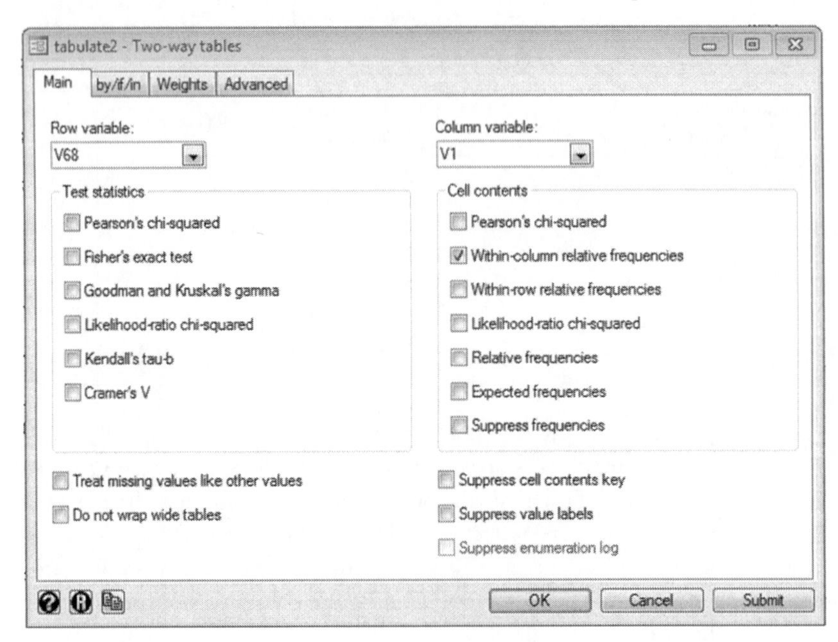

As you can see from this menu, the default is just to produce our original observed or actual frequencies. You can check boxes for any combination of percentages by row or column. You can also have the program calculate the "Expected" frequencies that are used in the calculation of the chi-square statistic. You can also run a variety of hypothesis tests. You can select the preferred test through the GUI menu by checking boxes in the main menu or by adding the following options to the end of the **tabulate** command (after a comma):

Option	Test
chi2	Pearson's chi-squared
exact[(#)]	Fisher's exact test
Gamma	Goodman and Kruskal's gamma
lrchi2	Likelihood-ratio chi-squared
Taub	Kendall's tau-b
V	Cramer's V

Note: Stata does not natively support the calculation of Goodman and Kruskal's lambda. In order to produce this statistic, you will need to download a user-contributed command. In this case, the **lambda** command can be installed from within Stata by entering the command "**ssc install lambda**." Use this command's help file for further instructions.

Example 4.4.3—Produce a chi-squared test for the relationship between gender and the party of one's House vote (again without sampling bias correction).

tabulate V68 V1, chi

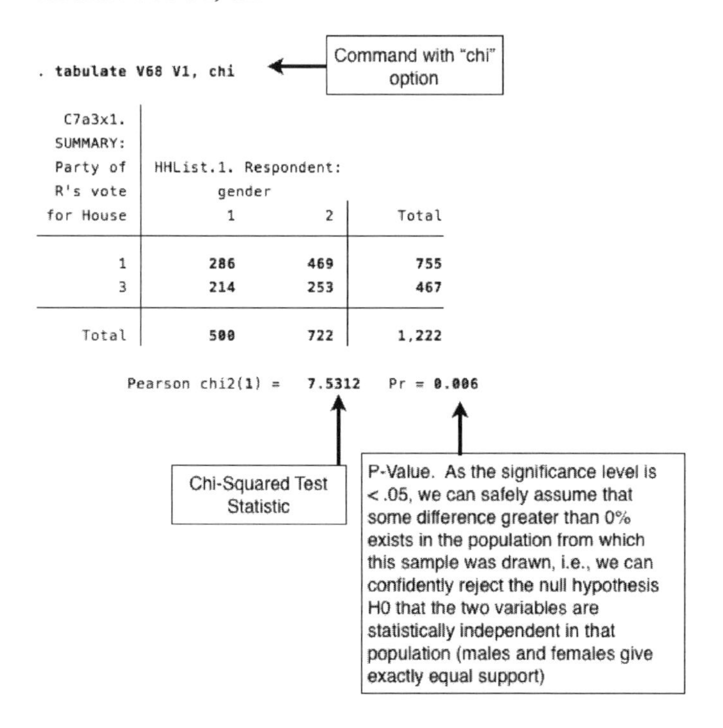

```
. tabulate V68 V1, chi
```

C7a3x1. SUMMARY: Party of R's vote for House	HHList.1. Respondent: gender 1	2	Total
1	286	469	755
3	214	253	467
Total	500	722	1,222

```
Pearson chi2(1) =   7.5312   Pr = 0.006
```


Caution:

A "significant difference" doesn't necessarily mean that your hypothesis is correct. What if you hypothesized that females were less likely to vote for Democrats than males? The chi-square statistic would still be the same, but in our example the data contradict our hypothesis. Reversing the number for males and females would produce the same result.

Like most commands, the **tabulate** command is compatible both with the **bysort**prefix and "if/in" statements. The **bysort** prefix would allow you to check to see if a third variable affected cross-classification. For example, adding **bysort V2:** to the beginning of the previous command would check for male-female differences in House voting by race. Alternatively, "if" statements could be added to the end of a command to check for gender differences only among whites (**tabulate V68 V1 if V2==1**). Either technique allows you to "control" for a third variable in order to test for a spurious relationship, explanatory connection, interaction, or specification effect and will produce a separate table for each valid value of that control variable.

Example 4.4.4—Determine whether gender differences in party House votes can be explained by one's views about the worth of the Iraq War (*V37*) using the **ANES2008A.dta** file. With two Iraq War view categories, two tables would be produced—House vote by gender for those who felt the Iraq War was worth the cost (*V37* = 1) and a separate table for those who thought it wasn't (*V37* = 2).

bysort V37: tabulate V68 V1

```
. bysort V37: tabulate V68 V1

------------------------------------------------------------------

-> V37 = 1

   C7a3x1. |
  SUMMARY: |
  Party of |  HHList.1. Respondent:
  R's vote |         gender
 for House |         1          2 |     Total
-----------+----------------------+----------
         1 |        19         33 |        52 
         2 |       105        123 |       228 
-----------+----------------------+----------
     Total |       124        156 |       280 


------------------------------------------------------------------

-> V37 = 2

   C7a3x1. |
  SUMMARY: |
  Party of |  HHList.1. Respondent:
  R's vote |         gender
 for House |         1          2 |     Total
-----------+----------------------+----------
         1 |       263        428 |       691 
         2 |       105        120 |       225 
-----------+----------------------+----------
     Total |       368        548 |       916 
```

According to these results, a gender gap does exist among respondents who felt the Iraq war was not worth the costs ($p = 0.022$), but not among those who think it was worth the costs ($p = 0.213$).

To achieve the same results using the GUI, repeat the previous instructions for producing a crosstabulation, but this time also click the tab that says "by/if/in." Check the box for "Repeat command by groups" and enter the pertinent variable, in this case *V37*.

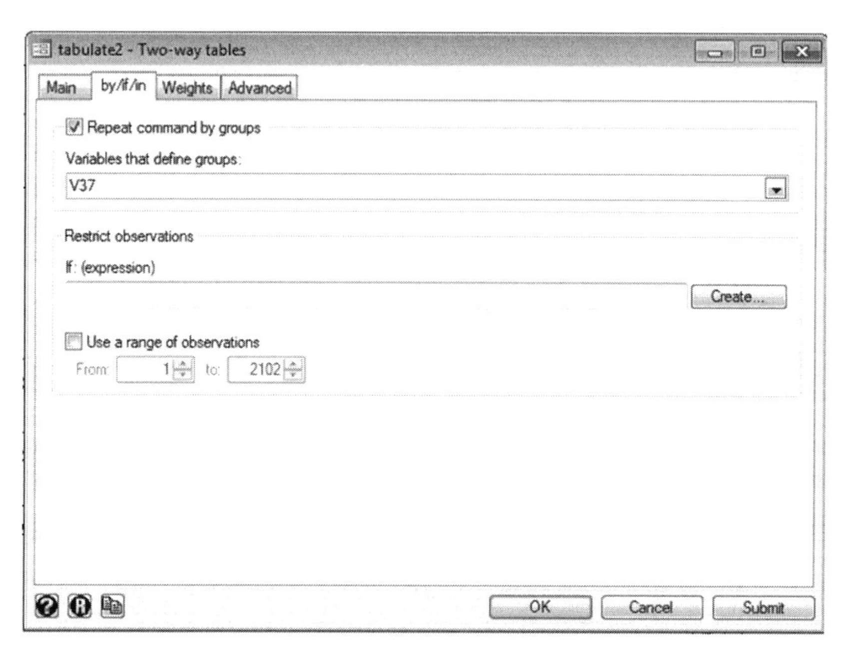

Caution:

Please make sure that if you have a control variable with many categories (e.g., age), you first recode it down into two or three categories—otherwise, you will wind up with a ridiculous number of tables. The number of separate tables produced will be equal to the number of categories of the control variable remaining after recoding. For example, if we wanted to use age (*V4*) as a control, but did not first recode it, we would have more than 70 separate tables: one for 17 year olds, one for 18 year olds, and so forth.

Example 4.4.5—Crosstabulate gender with the party of one's House vote using sampling weights (**ANES2008A.dta** file). Again, the **tabulate** command is compatible with the **svy** prefix. To obtain weighted estimates, simply begin your command with **svy:**

svy: tabulate V68 V1

The default table with sampling weights will estimate the proportion of cases that fall into each cell in the weighted sample. For example, approximately 23% of the weight-adjusted sample are males (*V1* = 1) that voted Democratic (*V68* = 1). If you prefer to obtain estimated totals, simply employ the "count" option with the **tabulate** command (**svy: tabulate V68 V1, count**).

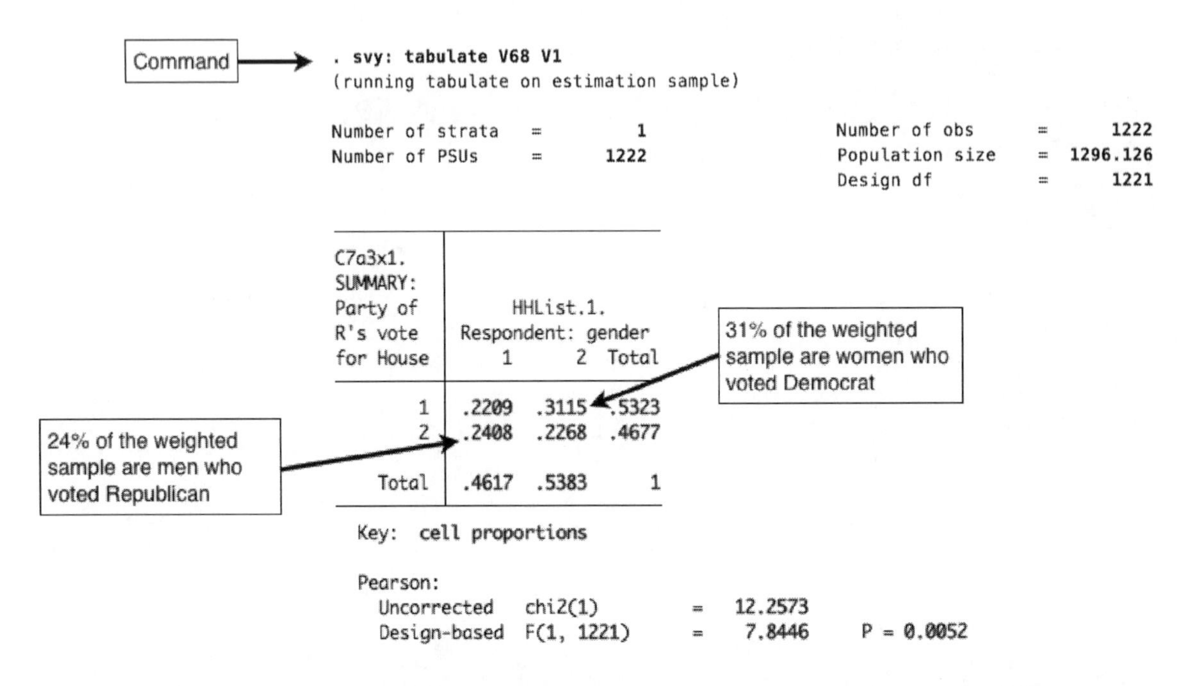
Command
31% of the weighted sample are women who voted Democrat
24% of the weighted sample are men who voted Republican

```
. svy: tabulate V68 V1
(running tabulate on estimation sample)

Number of strata   =         1          Number of obs     =       1222
Number of PSUs     =      1222          Population size   =   1296.126
                                        Design df         =       1221

-------------------------------------
C7a3x1.    |
SUMMARY:   |
Party of   |        HHList.1.
R's vote   |  Respondent: gender
for House  |      1        2  Total
-----------+-------------------------
         1 |  .2209    .3115  .5323
         2 |  .2408    .2268  .4677
           |
     Total |  .4617    .5383      1
-------------------------------------
  Key:  cell proportions

  Pearson:
    Uncorrected   chi2(1)         =   12.2573
    Design-based  F(1, 1221)      =    7.8446     P = 0.0052
```

Question:

Correcting for sampling bias, were females more likely to vote for Democratic House candidates than men?

Answer:

Yes, they were 10.1 percentage points more likely to do so (57.9–47.8).

Not all of the options available with the **tabulate** command will be available when correcting for sampling bias. Also, importantly, the option for producing the Pearson's chi-squared test statistic varies when using the **svy** prefix. To obtain this test statistic for weighted data, the correct option is "pearson," *not* "chi2."

To use the GUI interface with sampling correction, you will start with the "Statistics" pull-down menu and instead move your cursor to "Survey data analysis" and then "Tables." Choose the option for "Two-way tables." Options for measures of association are available under the "Test statistics" tab, but the Pearson's chi-squared statistic is produced by default.

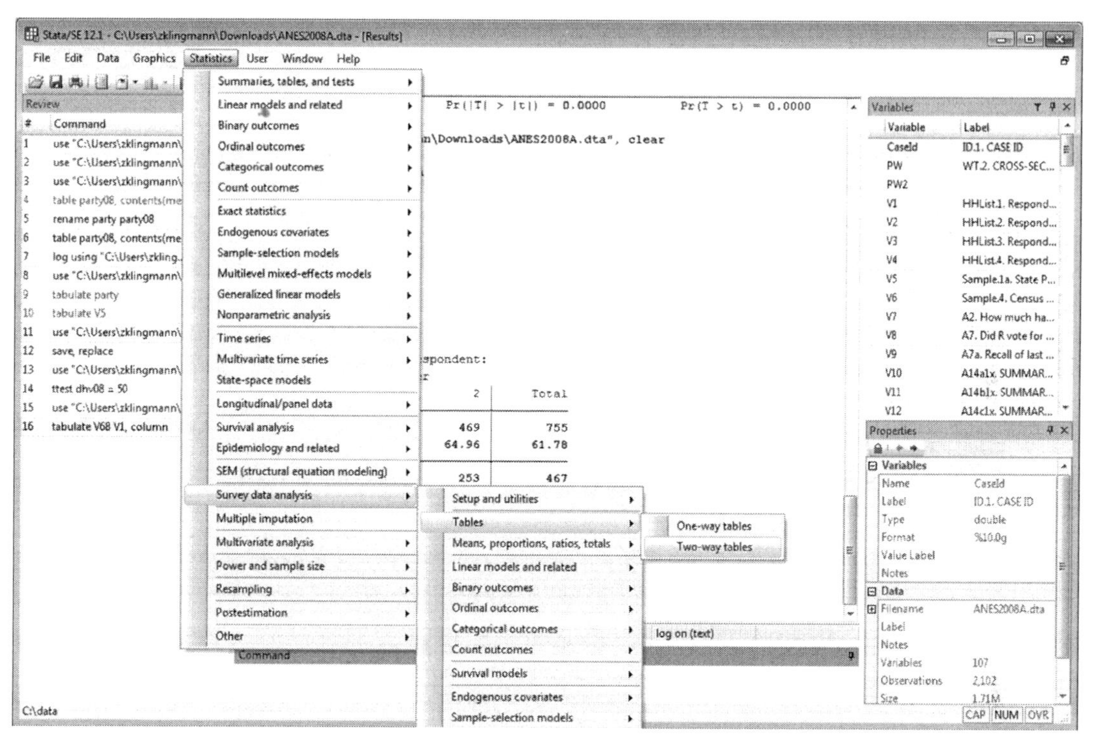

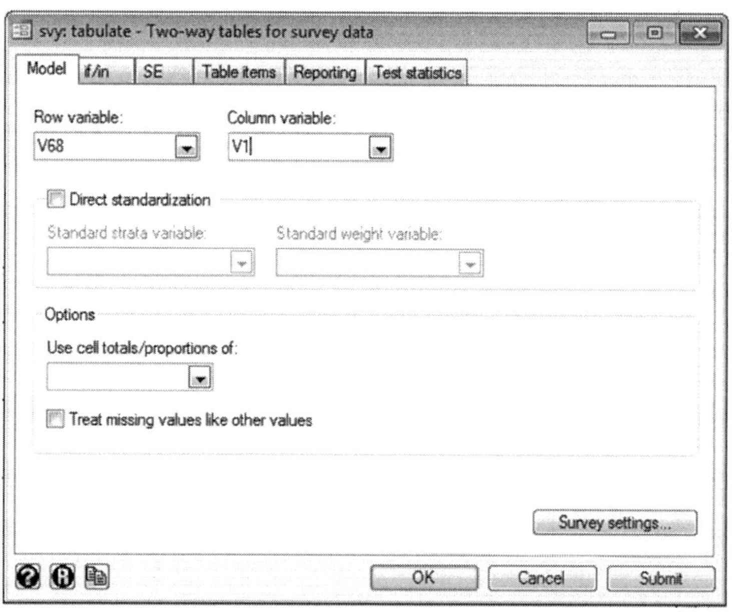

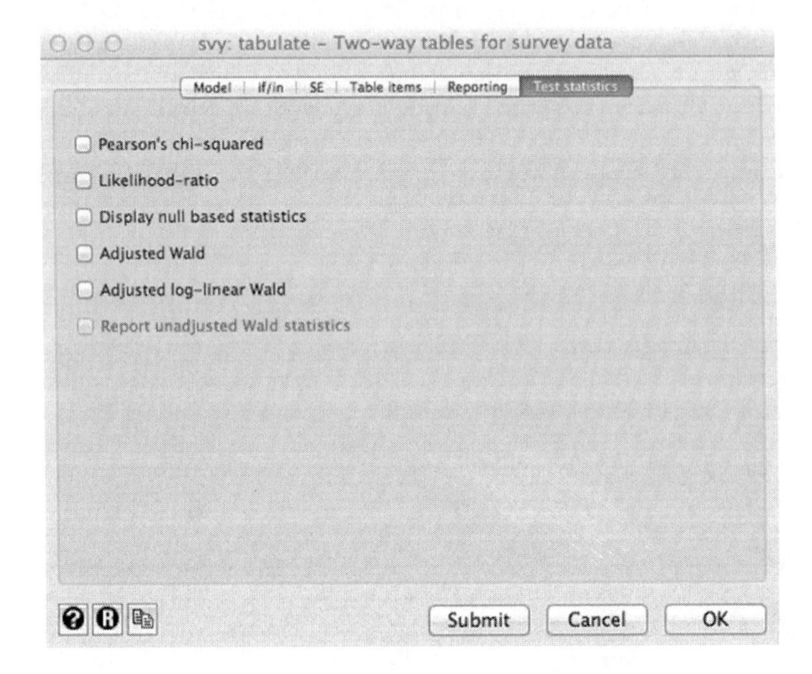

The **bysort** and **svy** prefix cannot be used at the same time. Instead, use an "if" statement to run tables by a single value of the third variable of interest and repeat for every value of that third variable. Through the GUI menu, this option can be accessed by clicking on the "if/in" tab.

Sample Exercises 4.4

ANES2012A

For each exercise, weight the sample by *PW2012*.

1. Were those who felt the election was going to be close (*V31*) more likely to vote (*V64*) than those who felt it would be won by "quite a bit"? Make sure to have the program calculate the relevant percentages (which you will then subtract), chi-square (so that you can test your observations against an expectation or null hypothesis of no difference in the population), and gamma. Interpret all figures. Note that, given the ordering of the independent and dependent variables, you should anticipate a negative gamma. Remember that because this is a two-by-two table, the "continuity correction" must be used for chi-square.
2. Repeat problem 1, but this time, make your independent variable *V32* (closeness in state). Compare your results.

3. Using a third, control variable, do either results differ much for men versus women?
4. Using a third, control variable (*V32*), how do *V31* and *V32* interact to affect turnout? Don't worry if the results seem a bit counterintuitive.
5. How does one's perception of financial status (*V20*) influence how one voted for president (*V66*)? Again, compute percentages and gamma. Does it seem that President Obama was rewarded/punished based on this financial evaluation?

Congress 2008–2012

1. For any year, using the variable on party spending you created earlier (problem 1 in "Congress 2008–2012" in "Sample Exercises 3.3" [Chapter 3, this volume]) as your independent variable (e.g., *dem08*) and the winning party (e.g., *party08*) as your dependent variable, answer the following question, using percentage differences, Cramer's V, and gamma. Note: if the statement is correct for your year, given the coding of the variables, gamma should be positive.

   Democrats were more likely to win the election if they outspent Republicans. Republicans were equally advantaged.

2. Is there any evidence that leads one to consider the previous relationship to be stronger in those districts with PCIs below the mean than above? Repeat the crosstabulation with the recoded PCI (problem 2 in "Congress 2008–2012" in "Sample Exercises 3.1" [Chapter 3, this volume]) for your year. If there is, what may be the reason?

EURO69

For each exercise, weight the sample by *W27*. If analyzing only one country or comparing just two countries against each other, use *W1*.

1. Were men or women (*V27*) more likely to feel that being in the EU meant a loss of cultural identity (*V10*)? Make sure to have the program calculate the relevant percentages (which you will then subtract), chi-square (so that you can test your observations against an expectation or null hypothesis of no difference in the population), and gamma. Interpret all figures. Remember that because this is a two-by-two table, the "continuity correction" must be used for chi-square. Again, why is such a small difference statistically significant?
2. Using your two-category Left-Right scale variable (recoded *V25* from problem 2 in "EURO69" in "Sample Exercises 3.1" [Chapter 3, this

volume]) as your independent variable and your computed *EUpolicy* variable (problem 1 in "EURO69" in "Sample Exercises 3.2" [Chapter 3, this volume]) as your dependent variable, is the following hypothesis confirmed or disconfirmed (at least for this survey)? Calculate and interpret percentage differences and interpret chi-square, Cramer's V, and gamma. Note that, given the ordering of the independent and dependent variables, you should anticipate a negative gamma.

Individuals who lean ideologically Left are less likely to support common EU policies than those who lean ideologically Right.

3. Using a third, control variable (*V27*), do either results differ much for men versus women?

CCES2012

For each exercise, weight the sample by WEIGHT.

1. Were those respondents who had served in the military or who had family members who served in the military (*V17*) more or less likely to agree (not a mistake) with U.S. intervention in Iraq (*V26*) and Afghanistan (*V27*)? Make sure to have the program calculate the relevant percentages (which you will then subtract), chi-square (so that you can test your observations against an expectation or null hypothesis of no difference in the population), lambda, and gamma. Interpret all figures. Note that, given the ordering of the independent and dependent variables, you should anticipate a negative gamma if they were more likely and a positive gamma if they were less likely.
2. Using a third, control variable, do either results differ much for men versus women?
3. Using your two-category "health insurance" variable (*V22*), were those with health insurance more likely to have excellent health and less likely to be in poor health? Can you think of another variable that might reduce the degree to which that relationship is confirmed? (Hint: Think about how some individuals automatically receive health insurance.)

Crossnational

1. Using a simple crosstabulation procedure, answer the following question:

Are countries that limit party spending (idea_lps) more likely to provide direct funding to them (idea_dpfp) than countries that do not limit spending?

Use percentage differences, gamma, and chi-square to help answer the question. The directional measures should be positive if the question is answered affirmatively.

2. Is there a difference in this relationship between countries with a unicameral and a bicameral legislature?

4.5 LINEAR REGRESSION

A regression tests for the linear relationship (direction and value) between a dependent (outcome) variable and one or more independent (potentially causal) variables. The regression equation is based on minimizing the sum of the squared differences between the observed values on the dependent variable and the values predicted by the calculated regression equation. For more information on linear regression, see Chapters 11 and 12 in *Understanding Political Science Statistics: Observations and Expectations in Political Analysis.* In Stata, the **regress** command (abbreviated to **reg** in all examples) will execute the simplest form of this statistical procedure. The syntax is as follows:

reg *dependentvariable varlist*

Example 4.5.1—To test whether there is a linear association between the proportion of individuals 65 and older (*per65*) in a district and the district's vote for Barack Obama (*obama*) using the **congress2008.dta** file.

reg obama per65

Note: This is the simplest representation of the procedure's commands. As always, check the help file for additional options.

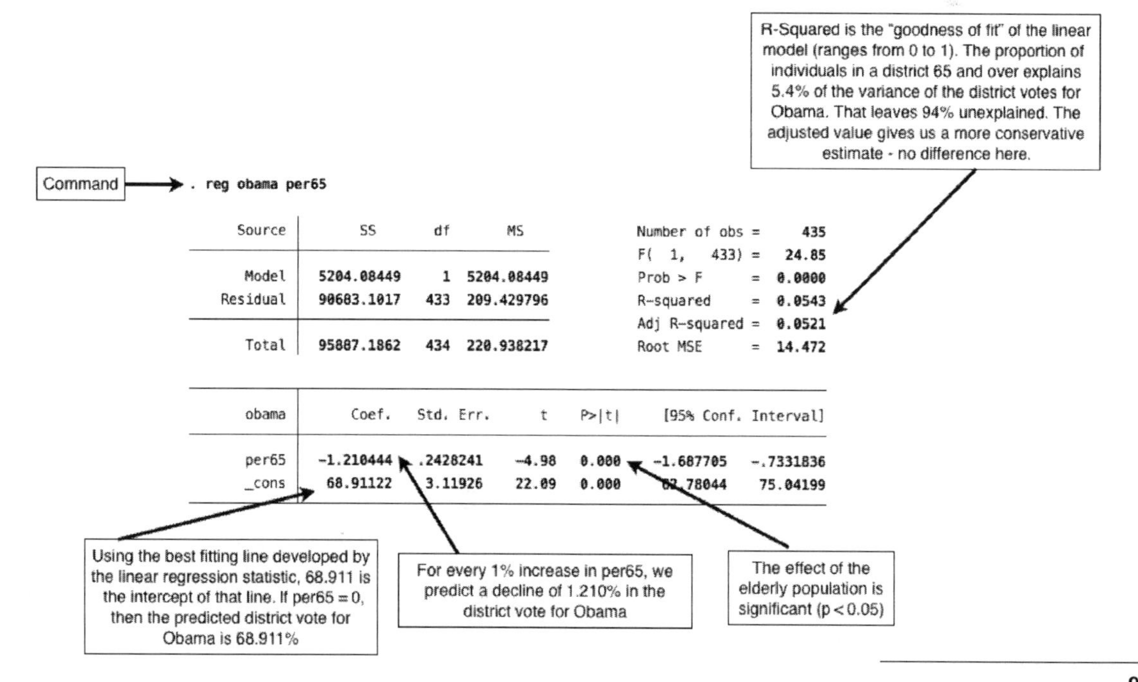

```
. reg obama per65

      Source |       SS       df       MS              Number of obs =     435
-------------+------------------------------           F(  1,   433) =   24.85
       Model |  5204.08449     1  5204.08449           Prob > F      =  0.0000
    Residual |  90603.1017   433  209.429796           R-squared     =  0.0543
-------------+------------------------------           Adj R-squared =  0.0521
       Total |  95807.1862   434  220.938217           Root MSE      =  14.472

------------------------------------------------------------------------------
       obama |      Coef.   Std. Err.      t    P>|t|     [95% Conf. Interval]
-------------+----------------------------------------------------------------
       per65 |  -1.210444   .2428241    -4.98   0.000    -1.687705   -.7331836
       _cons |   68.91122    3.11926    22.09   0.000     62.78044    75.04199
------------------------------------------------------------------------------
```

R-Squared is the "goodness of fit" of the linear model (ranges from 0 to 1). The proportion of individuals in a district 65 and over explains 5.4% of the variance of the district votes for Obama. That leaves 94% unexplained. The adjusted value gives us a more conservative estimate - no difference here.
Command
Using the best fitting line developed by the linear regression statistic, 68.911 is the intercept of that line. If per65 = 0, then the predicted district vote for Obama is 68.911%
For every 1% increase in per65, we predict a decline of 1.210% in the district vote for Obama
The effect of the elderly population is significant (p < 0.05)

We can use the information from this table to define the equation for the linear relationship between the elderly population and Obama's district vote share:

obama = 68.911%—1.210% x per65

Notice that the total sum of squares (original variation on *obama*) minus the regression sum of squares (explained by *per65*) equals the residual sum of squares. Also notice that if you perform the following calculation (Total – Residual)/Total you will come up with the R^2 value. Meaning? Like lambda, regression performs a proportional reduction of (squared) errors measurement. Knowing the variance on *per65* reduces your error in guessing the variance on *obama* by 5.4%.

Question:

Using the regression formula, what would you predict Obama's vote to be if the proportion of those 65 and older was 20%?

Answer:

68.911% – 1.210 × 20% = 44.911%

Example 4.5.2—Add the percentage of district individuals classified racially as black to the equation predicting vote for Obama. Do we improve our predictive power?

reg obama per65 black

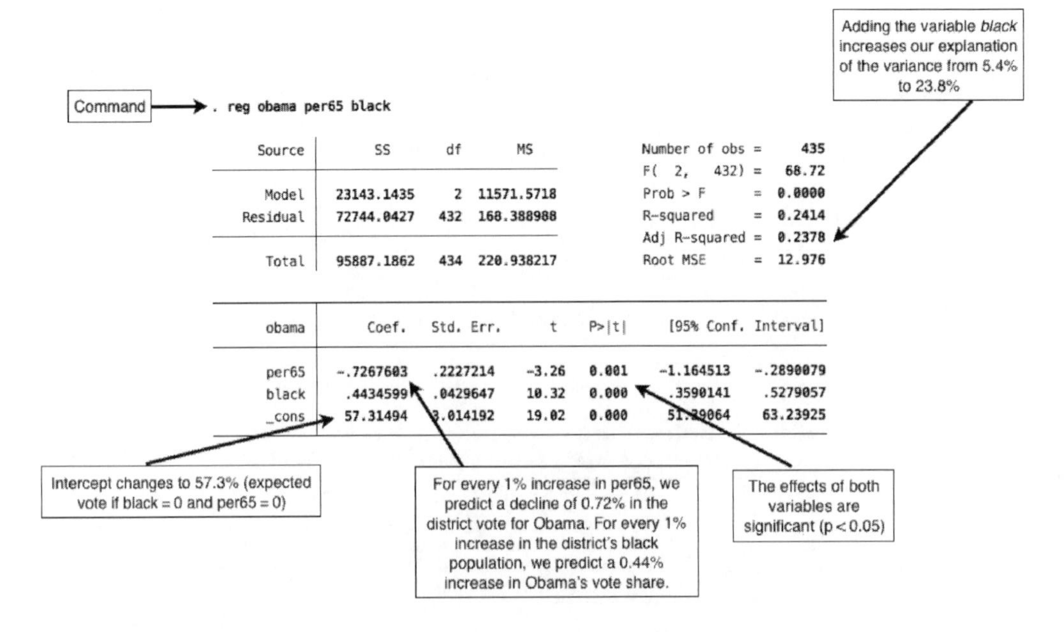

```
. reg obama per65 black
```

Source	SS	df	MS
Model	23143.1435	2	11571.5718
Residual	72744.0427	432	168.388988
Total	95887.1862	434	220.938217

Number of obs =	435
F(2, 432) =	68.72
Prob > F =	0.0000
R-squared =	0.2414
Adj R-squared =	0.2378
Root MSE =	12.976

obama	Coef.	Std. Err.	t	P>|t|	[95% Conf. Interval]	
per65	-.7267603	.2227214	-3.26	0.001	-1.164513	-.2890079
black	.4434599	.0429647	10.32	0.000	.3590141	.5279057
_cons	57.31494	3.014192	19.02	0.000	51.39064	63.23925

Command
Adding the variable black increases our explanation of the variance from 5.4% to 23.8%
Intercept changes to 57.3% (expected vote if black = 0 and per65 = 0)
For every 1% increase in per65, we predict a decline of 0.72% in the district vote for Obama. For every 1% increase in the district's black population, we predict a 0.44% increase in Obama's vote share.
The effects of both variables are significant (p < 0.05)

Question:

What is the predicted district vote for Obama if *per65* = 20% and black = 35%?

Answer:

58.28%

The regression GUI is straightforward. To produce this output using the GUI interface, click on the "Statistics" pull-down menu, scroll to "Survey data analysis," choose "Linear models and related," and then select "Linear regression."

Note: The regress command is compatible with the **svy** prefix. If your data are declared as survey data, you need only to begin the command with **svy:**

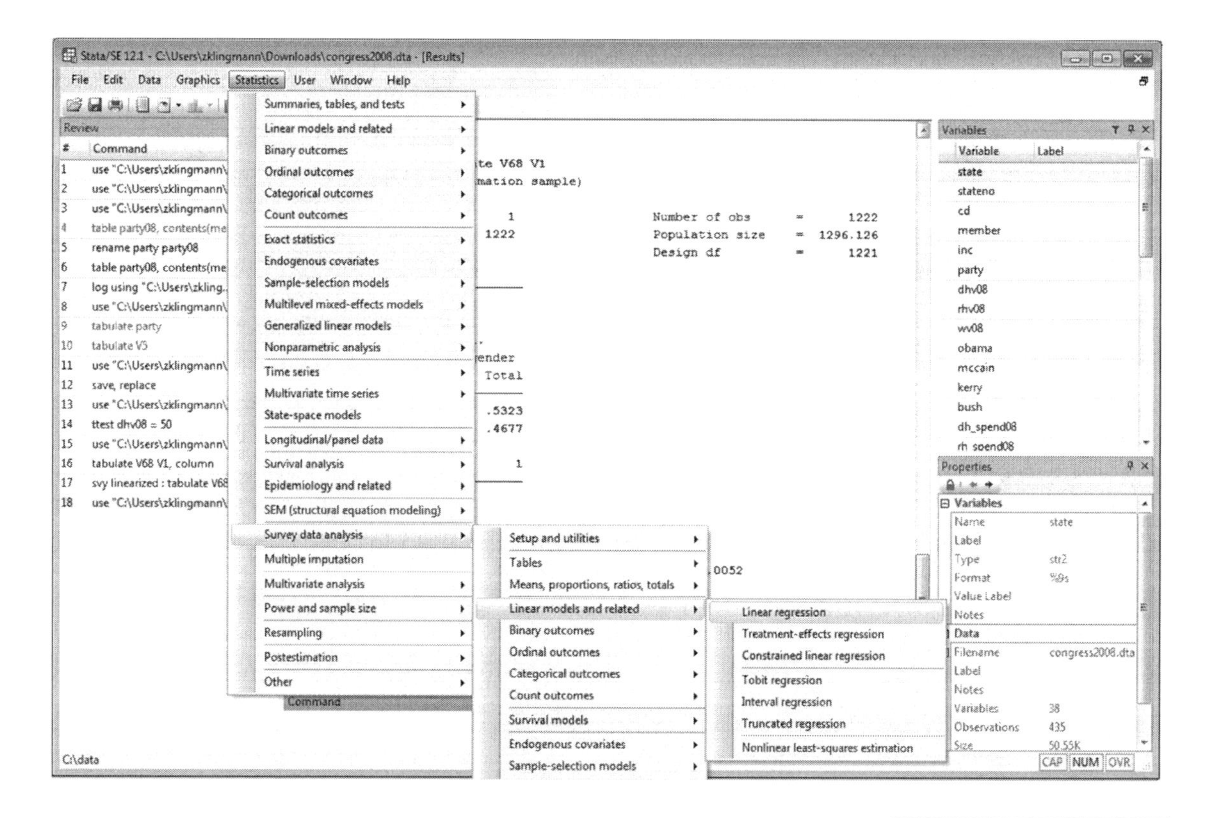

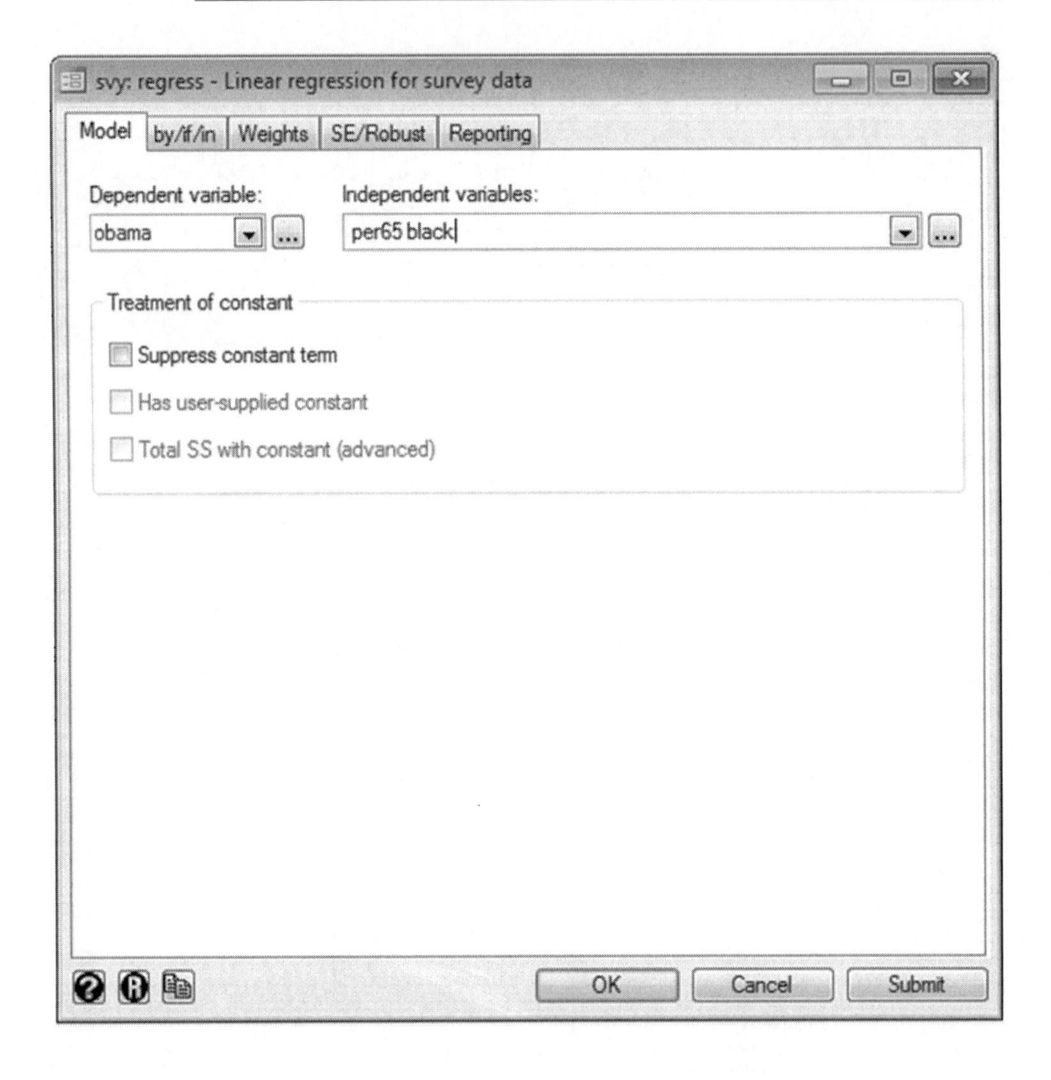

In the dialogue box, enter your dependent variable and independent variable. More than one variable can be listed as an independent variable. Click "OK" to enter.

Example 4.5.3—You can produce different regression outputs for different subsets of cases. For example, if you wished to see if the effects of *per65* on *obama* were different for districts won by Democrats and districts won by Republicans, you would employ the **bysort** prefix. If you have carried this out properly, you will produce two sets of results.

bysort party: regress obama per65

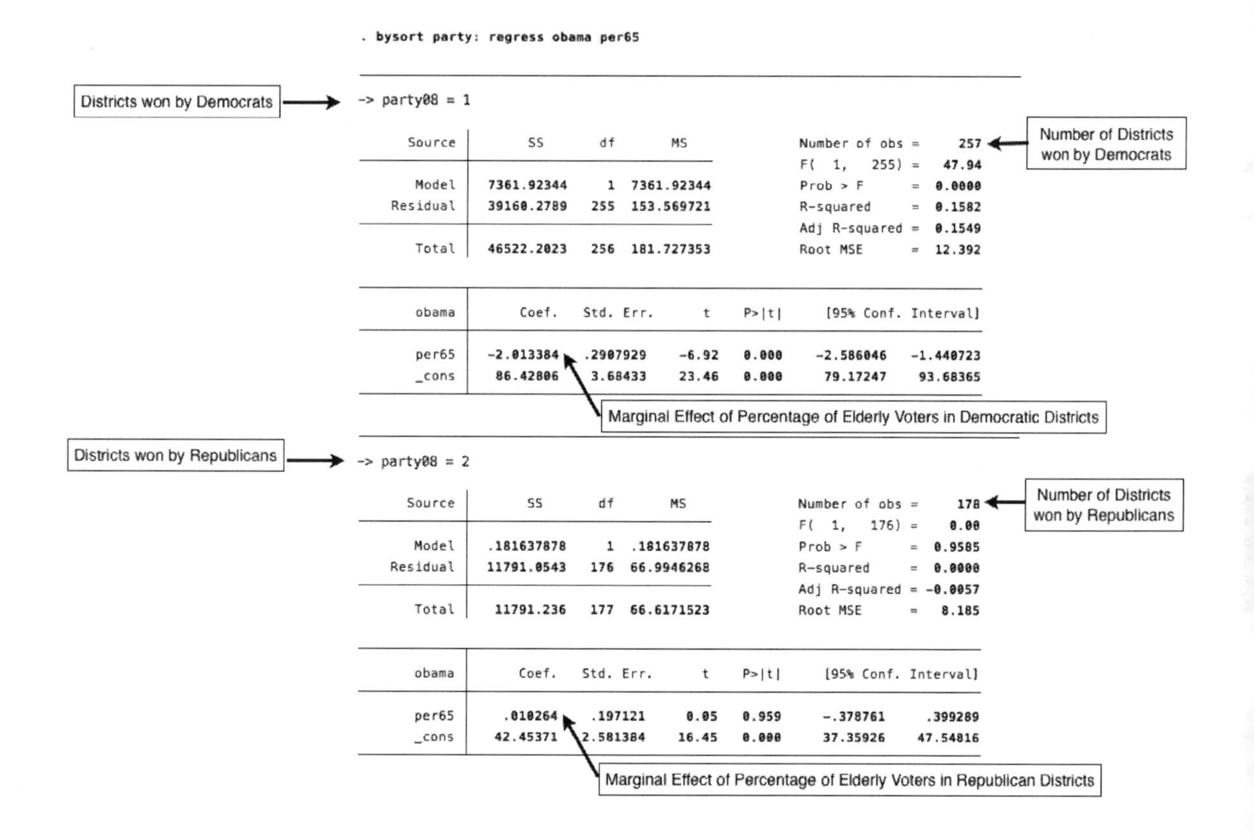

```
. bysort party: regress obama per65

-> party08 = 1

      Source |       SS       df       MS              Number of obs =     257
-------------+------------------------------           F(  1,   255) =   47.94
       Model |  7361.92344     1  7361.92344           Prob > F      =  0.0000
    Residual |  39160.2789   255  153.569721           R-squared     =  0.1582
-------------+------------------------------           Adj R-squared =  0.1549
       Total |  46522.2023   256  181.727353           Root MSE      =  12.392

------------------------------------------------------------------------------
       obama |      Coef.   Std. Err.      t    P>|t|     [95% Conf. Interval]
-------------+----------------------------------------------------------------
       per65 |  -2.013384   .2907929    -6.92   0.000    -2.586046   -1.440723
       _cons |   86.42806    3.68433    23.46   0.000     79.17247    93.68365
------------------------------------------------------------------------------

-> party08 = 2

      Source |       SS       df       MS              Number of obs =     178
-------------+------------------------------           F(  1,   176) =    0.00
       Model |  .181637878     1  .181637878           Prob > F      =  0.9585
    Residual |  11791.0543   176  66.9946268           R-squared     =  0.0000
-------------+------------------------------           Adj R-squared = -0.0057
       Total |   11791.236   177  66.6171523           Root MSE      =   8.185

------------------------------------------------------------------------------
       obama |      Coef.   Std. Err.      t    P>|t|     [95% Conf. Interval]
-------------+----------------------------------------------------------------
       per65 |    .010264    .197121     0.05   0.959     -.378761     .399289
       _cons |   42.45371   2.581384    16.45   0.000     37.35926    47.54816
------------------------------------------------------------------------------
```


Question:

Does *per65* better explain the variance of *obama* in Democratic or Republican districts? Why or why not?

The GUI directions for producing multiple regressions based on unique values of a third variable are straightforward. Simply click on the "by/if/in" tab in the regression pop-up window and select the box "Repeat command by groups." Enter the variable of interest in the "Variables that define groups" field and hit enter.

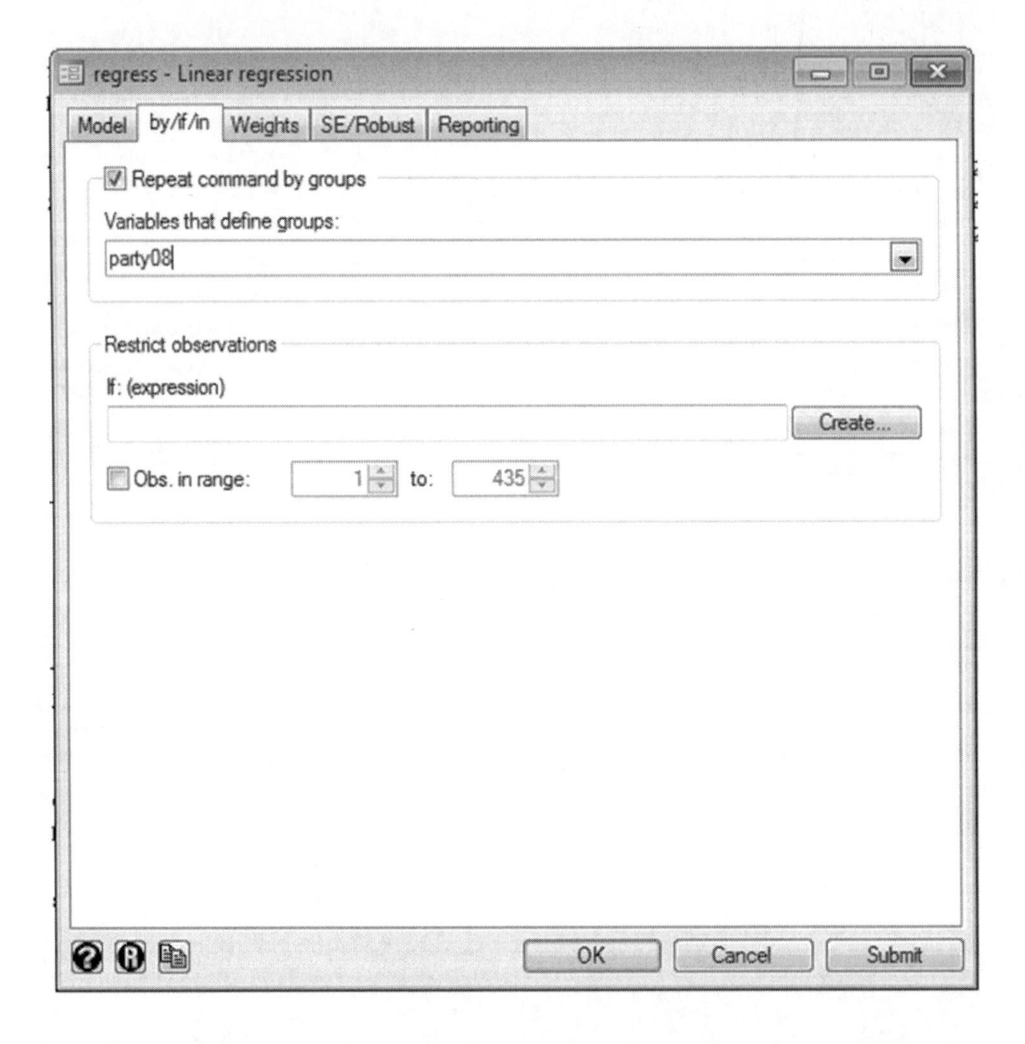

Note: Again, the **bysort** command is not compatible with the **svy** prefix. If you wish to compute separate regressions for unique categories of a third variable while accounting for sampling bias, it is best to employ an "if" statement and rerun the command for each unique category (e.g., **svy: regress DV IV if control==1**).

Plots

It is sometimes useful to visualize the linear relationship between two variables by producing a scatterplot. Stata's **twoway** command will allow you to make a variety of graphs that show the relationship between two variables, including scatterplots.

The syntax for the **twoway** graphing command for scatterplots is as follows:

twoway scatter *varname1 varname2*

Following convention, all examples will use the dependent variable as the first variable, the one to be represented on the y-axis.

Example 4.5.4—Using the **congress2008.dta** file, produce a scatterplot showing the relationship between the percentage of the population over 65 in a district (*per65*) and the vote for Obama (*obama*).

twoway scatter obama per65

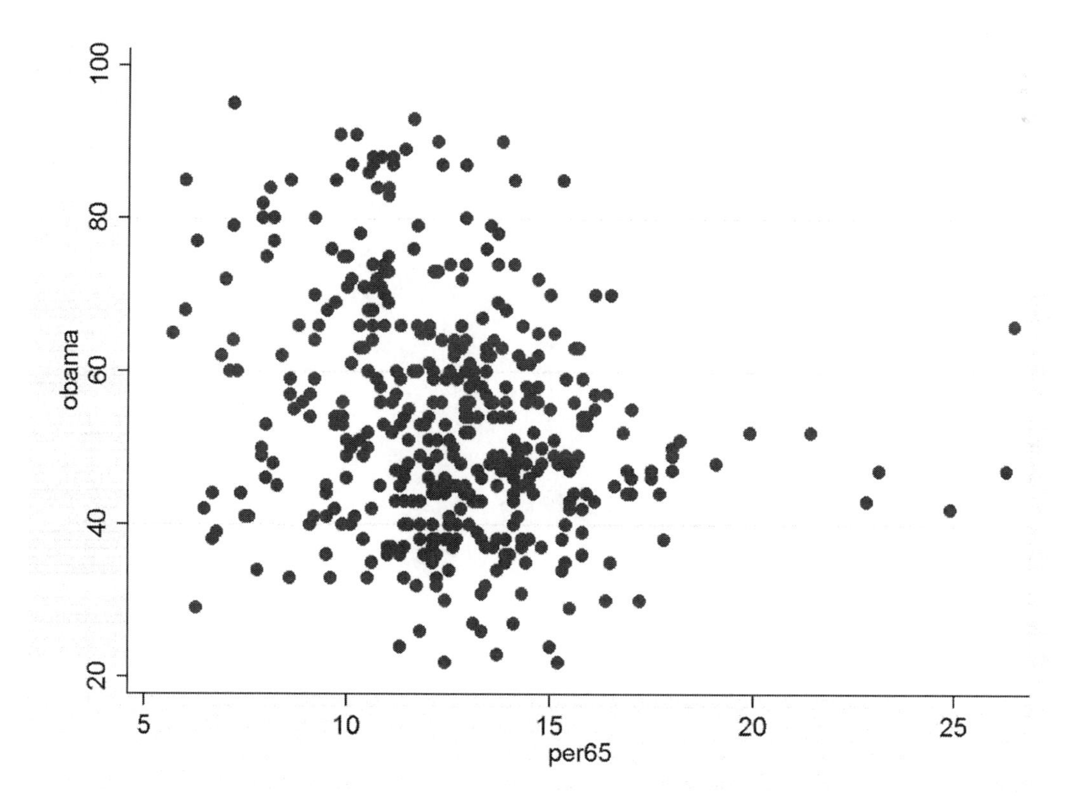

This graph could also be produced using the GUI interface. Go to the "Graphics" pull-down menu and select "Twoway graph (scatter, line, etc.)." In the "Plots" tab, click the button labeled "Create . . ." The scatterplot type will be selected as the default, so all you need to do is fill in the X (*per65*) and Y (*obama*) variables. Click "accept" and then "OK" to produce the graph.

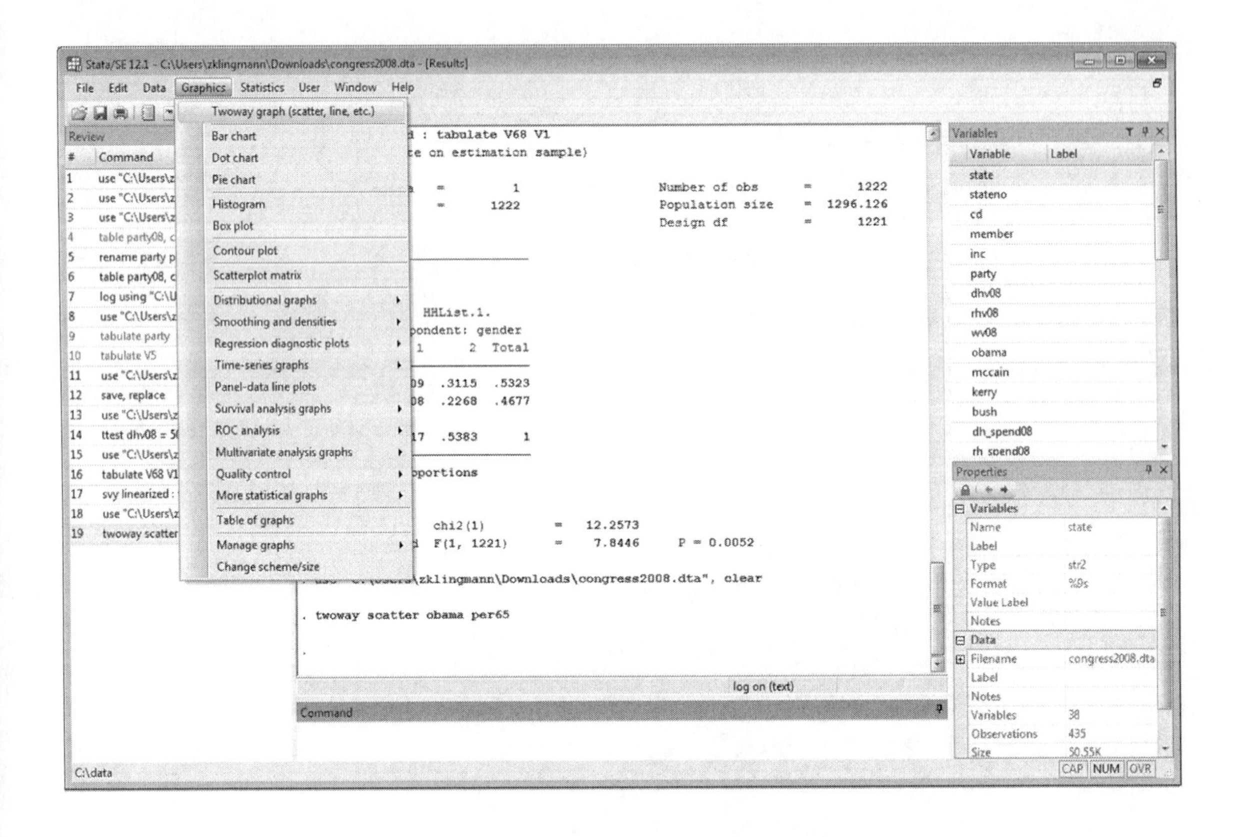

Stata/SE 12.1 - C:\Users\zklingmann\Downloads\congress2008.dta - [Results]
File
Edit
Data
Graphics
Statistics
User
Window
Help
Twoway graph (scatter, line, etc.)
Bar chart
Dot chart
Pie chart
Histogram
Box plot
Contour plot
Scatterplot matrix
Distributional graphs
Smoothing and densities
Regression diagnostic plots
Time-series graphs
Panel-data line plots
Survival analysis graphs
ROC analysis
Multivariate analysis graphs
Quality control
More statistical graphs
Table of graphs
Manage graphs
Change scheme/size
Review
Command
. twoway scatter obama per65
Number of obs = 1222
Population size = 1296.126
Design df = 1221
Variables
Variable
Label
state
stateno
cd
member
inc
party
dhv08
rhv08
wv08
obama
mccain
kerry
bush
dh_spend08
rh_spend08
Properties
Name
state
Type
str2
Format
%9s
Filename
congress2008.dta
Variables
38
Observations
435
log on (text)
C:\data

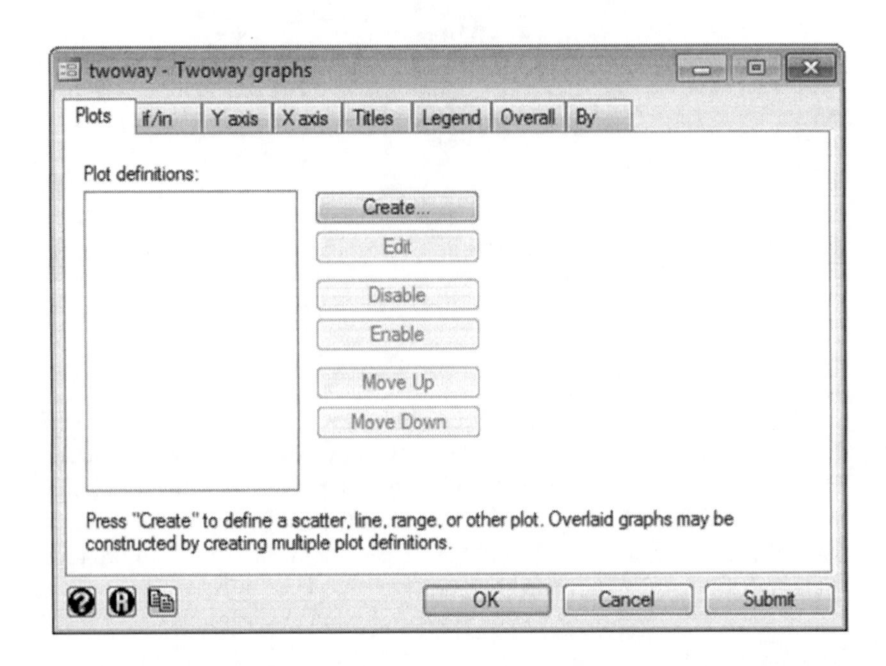

twoway - Twoway graphs
Plots
if/in
Y axis
X axis
Titles
Legend
Overall
By
Plot definitions:
Create...
Edit
Disable
Enable
Move Up
Move Down
Press "Create" to define a scatter, line, range, or other plot. Overlaid graphs may be constructed by creating multiple plot definitions.
OK
Cancel
Submit

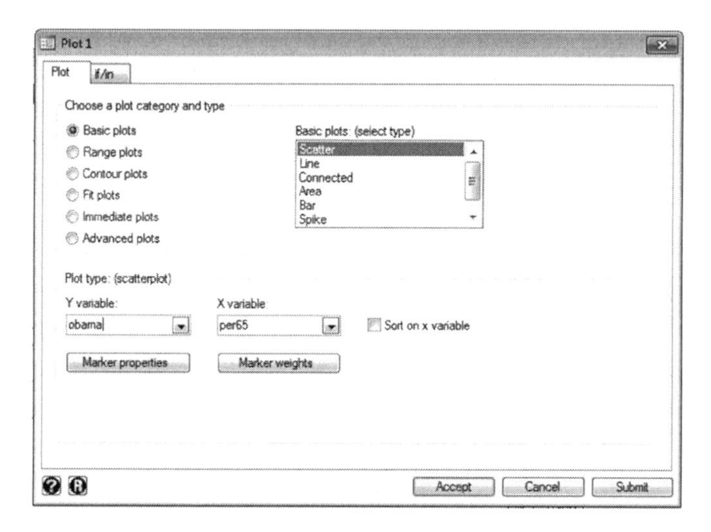

It is often useful to draw a line of best fit on scatterplots (a regression line). This line can be added to the scatterplot produced above in two ways. From the GUI interface, simply hit the "Create . . ." button a second time before clicking "OK." Under "Choose a plot category and type," select the option for "Fit plots," and select "Linear prediction." Clicking "Accept" and "OK" will add this second type of plot over your scatterplot.

Alternatively, the Stata command for a linear fit plot is **lfit**. Multiple two-way plots can be added in the same command. For, example, the following command will produce a scatterplot as well as a line of best fit for the relationship between the percentage of people over 65 in a district and the vote for President Obama in 2008:

twoway (scatter obama per65) (lfit obama per65)

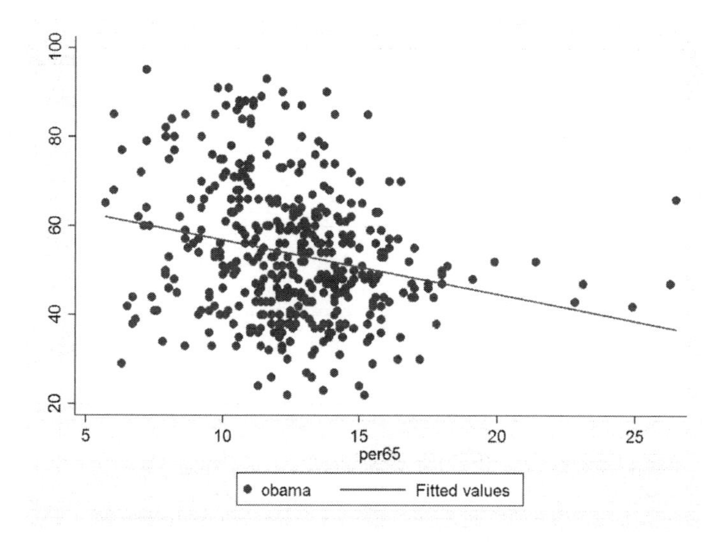

Notice that the equation for the regression line does not appear. If you want that to be placed within your chart as text you can click on the "Graph Editor" button at the top of the graph window and enter it manually. More instructions on how to use the graph editor are provided in Appendix A. You can alter your graph in a variety of ways in the graph editor (e.g., changing colors, changing marker shapes, or adding a graph title).

It is possible to overlay multiple graphs at once. For example, building on Example 4.5.4, you may want to visualize the relationship between Obama's vote share and the elderly population separately to House districts won by Republicans and Democrats. To achieve this end, simply add "if" statements to your graphing command as follows:

twoway (scatter obama per65 if party==1) (lfit obama per65 if party==1) (scatter obama per65 if party==2) (lfit obama per65 if party==2)

This will produce the following graph. You may want to use the graph editor to match the line of best fit with the color of the scatter markers.

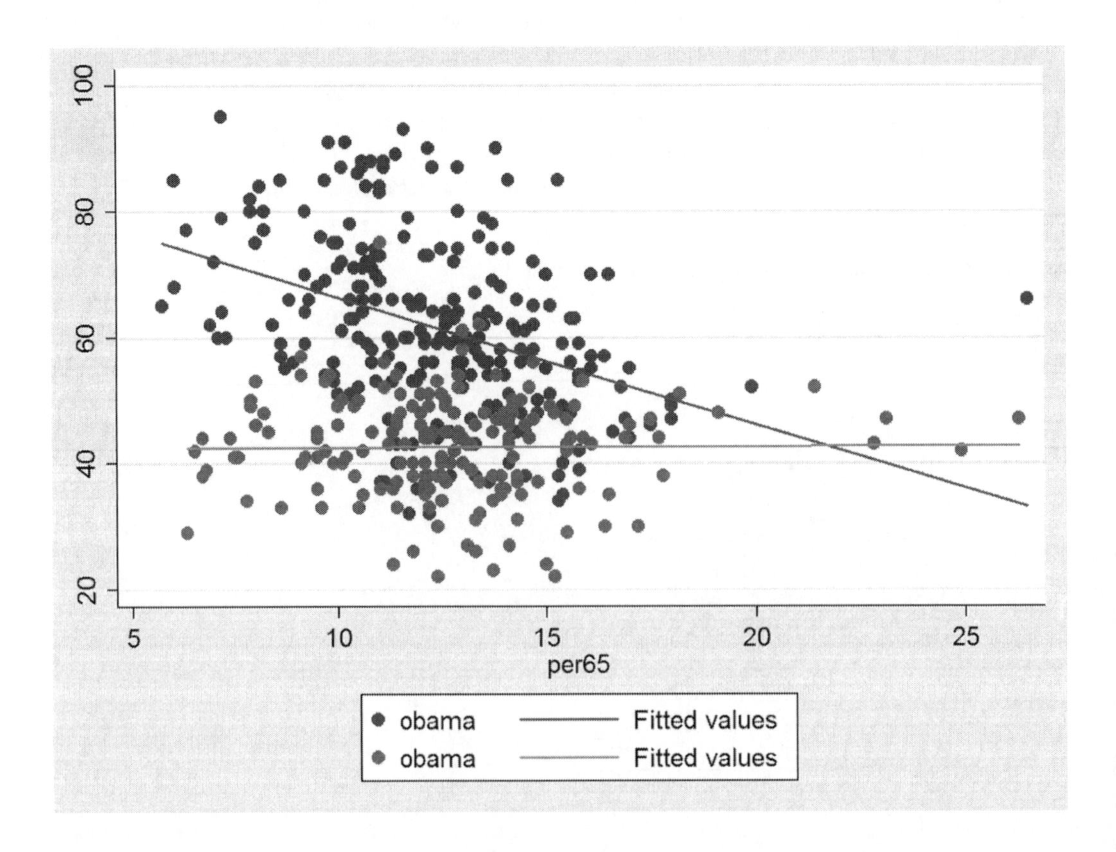

Sample Exercises 4.5

ANES2012A

For each exercise, weight the sample by *PW2012.*

1. Using a simple two-variable linear regression, do your results confirm or disconfirm the following hypothesis for 2012? Your answer should be "no," but interpret the unstandardized slope and R-square values. Also, is the slope significantly different from 0?

   The cooler one feels toward Big Business (V75B), the warmer one feels toward the Tea Party (V81T), and the relationship is negative and linear.

2. Follow up on problem 1 by adding in feelings toward blacks (*V78*). Interpret the individual unstandardized slopes and their t-values, compare the standardized ones, and interpret the R-square value. Does adding *V78* change the values much? Which of your two independent variables is more important in explaining variation on the Tea Party thermometer?
3. Follow up on problem 1; using an "if" statement, is the relationship different between those who are angry at President Obama (*V23*) or not? Now, enter *V23* as a separate independent, dummy variable. Interpret those results. Does *V23* or feelings toward big business better explain feelings toward the Tea Party?

Congress 2008–2012

1. Using a simple two-variable linear regression, do your results confirm or disconfirm the following hypothesis for any year? Interpret the unstandardized slope and R-square values. Remember that the unstandardized slope will seem extremely low, but that is only because the variation in dollars is much greater than marginal victory percentages.

   The more that Democrats spend in comparison to Republicans (spenddiff), the greater will be their winning margin over Republicans (windiff), and the relationship is positive and linear.

2. Using a simple two-variable regression, answer the following problem comparing results from 2008 and 2012:

   As the percentage of Hispanics in a district increases, so should the Democratic vote, and the relationship is positive and linear.

   You will first need to generate two new variables. The variable *demdiff* was already created in "Sample Exercises 3.2," problem 3 (*dhv12-dhv08*). You will also need to generate your independent variable (call it *hisdiff*) that equals *hispanic12-hispanic08*.

3. Follow up on problem 1; using an "if" statement, is the relationship different in those districts with PCIs below the mean than above? Now, enter that recoded PCI as a separate independent, dummy variable. Interpret those results. Does PCI or spending differences explain more of the variance of *windiff*? Discuss all relevant measures.

EURO69

For each exercise, weight the sample by *W27*. If analyzing only one country or comparing just two countries against each other, use *W1*.

1. Using a simple two-variable linear regression, do your results confirm or disconfirm the following hypothesis? Interpret the unstandardized slope and R-square values. Also, is the slope significantly different from 0?

   The older one is, the less likely one is to believe in the seriousness of global warming.

2. Follow up on problem 1; using an "if" statement, is the relationship different between Left- and Right-leaning individuals (recoded *V25*) or not? Now, enter *V25* as a separate independent, dummy variable. Interpret those results. Does ideology or age better explain perceptions about global warming? Discuss all measures.

CCES2012

For each exercise, weight the sample by the variable WEIGHT.

1. Using a simple two-variable linear regression, do your results confirm or disconfirm the following hypothesis for 2012? Your answer should be a cautioned "yes," but interpret the unstandardized slope and R-square values. Also, is the slope significantly different from 0?

   The older one is (V5), the more likely one is to prefer solving state budget deficits with cuts than taxes (V60), and the relationship is positive and linear.

2. Follow up on problem 1; using an "if" statement, is the relationship different between men and women (*V1*)? Why or why not? Now, enter *V1* as a separate independent, dummy variable. Interpret those results. Does gender or age better explain one's allocation choice for solving budget deficits?

3. Follow-up question: Is there a linear relationship between income and candidate proximity (use *proximity*, not *proximity2*)? Using regression, fully explain your answer.

Note: Some might balk at using *V14* (Family Income) in a regression analysis, as the 15 categories are not truly interval. The midpoints are not equally spaced, nor are the proportions in each category roughly equal.

Crossnational

1. Using a simple two-variable linear regression, is the following hypothesis confirmed or disconfirmed?

   There is a positive, linear relationship between health expenditures per capita and life expectancy.

   Interpret the unstandardized slope and R-square values.

2. Special combination:

   Step 1: Using the generate command, calculate the difference between male and female literacy rates (*wdi_litm* – *wdi_litf*). Call the new variable *litdiff*. The higher the value, the greater the literacy of men compared to women.
   Step 2: Is there a negative, linear relationship between *litdiff* and the percentage of seats held by women in the lower House (*idea_swlh*)?

3. Conduct a multivariate regression procedure, with voter turnout for parliament as the dependent variable (*idea_vtvap_pa*) and total literacy rate as one dependent variable and compulsory voting (*cvote_l*) as the second, dummy variable. Which independent variable is more important in explaining voting turnout? Interpret the different slopes and R-square value.
4. Following up on problem 3, is the relationship between literacy and turnout subdued when voting is compulsory?

Appendix A

Editing Graphs

Graphing data is an excellent way to communicate descriptive statistics and basic forms of analysis. Stata has a variety of graphing capabilities, including commands for bar charts, dot charts, pie charts, box plots, histograms, line plots, and scatterplots. In addition, Stata's sophisticated graph editing feature allows you to easily customize all of your produced graphs.

Stata's Graph Editor is a user-friendly way to manipulate graphics. To start the graph editor, produce a graph and go to "File" > "Start Graph Editor." Depending on your version of Stata, you may alternatively simply click on the "Graph Editor" button on the graph's toolbar. When you open the graph editor, it will look like this:

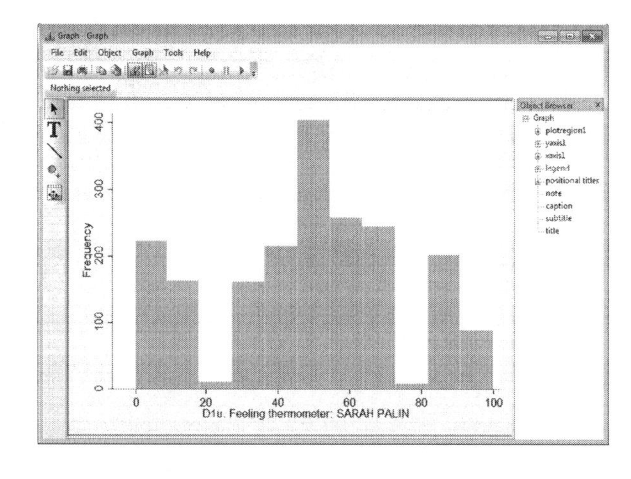

The graph editor provides a number of features. In the upper-left corner of the graph, there are five tools. The following table explains the functions of each tool:

Tool	Function
(Arrow)	Select Objects
T	Add Text
(Line)	Add Lines
(Marker +)	Add a Marker
(Layout)	Change Graph Layout

Selecting objects is a particularly useful tool in the graph editor. This tool will allow you to double-click on any object in the graph, pulling up a full menu of properties. For example, double-clicking on a slice of a pie graph would allow you to change its color, fill intensity, or pattern. Likewise, double-clicking on the legend of a graph will allow you to change aspects such as the labels and font size. In this manner, you can also manually change axis properties or the graph title. All graph objects can be hidden, deleted, or locked into place by right-clicking them. Alternatively, all of the aforementioned changes can be completed by browsing and double-clicking (or right-clicking) on objects through the left-hand "browser" of the graph editor.

The graph recorder is also a useful graphing tool when you are making multiple, similar graphs. The graph recorder allows you to create macros that will edit a batch of graphs in an identical fashion. To start the graph recorder, simply hit the "record" button in the graph editor. Edit the graph as desired and hit the "record" button again to stop the recording. Stata will prompt you to save your graph recording. When you want to alter a different graph in the same manner, simply enter the graph editor for the new graph and hit the "play" button. This will allow you to access your saved graph recording and will make all recorded changes automatically.

Appendix B

Data Codebooks

CODEBOOKS FOR DATA FILES (STATA.DTA FILES)

ANES2008A—a subset of the 2008 American National Election Studies—all respondents

ANES2008S—a subset of ANES2008A suitable for use with the student version of SPSS and Stata/SE

ANES2012A—a subset of the 2012 American National Election Studies—all respondents

ANES2012S—a subset of ANES2012A suitable for use with the student version of SPSS and Stata/SE

congress2008—a selection of political and demographic data for all 435 congressional districts

CONGRESS2008-2012—a comprehensive file tracking changes during the 2010 midterm and post-redistricting U.S. House (2014 results will be added when available)

EURO69—a subset of the March–May 2008 (EB69:2) data set—all respondents from then current EU member nations

EURO69D, EURO69H, EURO69I—single nation (Denmark, Hungary, Italy) data files suitable for use with the student version of SPSS and Stata/SE

CCES2012A—a subset of the 2012 Cooperative Congressional Election Study—all respondents

CCES2012I, CCES2012M—single state (Indiana, Maryland) data files suitable for use with the student version of SPSS and Stata/SE

CROSSNAT—a multinational file containing country-specific political, economic, and demographic variables

NOTE: Value labels, with the exception of state or country names, have been eliminated from these files. Although the author of this manual understands the clarity provided by labels, they can also create confusion when variables are recoded. Students can enter labels into their output once converted to a word processing program.

For example, look at *V10* in the *ANES 2008* codebook. If a student recodes that variable into three categories (approve, neither, disapprove), the labels will still read:

1. Approve strongly
2. Approve not strongly
3. Neither/Don't know (DK)

B1: ANES 2008 CODEBOOK

NOTE: Two data files are associated with this codebook.

ANES2008A.dta includes all of the following variables and all of the survey respondents (*N* = 2,012).

ANES2008S.dta includes only the variables whose names are in italics and only those respondents who claim to have voted for the House of Representatives (*N* = 1,256). This data set can be analyzed with the reduced, student version of SPSS and Stata Small.

Note that you will not be able to answer any questions about why someone voted (or not), as non-voters have been eliminated.

Variable Name	Variable Label Value. Value Label
PW	SAMPLE WEIGHT—POST-ELECTION 0. No post-election interview
PW2	WEIGHT ADJUSTED FOR UNINTENTIONAL OVERSAMPLING OF WOMEN

PRE-ELECTION INTERVIEW PHASE:

V1	GENDER 1. Male 2. Female

V2 RACE
1. White
2. Black/African-American
3. Other

V3 LATINO
1. Latino
2. Not Latino

V4 AGE (actual coded) Mean = 46.5 Median = 46.0
17. 17 years old (18 by Oct. 30, 2008)
18. 18 years old
.
.
90. 90 years old or older

V5 State Postal Code (e.g., AK = Alaska)

V6 CENSUS REGION
1. Northeast
2. North Central
3. South
4. West

V7 How much has R (survey respondent) thought about election for president?
1. Quite a lot
2. Only a little

V8 Did R vote for president in 2004?
1. Yes, voted
2. No, didn't vote

V9 Recall of last (2004) presidential vote choice
1. John Kerry
2. George W. Bush

V10 Approve/disapprove president handling job
1. Approve strongly
2. Approve not strongly
3. Neither/DK
4. Disapprove not strongly
5. Disapprove strongly

V11 Approve/disapprove president handling economy
1. Approve strongly
2. Approve not strongly
3. Neither/DK
4. Disapprove not strongly
5. Disapprove strongly

V12 Approve/disapprove president handling foreign relations
1. Approve strongly
2. Approve not strongly
3. Neither/DK
4. Disapprove not strongly
5. Disapprove strongly

V13 Approve/disapprove president handling health care
1. Approve strongly
2. Approve not strongly
3. Neither/DK
4. Disapprove not strongly
5. Disapprove strongly

V14 Approve/disapprove president handling war in Iraq
1. Approve strongly
2. Approve not strongly
3. Neither/DK
4. Disapprove not strongly
5. Disapprove strongly

I'd like to get your feelings toward some of our political leaders and other people who are in the news these days. I'll read the name of a person and I'd like you to rate that person using something we call the feeling thermometer. Ratings between 50 degrees and 100 degrees mean that you feel favorable and warm toward the person. Ratings between 0 degrees and 50 degrees mean that you don't feel favorable toward the person and that you don't care too much for that person. You would rate the person at the 50-degree mark if you don't feel particularly warm or cold toward the person. If we come to a person whose name you don't recognize, you don't need to rate that person. Just tell me, and we'll move on to the next one.

V15 Feeling Thermometer: president (G. W. Bush)
Mean = 40.6 Median = 40.0

V16 Feeling Thermometer: Democratic presidential candidate Mean = 57.7 Median = 60.0

V17 Feeling Thermometer: Republican presidential candidate Mean = 51.9 Median = 50.0

V18 Feeling Thermometer: Democratic Party
Mean = 56.9 Median = 60.0

V19 Feeling Thermometer: Republican Party
Mean = 48.1 Median = 50.0

V20 R better/worse off than 1 year ago
1. Better
2. The Same
3. Worse

V21 Will R be financially better/worse off one year from now?
1. Better
2. The Same
3. Worse

V22 Does R have health insurance?
1. Yes
2. No

V23 Affect for Democratic presidential candidate: angry
0. Yes
1. No

V24 Affect for Democratic presidential candidate: hopeful
0. No
1. Yes

V25 Affect for Democratic presidential candidate: afraid
0. Yes
1. No

V26 Affect for Democratic presidential candidate: proud
0. No
1. Yes

V27 Affect for Republican presidential candidate: angry
0. Yes
1. No

V28 Affect for Republican presidential candidate: hopeful
0. No
1. Yes

V29 Affect for Republican presidential candidate: afraid
0. Yes
1. No

V30 Affect for Republican presidential candidate: proud
0. No
1. Yes

V31 Will presidential race be close or will (winner) win by a lot?
1. Will be close
2. Win by quite a bit

V32 Will presidential race be close in state?
1. Will be close
2. Win by quite a bit

V33 Economy better/worse in last year
1. Much better
2. Somewhat better
3. Stayed about the same
4. Somewhat worse
5. Much worse

V34 Which party better: handling nation's economy
1. Democrats
2. Either/Neither/DK
3. Republicans

V35 During last year, U.S. position in world weaker/stronger
1. Weaker
2. Stayed about the same
3. Stronger

V36 Party ID Summary
0. Strong Democrat
1. Weak Democrat
2. Independent-leaning Democrat
3. Independent
4. Independent-leaning Republican

5. Weak Republican
6. Strong Republican

V37 Was Iraq war worth the cost
1. Worth it
2. Not worth it

V38 Iraq war increased or decreased threat of terrorism
1. Increased
2. Kept about the same
3. Decreased

V39 Government assistance to blacks scale: self-placement
1. Government should help blacks
2.
3.
4. Neutral
5.
6.
7. Blacks should help themselves

V40 Federal Budget Spending: Social Security
1. Increased
2. Kept about the same
3. Decreased

V41 Federal Budget Spending: public schools
1. Increased
2. Kept about the same
3. Decreased

V42 Federal Budget Spending: foreign aid
1. Increased
2. Kept about the same
3. Decreased

V43 Federal Budget Spending: aid to the poor
1. Increased
2. Kept about the same
3. Decreased

V44 Federal Budget Spending: border security
1. Increased
2. Kept about the same
3. Decreased

V45	Federal Budget Spending: war on terrorism 1. Increased 2. Kept about the same 3. Decreased
V46	Favor/oppose death penalty 1. Favor 2. Oppose
V47	Should federal government make it more difficult to buy a gun? 1. More difficult 2. Keep rules about the same/make it easier
V48	Black president makes R uncomfortable 1. Extremely uncomfortable 2. Very uncomfortable 3. Moderately uncomfortable 4. Slightly uncomfortable 5. Not uncomfortable at all
V49	Black president makes R pleased 1. Extremely pleased 2. Very pleased 3. Moderately pleased 4. Slightly pleased 5. Not pleased at all
V50	Hope that U.S. has African-American president 0. No 1. Yes
V51	U.S. ready for African-American president 0. No 1. Yes
V52	U.S. more or less secure than when president took office 1. More secure 2. No change 3. Less secure
V53	Is religion important part of R's life? 1. Important 2. Not important

V54 Consider self born again
1. Yes
2. No

V55 Stereotype: whites hardworking
1. Hardworking
2.
3.
4. Neutral
5.
6.
7. Lazy

V56 Stereotype: blacks hardworking
1. Hardworking
2.
3.
4. Neutral
5.
6.
7. Lazy

V57 Stereotype: whites intelligent
1. Intelligent
2.
3.
4. Neutral
5.
6.
7. Unintelligent

V58 Stereotype: blacks intelligent
1. Intelligent
2.
3.
4. Neutral
5.
6.
7. Unintelligent

V59 Position on gay marriage
1. Should be allowed
2. Should not be allowed to marry but allow civil union, etc.
3. Should not be allowed

V60 Marital status

1. Married
2. Divorced
3. Separated
4. Widowed
5. Never married
6. Partnered, not married {volunteered}

V61 Highest grade of school or year of college completed

1. <HS
2. HS
3. Some college, associates, no bachelor's
4. Bachelor's degree
5. >Bachelor's

V62 Household income (categories are the *numbers* 1–25)

1. None or less than $2,999
2. $3,000–$4,999
3. $5,000–$7,499
4. $7,500–$9,999
5. $10,000–$10,999
6. $11,000–$12,499
7. $12,500–$14,999
8. $15,000–$16,999
9. $17,000–$19,999
10. $20,000–$21,999
11. $22,000–$24,999
12. $25,000–$29,999
13. $30,000–$34,999
14. $35,000–$39,999
15. $40,000–$44,999
16. $45,000–$49,999
17. $50,000–$59,999
18. $60,000–$74,999
19. $75,000–$89,999
20. $90,000–$99,999
21. $100,000–$109,999
22. $110,000–$119,999
23. $120,000–$134,999
24. $135,000–$149,999
25. $150,000 and over

POST-ELECTION INTERVIEW PHASE:

V63	How often trust the media to report news fairly? 1. Just about always 2. Most of the time 3. Only some of the time 4. Almost never
V64	Did R vote in 2008 election? 1. Non-voter 2. Voter
V65	Did R vote on Election Day or before Election Day? 1. Election Day 2. Sometime before this
V66	For whom did R vote for president 1. Barack Obama 2. John McCain
V67	NON-VOTER: Who did R prefer for president 1. Barack Obama 2. John McCain
V68	Party of R's vote for House 1. Democratic candidate 2. Republican candidate
V69	SUMMARY: Party of R's vote for Senate* 1. Democratic candidate 2. Republican candidate
V70	PERSONAL OPTIMISM 1. Very optimistic 2. Somewhat optimistic 3. Lean toward being optimistic 4. Do not lean either way 5. Lean toward being pessimistic 6. Somewhat pessimistic 7. Very pessimistic
V71	Feeling thermometer: JOE BIDEN Mean = 58.0 Median = 60.0

V72 Feeling thermometer: SARAH PALIN
Mean = 51.3 Median = 50.0

V73 Feeling thermometer: HISPANICS
Mean = 65.3 Median = 60.0

V74 Feeling thermometer: CHRISTIAN FUNDAMENTALISTS
Mean = 56.3 Median = 50.0

*Note: Roughly two-thirds of the states have a Senate race every electoral cycle. Responses from individuals in this subset may be somewhat different from those in the entire sample depending on which states held Senate races in 2008.

V75 Feeling thermometer: LIBERALS
Mean = 54.7 Median = 50.0

V76 Feeling thermometer: CONSERVATIVES
Mean = 60.3 Median = 60.0

V77 Feeling thermometer: GAY MEN AND LESBIANS
Mean = 49.4 Median = 50.0

V78 Feeling thermometer: BLACKS
Mean = 68.8 Median = 70.0

V79 Feeling thermometer: ILLEGAL IMMIGRANTS
Mean = 39.4 Median = 40.0

V80 Feeling thermometer: WHITES
Mean = 73.0 Median = 70.0

V81 Feeling thermometer: MUSLIMS
Mean = 50.4 Median = 50.0

V82 Know party with most members in House before election
1. Democrats
2. DK
3. Republicans

V83 Know party with most members in Senate before election
1. Democrats
2. DK
3. Republicans

V84 U.S. policy goal: bring democracy to world
1. Very important
2. Somewhat important
3. Not important at all

V85 U.S. policy goal: control illegal immigration
1. Very important
2. Somewhat important
3. Not important at all

V86 U.S. policy goal: combat international terrorism
1. Very important
2. Somewhat important
3. Not important at all

V87 What should immigration levels be
1. Increased a lot
2. Increased a little
3. Left the same as it is now
4. Decreased a little
5. Decreased a lot

V88 How likely immigration take away jobs
1. Extremely likely
2. Very likely
3. Somewhat likely
4. Not at all likely

V89 Need strong government for complex problems OR free market
1. Need a strong government to handle complex economic problems
2. Free market can handle without government involvement

V90 Hope the U.S. has a woman present in R's lifetime
1. Hope the U.S. has a woman president
2. Do not hope either way
3. Hope the U.S. does not have a woman president

V91 Important differences in what major parties stand for
1. Yes, differences
2. No, no differences

V92 Do women miss out on jobs because of discrimination
1. Agree strongly
2. Agree somewhat
3. Neither agree nor disagree
4. Disagree somewhat
5. Disagree strongly

V93 World is changing and we should adjust
1. Agree strongly
2. Agree somewhat
3. Neither agree nor disagree
4. Disagree somewhat
5. Disagree strongly

V94 Newer lifestyles breaking down society
1. Agree strongly
2. Agree somewhat
3. Neither agree nor disagree
4. Disagree somewhat
5. Disagree strongly

V95 Should be more tolerant of other moral standards
1. Agree strongly
2. Agree somewhat
3. Neither agree nor disagree
4. Disagree somewhat
5. Disagree strongly

V96 More emphasis on traditional family ties
1. Agree strongly
2. Agree somewhat
3. Neither agree nor disagree
4. Disagree somewhat
5. Disagree strongly

V97 Government run by a few big interests or for benefit of all
1. Government run by a few big interests
2. Government run for the benefit of all

V98	Does government waste much tax money? 1. Wastes a lot 2. Wastes some 3. Doesn't waste very much
V99	How many in government are crooked? 1. Quite a few are crooked 2. Not very many are crooked 3. Hardly any are crooked
V100	R likes responsibility for handling a lot of thinking 1. Likes 2. Neither likes nor dislikes 3. Dislikes
V101	R prefers simple problems or complex problems 1. Simple 2. Complex
V102	Like-dislike: Democratic Party 0. Strongly dislike 1. 2. 3. 4. 5. Neutral 6. 7. 8. 9. 10. Strongly like
V103	Like-dislike: Republican Party 0. Strongly dislike 1. 2. 3. 4. 5. Neutral 6. 7. 8. 9. 10. Strongly like

V104	How satisfied is R with life? 1. Extremely satisfied 2. Very satisfied 3. Moderately satisfied 4. Slightly satisfied 5. Not satisfied at all

B2: ANES 2012 CODEBOOK

NOTE: Two data files are associated with this codebook.

ANES2012A.dta includes all of the following variables and all of the face-to-face (not web) survey respondents (N = 2,054).
ANES2012S.dta includes only the variables whose names are in italics and only those respondents who were interviewed face-to-face (not web) and who claim to have voted in the general election for the House of Representatives (N = 1,079).

This data set can be analyzed with the reduced, student version of SPSS and Stata Small.

Note that you will not be able to answer any questions about why someone voted (or not), as non-voters have been eliminated.

Variable Name	Variable Label Value. Value Label
PW2012	SAMPLE WEIGHT—POST-ELECTION 0. No post-election interview
V1	GENDER 1. Male 2. Female
V2R	RACE 1. White non-Hispanic 2. Black non-Hispanic 3. Hispanic 4. Other non-Hispanic
V3	LATINO 1. Latino 2. Not Latino

V4	AGE (actual coded—based on year of birth) Mean = 47.25 Median = 47.0 17. 17 years old 18. 18 years old . . 90. 90 years old or older
V5	State Postal Code (e.g., AK = Alaska)
V8	Did R vote for president in 2008 1. Yes, voted 2. No, didn't vote
V9	Recall of last (2008) presidential vote choice 1. Barack Obama 2. John McCain
V10	Approve/disapprove president handling job 1. Approve strongly 2. Approve not strongly 3. Neither/DK 4. Disapprove not strongly 5. Disapprove strongly
V11	Approve/disapprove president handling economy 1. Approve strongly 2. Approve not strongly 3. Neither/DK 4. Disapprove not strongly 5. Disapprove strongly
V12	Approve/disapprove president handling foreign relations 1. Approve strongly 2. Approve not strongly 3. Neither/DK 4. Disapprove not strongly 5. Disapprove strongly
V13	Approve/disapprove president handling health care 1. Approve strongly 2. Approve not strongly 3. Neither/DK

4. Disapprove not strongly
5. Disapprove strongly

V14 Approve/disapprove president handling war in Afghanistan
1. Approve strongly
2. Approve not strongly
3. Neither/DK
4. Disapprove not strongly
5. Disapprove strongly

I'd like to get your feelings toward some of our political leaders and other people who are in the news these days. I'll read the name of a person, and I'd like you to rate that person using something we call the feeling thermometer. Ratings between 50 degrees and 100 degrees mean that you feel favorable and warm toward the person. Ratings between 0 degrees and 50 degrees mean that you don't feel favorable toward the person and that you don't care too much for that person. You would rate the person at the 50-degree mark if you don't feel particularly warm or cold toward the person. If we come to a person whose name you don't recognize, you don't need to rate that person. Just tell me, and we'll move on to the next one.

V15 Feeling Thermometer: George W. Bush
Mean = 46.0 Median = 50.0

V16 Feeling Thermometer: Democratic presidential candidate Mean= 57.3 Median = 60.0

V17 Feeling Thermometer: Republican presidential candidate Mean = 48.6 Median = 50.0

V18 Feeling Thermometer: Democratic Party
Mean = 55.3 Median = 60.0

V19 Feeling Thermometer: Republican Party
Mean = 47.2 Median = 50.0

V20 R better/worse off than 1 year ago
1. Better
2. The Same
3. Worse

V21 Will R be financially better/worse off one year from now?
1. Better
2. The Same
3. Worse

V22	Does R have health insurance? 1. Yes 2. No
V23	Affect for Democratic presidential candidate: angry 0. Yes 1. No
V24	Affect for Democratic presidential candidate: hopeful 0. No 1. Yes
V25	Affect for Democratic presidential candidate: afraid 0. Yes 1. No
V26	Affect for Democratic presidential candidate: proud 0. No 1. Yes
V27	Affect for Republican presidential candidate: angry 0. Yes 1. No
V28	Affect for Republican presidential candidate: hopeful 0. No 1. Yes
V29	Affect for Republican presidential candidate: afraid 0. Yes 1. No
V30	Affect for Republican presidential candidate: proud 0. No 1. Yes
V31	Will presidential race be close or will (winner) win by a lot? 1. Will be close 2. Win by quite a bit
V32	Will presidential race be close in state? 1. Will be close 2. Win by quite a bit

V33 Economy better/worse in last year
1. Much better
2. Somewhat better
3. Stayed about the same
4. Somewhat worse
5. Much worse

V34 Which party better: handling nation's economy
1. Democrats
2. Either/neither
3. Republicans

V35 During last year, U.S. position in world weaker/stronger
1. Weaker
2. Stayed about the same
3. Stronger

V36 Party ID Summary
0. Strong Democrat
1. Weak Democrat
2. Independent-leaning Democrat
3. Independent
4. Independent-leaning Republican
5. Weak Republican
6. Strong Republican

V37 Was Afghanistan war worth the cost?
1. Worth it
2. Not worth it

V38 Afghanistan war increased or decreased threat of terrorism
1. Increased
2. Kept about the same
3. Decreased

V38R Approve/disapprove government efforts to reduce terrorism
1. Approve
2. Neither approve/disapprove
3. Disapprove

V38T

Favor or oppose torture for suspected terrorists
1. Favor
2. Neither favor/oppose
3. Oppose

V39

Government assistance to blacks scale: self-placement
1. Government should help blacks
2.
3.
4. Neutral
5.
6.
7. Blacks should help themselves

V40

Federal Budget Spending: Social Security
1. Increased
2. Kept about the same
3. Decreased

V41

Federal Budget Spending: public schools
1. Increased
2. Kept about the same
3. Decreased

V42E

Federal Budget Spending: the environment
1. Increased
2. Kept about the same
3. Decreased

V43

Federal Budget Spending: aid to the poor
1. Increased
2. Kept about the same
3. Decreased

V44S

Federal Budget Spending: science and technology
1. Increased
2. Kept about the same
3. Decreased

V45S

Federal Budget Spending: child care
1. Increased
2. Kept about the same
3. Decreased

V46 Favor/oppose death penalty
1. Favor
2. Oppose

V47 Should federal government make it more difficult to buy a gun?
1. More difficult
2. Keep rules about the same/make it easier

V48T Do you support, oppose, or neither support nor oppose the Tea Party movement?
1. Support
2. Neither support nor oppose
3. Oppose

V52 U.S. more or less secure than when president took office
1. More secure
2. No change
3. Less secure

V53 Is religion important part of R's life?
1. Important
2. Not important

V54 Consider self born again
1. Yes
2. No

V55 Stereotype: whites hardworking
1. Hardworking
2.
3.
4. Neutral
5.
6.
7. Lazy

V56 Stereotype: blacks hardworking
1. Hardworking
2.
3.
4. Neutral
5.
6.
7. Lazy

V57

Stereotype: whites intelligent
1. Intelligent
2.
3.
4. Neutral
5.
6.
7. Unintelligent

V58

Stereotype: blacks intelligent
1. Intelligent
2.
3.
4. Neutral
5.
6.
7. Unintelligent

V59

Position on gay marriage
1. Should be allowed
2. Should not be allowed to marry but allow civil union, etc.
3. Should not be allowed

V60

Marital status
1. Married
2. Divorced
3. Separated
4. Widowed
5. Never married
6. Partnered, not married {VOL}

V61

Highest grade of school or year of college completed
1. <HS
2. HS
3. Some college, associates, no bachelor's
4. Bachelor's degree
5. >Bachelor's

V62A

Household income (categories are the *numbers* 1–25)
01. Under $5,000
02. $5,000–$9,999
03. $10,000–$12,499

04. $12,500–$14,999
05. $15,000–$17,499
06. $17,500–$19,999
07. $20,000–$22,499
08. $22,500–$24,999
09. $25,000–$27,499
10. $27,500–$29,999
11. $30,000–$34,999
12. $35,000–$39,999
13. $40,000–$44,999
14. $45,000–$49,999
15. $50,000–$54,999
16. $55,000–$59,999
17. $60,000–$64,999
18. $65,000–$69,999
19. $70,000–$74,999
20. $75,000–$79,999
21. $80,000–$89,999
22. $90,000–$99,999
23. $100,000–$109,999
24. $110,000–$124,999
25. $125,000–$149,999
26. $150,000–$174,999
27. $175,000–$249,999
28. $250,000 or more

V63J — Electoral integrity: is journalist coverage fair
1. Very often
2. Fairly often
3. Not often
4. Not at all often

V63T — Does federal government pose a threat to citizens
1. Yes
2. No

V63R — Electoral integrity: do the rich buy elections
1. Very often
2. Fairly often
3. Not often
4. Not at all often

POST-ELECTION INTERVIEW PHASE:

V64 Did R vote in 2012 election
1. Non-voter
2. Voter

V66 For whom did R vote for president
1. Barack Obama
2. W. Mitt Romney

V68 Party of R's vote for House
1. Democratic candidate
2. Republican candidate

V69 SUMMARY: Party of R's vote for Senate*
1. Democratic candidate
2. Republican candidate

*Note: Roughly two-thirds of the states have a Senate race every electoral cycle. Responses from individuals in this subset may be somewhat different from those in the entire sample depending on which states held Senate races in 2012.

V71 Feeling thermometer: JOE BIDEN
Mean = 54.0 Median = 50.0

V72 Feeling thermometer: PAUL RYAN
Mean = 51.2 Median = 50.0

V74 Feeling thermometer: CHRISTIAN FUNDAMENTALISTS
Mean = 53.4 Median = 50.0

V75 Feeling thermometer: LIBERALS
Mean = 52.1 Median = 50.0

V75B Feeling thermometer: BIG BUSINESS
Mean = 53.4 Median = 50.0

V76 Feeling thermometer: CONSERVATIVES
Mean = 57.7 Median = 60.0

V77 Feeling thermometer: GAY MEN AND LESBIANS
Mean = 53.7 Median = 50.0

V78	Feeling thermometer: BLACKS Mean = 66.3 Median = 70.0
V79	Feeling thermometer: ILLEGAL IMMIGRANTS Mean = 40.0 Median = 40.0
V80	Feeling thermometer: WHITES Mean = 72.5 Median = 70.0
V81	Feeling thermometer: MUSLIMS Mean = 47.9 Median = 50.0
V81M	Feeling thermometer: MORMONS Mean = 52.5 Median = 50.0
V81T	Feeling thermometer: TEA PARTY Mean = 46.2 Median = 50.0
V82	Know party with most members in House before election 1. Democrats 2. DK 3. Republicans
V83	Know party with most members in Senate before election 1. Democrats 2. DK 3. Republicans
V87	What should immigration levels be 1. Increased a lot 2. Increased a little 3. Left the same as it is now 4. Decreased a little 5. Decreased a lot
V88	How likely immigration take away jobs 1. Extremely likely 2. Very likely 3. Somewhat likely 4. Not at all likely

V88P — U.S. government policy toward unauthorized immigrants
1. Make all unauthorized immigrants felons and send them back to their home country.
2. Have a guest worker program that allows unauthorized immigrants to remain.
3. Allow unauthorized immigrants to remain in the United States . . . certain requirements
4. Allow unauthorized immigrants to remain in the United States . . . without penalties

V88C — Allow citizenship to some illegal aliens
1. Favor
2. Neither favor/oppose
3. Oppose

V89 — Need strong government for complex problems OR free market
1. Need a strong government to handle complex economic problems
2. Free market can handle without government involvement

V90W — Woman president in next 20 years—good or bad
1. Good
2. Neither good/bad
3. Bad

V91 — Important differences in what major parties stand for
1. Yes, differences
2. No, no differences

V92H — Discrimination against women
1. Not a problem at all
2. A minor problem
3. A moderately serious problem
4. A very serious problem
5. An extremely serious problem

V93 — World is changing and we should adjust
1. Agree strongly
2. Agree somewhat

3. Neither agree nor disagree
4. Disagree somewhat
5. Disagree strongly

V94 Newer lifestyles breaking down society
1. Agree strongly
2. Agree somewhat
3. Neither agree nor disagree
4. Disagree somewhat
5. Disagree strongly

V95 Should be more tolerant of other moral standards
1. Agree strongly
2. Agree somewhat
3. Neither agree nor disagree
4. Disagree somewhat
5. Disagree strongly

V96 More emphasis on traditional family ties
1. Agree strongly
2. Agree somewhat
3. Neither agree nor disagree
4. Disagree somewhat
5. Disagree strongly

V97 Government run by a few big interests or for benefit of all
1. Government run by a few big interests
5. Government run for the benefit of all

V98 Does government waste much tax money
Note: pre-election
1. Wastes a lot
2. Wastes some
3. Doesn't waste very much

V99C How many in government are corrupt
1. All
2. Most
3. About half
4. A few
5. None

V99P How often can people be trusted
1. Always
2. Most of the time

3. About half of the time
4. Some of the time
5. Never

V99E Elections make government pay attention
1. A good deal
2. Some
3. Not much

V99D Makes a difference whom one votes for
1. Won't make a difference
2.
3.
4.
5. Can make a big difference

V102 Like-dislike: Democratic Party
0. Strongly dislike
1.
2.
3.
4.
5. Neutral
6.
7.
8.
9.
10. Strongly like

V103 Like-dislike: Republican Party
0. Strongly dislike
1.
2.
3.
4.
5. Neutral
6.
7.
8.
9.
10. Strongly like

V104 How satisfied is R with life
1. Extremely satisfied
2. Very satisfied

3. Moderately satisfied
4. Slightly satisfied
5. Not satisfied at all

V105 Is global warming happening or not
1. Has probably been happening
2. Probably hasn't been happening

V106 (7-point scale) liberal/conservative self-placement
Note: pre-election
1. Extremely liberal
2. Liberal
3. Slightly liberal
4. Moderate/middle of the road
5. Slightly conservative
6. Conservative
7. Extremely conservative
-1. Haven't thought much about this

B3: CONGRESS 2008 CODEBOOK

Variable Name	Variable Label Value. Value Label	
state	ANES POSTAL CODE ABBREVIATION	
stateno	Number of state if listed alphabetically	
cd	Congressional district number	
member	Name of district winner	
inc08	Incumbency status of election[1] 1. Democratic incumbent 2. Republican Incumbent 3. Open seat—previously held by Democrat 4. Open seat—previously held by Republican	
party08	Winning Party 2008 1. Democratic 2. Republican	
dhv08	Percentage won by Democratic candidate	
rhv08	Percentage won by Republican candidate	
wv08	Percentage won by winning candidate	
		National[2]
obama	District vote for Obama[3]	52.93%
mccain	District vote for McCain	45.65%

kerry	District vote for Kerry (2004)	48.27%
bush	District vote for Bush (2004)	50.73%
dhspend_08	Expenditures for Democratic House candidate[4]	
rhspend_08	Expenditures for Republican House candidate	
seniority08	Number of years served by incumbent	
pu08	Party Unity Score 2008[5]	
pu09	Party Unity Score 2009	
ps08a	Presidential Support Score All[6]	
ps08n	Presidential Support Score Non-unanimous Votes Only	
acu08	American Conservative Union Rating 2008[7]	
acu09	American Conservative Union Rating 2009	
dwnom110	DW-NOMINATE SCORE 110th Congress[8]	
dwnom111	DW-NOMINATE SCORE 111th Congress	

		National[2]
totpop	Total population estimate for district[9]	685,453
medianage	Median age of district resident	36.40
white	Percentage whites in district	74.13%
black	Percentage blacks in district	12.37%
hispanic	Percentage Hispanic in district	14.73%
per65	Percentage 65 and older	12.47%
lt18	Percentage under 18	25.00%
college	Percentage 25 years or older completing college or advanced degree	27.00%
pci	Per capita income	$26,178
mv	Median value of owner-occupied dwelling	$181,800
mhi	Median household income	$50,007
hgini	Gini index based on households (measure of income inequality)[10]	.465
mfo	Median family income	$60,374
vet18	Percentage of those 18 and over who are veterans (male and female)	10.44%

NOTES AND SOURCES

1 To avoid confusion when using certain variables (*seniority08, pu08, ps08a, ps08n, acu08, dwnom110*), data were eliminated for those members of Congress who did not run for reelection in the general election (a few were eliminated in primaries). These correspond to *inc08* categories 3 and 4.

2 Other than *totpop*, these figures will not necessarily be exactly the same as the means calculated from the 435 districts. Why? By 2005–2007, districts were not of equal population size. They each, therefore, carry

different weight in the calculation of the true population figures. These figures also include Washington, D.C., and Puerto Rico, both of which have no House representation (other than a delegate).

3 Presidential vote by district: http://www.swingstateproject.com/showDiary.do?diaryId=4161.
Presidential vote 2008—national: http://www.fec.gov/pubrec/fe2008/tables2008.pdf.
Presidential vote 2004—national: http://www.fec.gov/pubrec/fe2004/tables.pdf.

4 Finance data: http://fec.gov/DisclosureSearch/mapHSApp.do?election_yr=2008.

5 Party unity scores courtesy of Keith Poole.

6 Presidential support scores courtesy of George C. Edwards III. Unlike the standard *Congressional Quarterly* support scores, Dr. Edwards, among other modifications, includes paired votes in each member's calculation. The first score represents the proportion of times that a member sided with the president on all roll call votes on which President Bush had declared a position. The second only includes those roll call votes that were non-unanimous. The latter will increase the mean difference between Democrats and Republicans.

7 American Conservative Union scores:
http://www.conservative.org/ratings/ratingsarchive/2008/2008house.htm.
http://www.conservative.org/ratings/ratingsarchive/2009/House Ratings.htm.

8 Description: Based on a multidimensional scaling of roll calls, House members are ranked from most liberal (negative score) to most conservative (positive score). Only the first dimension, corresponding to economic issues, is used. Scores courtesy of Keith Poole.

DWNOM110: Legislator's DW-NOMINATE score for the 110th Congress (2007–2008), 1st dimension only (from http://www.voteview.com/dwnomin.htm; Legislator Estimates 1st to 111th Houses Excel file).

DWNOM111: Legislator's DW-NOMINATE score for the 111th Congress (2009–2010), 1st dimension only (from http://www.voteview.com/dwnomin.htm; Legislator Estimates 1st to 111th Houses Excel file).

9 Demographic data: 2005–2007 American Community Survey 3-Year Estimates.
http://factfinder.census.gov/servlet/GCTGeoSearchByListServlet?ds_name=ACS_2007_3YR_G00_&_lang=en&_ts=320436047885.

10 Based on the Lorenz curve, a score of 0.0 means perfect equality of household incomes, and 1.00 perfect inequality. It corresponds to the area between the Lorenz income distribution curve and the line of perfect equality.

B4: CONGRESS 2008–2012 CODEBOOK

(Not suitable for the Student version of SPSS or SMALL STATA.)

Variable Name	Variable Label Value. Value Label
state	ANES POSTAL CODE ABBREVIATION
stateno	Number of state if listed alphabetically
cd08	Congressional district number 2008–2010 elections
cd12	Congressional district number 2012
member08	Name of district winner 2008
member10	Name of district winner 2010
member12	Name of district winner 2012
inc08	Incumbency status of 2008 election[1]
inc10	Incumbency status of 2010 election
inc12	Incumbency status of 2012 election
	1. Democratic incumbent
	2. Republican Incumbent
	3. Open seat—previously held by Democrat
	4. Open seat—previously held by Republican
party08	Winning Party 2008
party10	Winning Party 2010
party12	Winning Party 2012
	1. Democratic
	2. Republican
dhv08	Percentage won by Democratic candidate in 2008 (of all votes)[1]
dhv10	Percentage won by Democratic candidate in 2010
dhv12	Percentage won by Democratic candidate in 2012
rhv08	Percentage won by Republican candidate in 2008
rhv10	Percentage won by Republican candidate in 2010
rhv12	Percentage won by Republican candidate in 2012
wv08	Percentage won by winning candidate in 2008
wv10	Percentage won by winning candidate in 2010
wv12	Percentage won by winning candidate in 2012
obama08	District's 2008 vote for Obama, 2008–2010 districts[2]
obama08a	District's 2008 vote for Obama, 2012 districts
obama2012	District's 2012 vote for Obama (only use with 2012 data)
mccain08	District's 2008 vote for McCain, 2008–2010 districts
mccain08a	District's 2012 vote for McCain, 2012 districts
romney2012	District's 2012 vote for Romney, 2012 districts (only use with 2012 data)

kerry04	District vote for Kerry (2004) (only use with 2008–2010 data)
bush04	District vote for Bush (2004) (only use with 2008–2010 data)
dh_spend08	2008 Expenditures for Democratic House candidate[3]
dh_spend10	2010 Expenditures for Democratic House candidate
dh_spend12	2012 Expenditures for Democratic House candidate
rh_spend08	2008 Expenditures for Republican House candidate
rh_spend10	2010 Expenditures for Republican House candidate
rh_spend12	2012 Expenditures for Republican House candidate
dhc08	2008 Total Contributions to Democratic House candidate
dhc10	2010 Total Contributions to Democratic House candidate
dhc12	2012 Total Contributions to Democratic House candidate
rhc08	2008 Total Contributions to Republican House candidate
rhc10	2010 Total Contributions to Republican House candidate
rhc12	2012 Total Contributions to Republican House candidate
dhind08	2008 Total Contributions to Democratic candidate from individuals
dhind10	2010 Total Contributions to Democratic candidate from individuals
dhind12	2012 Total Contributions to Democratic candidate from individuals
rhind08	2008 Total Contributions to Republican candidate from individuals
rhind10	2010 Total Contributions to Republican candidate from individuals
rhind12	2012 Total Contributions to Republican candidate from individuals
dhind08a	2008 Total Contributions ≤ $200 to Democratic candidate from individuals
dhind10a	2010 Total Contributions ≤ $200 tor Democratic candidate from individuals
dhind12a	2012 Total Contributions ≤ $200 to Democratic candidate from individuals
rhind08a	2008 Total Contributions ≤ $200 to Republican candidate from individuals
rhind10a	2010 Total Contributions ≤ $200 to Republican candidate from individuals

rhind12a	2012 Total Contributions ≤ $200 to Republican candidate from individuals
dhp08	2008 Total Contributions to Democratic candidate from party committees
dhp10	2010 Total Contributions to Democratic candidate from party committees
dhp12	2012 Total Contributions to Democratic candidate from party committees
rhp08	2008 Total Contributions to Republican candidate from party committees
rhp10	2010 Total Contributions to Republican candidate from party committees
rhp12	2012 Total Contributions to Republican candidate from party committees
dho08	2008 Total Contributions to Democratic candidate from other committees, mainly PACs
dho10	2010 Total Contributions to Democratic candidate from other committees, mainly PACs
dho12	2012 Total Contributions to Democratic candidate from other committees, mainly PACs
rho08	2008 Total Contributions to Republican candidate from other committees, mainly PACs
rho10	2010 Total Contributions to Republican candidate from other committees, mainly PACs
rho12	2012 Total Contributions to Republican candidate from other committees, mainly PACs
seniority08	Number of years served by incumbent in 2008
seniority10	Number of years served by incumbent in 2010
seniority12	Number of years served by incumbent in 2012
seniority14	Number of years served by incumbent in 2014
pu08	Party Unity Score 2008[4]
pu09	Party Unity Score 2009
pu10	Party Unity Score 2010
pu11	Party Unity Score 2011
pu12	Party Unity Score 2012
ps08a	Presidential Support Score All, 2008[5]
ps09a	Presidential Support Score All, 2009
ps10a	Presidential Support Score All, 2010
ps11a	Presidential Support Score All, 2011
ps12a	Presidential Support Score All, 2012
ps08n	Presidential Support Score Non-unanimous Votes Only, 2008
ps09n	Presidential Support Score Non-unanimous Votes Only, 2009

ps10n	Presidential Support Score Non-unanimous Votes Only, 2010
ps11n	Presidential Support Score Non-unanimous Votes Only, 2011
ps12n	Presidential Support Score Non-unanimous Votes Only, 2012
acu08	American Conservative Union Rating 2008[6]
acu09	American Conservative Union Rating 2009
acu10	American Conservative Union Rating 2010
acu11	American Conservative Union Rating 2011
acu12	American Conservative Union Rating 2012
acu13	American Conservative Union Rating 2013
dwnom110	DW-NOMINATE SCORE 110th Congress[7]
dwnom111	DW-NOMINATE SCORE 111th Congress
dwnom112	DW-NOMINATE SCORE 112th Congress
totpop08	Total population estimate for district[8]
medianage08	Median age of district resident
white08	Percentage whites in district
black08	Percentage blacks in district
hispanic08	Percentage Hispanic in district
per6508	Percentage 65 and older
lt1808	Percentage under 18
college08	Percentage 25 years or older completing college or advanced degree
pci08	Per capita income
mv08	Median value of owner-occupied dwelling
mhi08	Median household income
mfi08	Median family income
vet1808	Percentage of those 18 and over who are veterans (male and female)
totpop10	Total population estimate for district
medianage10	Median age of district resident
white10	Percentage whites in district
black10	Percentage blacks in district
hispanic10	Percentage Hispanic in district
per6510	Percentage 65 and older
lt1810	Percentage under 18
college10	Percentage 25 years or older completing college or advanced degree
pci10	Per capita income
mv10	Median value of owner-occupied dwelling
mhi10	Median household income
mfi10	Median family income
vet1810	Percentage of those 18 and over

totpop12	Total population estimate for district
medianage12	Median age of district resident
white12	Percentage whites in district
black12	Percentage blacks in district
hispanic12	Percentage Hispanic in district
per6512	Percentage 65 and older
lt1812	Percentage under 18
college12	Percentage 25 years or older completing college or advanced degree
pci12	Per capita income
mv12	Median value of owner-occupied dwelling
mhi12	Median household income
mfi12	Median family income
vet1812	Percentage of those 18 and over who are veterans (male and female)

NOTES AND SOURCES

1 All percentages are of total votes cast, not just two party. To obtain the percentage of the two-party vote (within rounding error), divide *dhv*/(*dhv* + *rhv*), and so forth. When two candidates of the same party (CA in 2012 and LA) ran against each other, these data were eliminated.

2 Presidential vote by district:

http://www.swingstateproject.com/showDiary.do?diaryId=4161.
http://www.dailykos.com/story/2012/11/19/1163009/-Daily-Kos-Elections-presidential-results-by-congressional-district-for-the-2012-2008-elections.
Presidential vote 2008—national: http://www.fec.gov/pubrec/fe2008/tables2008.pdf.
Presidential vote 2004—national: http://www.fec.gov/pubrec/fe2004/tables.pdf.

3 Finance data: http://fec.gov/DisclosureSearch/mapHSApp.do?election_yr=2008, 2010, 2012.

4 Party unity scores courtesy of Keith Poole.

5 Presidential support scores courtesy of George C. Edwards III. Unlike the standard *Congressional Quarterly* support scores, Dr. Edwards, among other modifications, includes paired votes in each member's calculation. The first score represents the proportion of times that a member sided with the president on all roll call votes on which President Bush had declared a position. The second only includes those roll call votes that were non-unanimous. The latter will increase the mean difference between Democrats and Republicans.

6 American Conservative Union scores:

http://conservative.org/ratingsarchive/uscongress/2009, 2010, 2011, 2012.

7 Description: Based on a multidimensional scaling of roll calls, House members are ranked from most liberal (negative score) to most conservative (positive score). Only the first dimension, corresponding to economic issues, is used. Scores courtesy of Keith Poole.

Legislator Estimates 1st to 112th Houses: //www.voteview.com/dwnomin.htm.

8 Demographic data: 2006–2008 American Community Survey 3-Year Estimates.

2008–2010 American Community Survey 3-Year Estimates.
2010–2012 American Community Survey 3-Year Estimates.
2010–2012 American Community Survey should only be used for the 113th Congress.
The Census Bureau recommends only making comparisons with non-overlapping 3-year estimates. Therefore, one is cautioned to only compare the 2006–2008 with the 2010–2012 data.
Source: http://factfinder2.census.gov.

B5: EUROBAROMETER 69:2 CODEBOOK

NOTE: Four data files are associated with this codebook.

EURO69.dta includes all of the survey respondents (*N* = 26,661) from the 27 EU nations (March–May 2008).
Respondents who were part of the split sample question file were eliminated.
Weight variable *W27* should be used because it adjusts for different country populations.

The following data sets can be analyzed with the reduced, student version of SPSS and Stata Small.
Weight variable *W1* should be used with each.

EURO69I.dta includes only respondents from Italy (*N* = 1,022).
EURO69H.dta includes only respondents from Hungary (*N* = 1,000).
EURO69D.dta includes only respondents from Denmark (*N* = 1,005).

Variable Name **Variable Label Value.**
Value Label

country Numerical Country Code[1]

1. Belgium	8. France	15. Sweden
2. Denmark	9. Ireland	16. Great Britain
3. Germany (west)	10. Italy	17. Northern Ireland
4. Germany (east)	11. Luxembourg	18. Cyprus
5. Greece	12. Netherlands	19. Czech Republic
6. Spain	13. Austria	20. Estonia
7. Finland	14. Portugal	21. Hungary
22. Latvia	25. Poland	28. Bulgaria
23. Lithuania	26. Slovakia	29. Romania
24. Malta	27. Slovenia	

W1 WEIGHT ADJUSTS FOR DEMOGRAPHIC INEQUALITIES IN SAMPLING FOR INDIVIDUAL COUNTRIES (only use with single country subsets or when comparing individual; countries with each other)

W27 W1 PLUS ADJUSTMENT FOR COUNTRY POPULATIONS (27 EU member nations existing at the time; use when analyzing the entire EU)

V1 QA3 LIFE SATISFACTION[2]
1. Very satisfied
2. Fairly satisfied
3. Not very satisfied
4. Not at all satisfied
5. DK[3] (0.5%)

V2 QA4A EXPECTATIONS NEXT 12 MONTHS: LIFE IN GENERAL
1. Better
2. Same
3. Worse

V3 QA4A EXPECTATIONS N12M: ECONOMIC SITUATION IN YOUR COUNTRY
1. Better
2. Same
3. Worse

V4	QA4A EXPECTATIONS N12M: FINANCIAL SITUATION OF YOUR HOUSEHOLD 1. Better 2. Same 3. Worse
V5	QA4A EXPECTATIONS N12M: EMPLOYMENT SITUATION IN YOUR COUNTRY 1. Better 2. Same 3. Worse
V6	QA7A COUNTRY'S EU MEMBERSHIP—GOOD/BAD 1. A good thing 2. Neither good nor bad 3. A bad thing
V7	QA8A EU MEMBERSHIP—COUNTRY BENEFITED FROM 1. Benefited 2. Not benefited
V8	QA11A PRESENT DIRECTION—COUNTRY 1. Going in the right direction 2. Neither/DK 3. Going in the wrong direction
V9	QA11A PRESENT DIRECTION—EUROPEAN UNION 1. Going in the right direction 2. Neither (volunteered)/DK 3. Going in the wrong direction
V10	QA14 EU MEANING: LOSS OF CULTURAL IDENTITY 0. Not mentioned 1. Mentioned
V11	QA15A EU STATEMENTS: PERSONAL VOICE COUNTS IN EU 1. Tend to agree 2. DK 3. Tend to disagree

V12 QA15A EU STATEMENTS: PERSONAL VOICE COUNTS IN COUNTRY
1. Tend to agree
2. DK
3. Tend to disagree

V13 QA15A EU STATEMENTS: MY COUNTRY'S VOICE COUNTS IN EU
1. Tend to agree
2. DK
3. Tend to disagree

V14 QA27 HOUSEHOLD PURCHASING POWER—LAST 5 YEARS
1. Improved
2. Stayed about the same
3. Got worse

V15 QA29 LIFE FOR THE NEXT GENERATION WILL BE
1. Easier
2. More difficult
3. Neither

V16 QA37 EU PROPOSALS: SINGLE CURRENCY FOR ALL COUNTRIES IN EU
1. For
2. DK
3. Against

V17 QA37 EU PROPOSALS: A COMMON FOREIGN POLICY AMONG ALL EU COUNTRIES
1. For
2. DK
3. Against

V18 QA37 EU PROPOSALS: A COMMON DEFENCE AND SECURITY POLICY AMONG ALL EU COUNTRIES
1. For
2. DK
3. Against

V19 QA47A GLOBALIZATION IS AN OPPORTUNITY FOR ECONOMIC GROWTH
1. Strongly agree
2. Somewhat agree
3. DK
4. Somewhat disagree
5. Strongly disagree

V20 QA47A GLOBALIZATION PRESENTS A THREAT TO OUR NATIONAL CULTURE
1. Strongly agree
2. Somewhat agree
3. DK
4. Somewhat disagree
5. Strongly disagree

V21 QC2 EUROPEAN ELECTIONS IN 2009—INTEREST
1. Very interested
2. Somewhat interested
3. Somewhat disinterested
4. Very disinterested

V22 QC3 EUROPEAN ELECTIONS—INTENTION TO VOTE (10-point scale)
1. Definitely will not vote
2.
3.
4.
5.
6.
7.
8.
9.
10. Definitely will vote

V23 QD1A IMMIGRANTS CONTRIBUTE A LOT TO OUR COUNTRY
1. Totally agree
2. Tend to agree
3. DK
4. Tend to disagree
5. Totally disagree

V24 QE2T GLOBAL WARMING/CLIMATE CHANGE—PERCEPTION (10-point scale)

1. Not a serious problem at all
2.
3.
4.
5.
6.
7.
8.
9.
10. An extremely serious problem

V25 D1 LEFT-RIGHT IDEOLOGICAL PLACEMENT (10-point scale)

1. Left
2.
3.
4.
5.
6.
7.
8.
9.
10. Right
11. Refused to answer (8.3%)
12. DK (11.1%)

V26 D7 MARITAL STATUS

1. Married
2. Remarried
3. Unmarried, living with partner
4. Unmarried, have never lived with partner
5. Unmarried, previously lived with partner
6. Divorced
7. Separated
8. Widowed

V27 D10 SEX

1. Male
2. Female

V28 D11 AGE (actual years coded)
Mean = 48.3 Median = 48.0
15. Fifteen years old
16.
.
.
.
98. Ninety-eight years old

V29 D25 TYPE OF COMMUNITY
1. Rural area or village
2. Small or middle-sized town
3. Large town

V30 D41 NATIONAL BACKGROUND: RESPONDENT WAS BORN
1. In current country
2. In another EU country
3. In Europe, but not in the EU
4. In Asia, Africa, or Latin America
5. In Northern America, Japan, or Oceana

V31 D42 NATIONAL BACKGROUND: PARENTS
1. Both parents born in current country
2. One in current country, one in another EU country
3. Both in another EU country
4. One in current country, one outside of the EU
5. One in another EU country, one outside of EU
6. Refused to answer/DK (.2%)

NOTES

1 Country codes can be used to create aggregated or country-specific variables. For example, a variable listing the type of electoral system that a country has can be added. Here are the specific possibilities:

Single Member District/Winner Take All

First past the post: Great Britain (including Northern Ireland)
Two-round: France
Single Transferable Vote: Ireland, Malta

Mixed (combination of proportional and single-member district)

Mixed member: Germany (both), Hungary
Parallel: Lithuania

Proportional Representation-List: all others
Source: The International Institute for Democracy and Electoral Assistance http://www.idea.int/esd/glossary.cfm#N

2 Question code (e.g., QA3) corresponds to original survey entry.
3 "DK" (don't know) was included in most issue items as it often is the response of a sizeable proportion of the sample, sometimes exceeding 15%. These respondents have been added to or included as a middle category. You may wish to eliminate these respondents by recoding their category to **SYSMIS** (**RECODE**, Form 1.1)

B6: CCES 2012 CODEBOOK

NOTE: Three data files are associated with this codebook.

CCES2012A.dta includes all of the following variables and all of the survey respondents ($N = 54{,}535$).
CCES2012I.dta includes only the variables whose names are in italics and only those respondents from Indiana ($N = 1{,}020$). This data set can be analyzed with the reduced, student version of SPSS and Stata Small.
CCES2012M.dta includes only the variables whose names are in italics and only those respondents from Maryland ($N = 1{,}062$). This data set can be analyzed with the reduced, student version of SPSS and Stata Small.

WEIGHT Common Content Weight
STATE STATE NUMBER (listed at end of codebook)
CD112 Congressional District Number, 112th Congress
CD113 Congressional District Number, 113th Congress

V1 GENDER
1. Male
2. Female

V2 EDUCATION
1. No HS
2. High school graduate
3. Some college
4. 2-year

5. 4-year
6. Post-grad

V3 RACE/ETHNICITY (self best description)
1. White
2. Black
3. Hispanic
4. Asian
5. Native American
6. Mixed
7. Middle Eastern
8. Other

V4 HISPANIC
1. Yes
2. No

V5 AGE (based on birth year)

V6 MARITAL STATUS
1. Married
2. Separated
3. Divorced
4. Widowed
5. Single
6. Domestic partnership

V7 REGISTERED (to vote)
1. Yes
2. No

V8 PARTY ID
1. Strong Democrat
2. Not very strong Democrat
3. Lean Democrat
4. Independent
5. Lean Republican
6. Not very strong Republican
7. Strong Republican

V9 BORN AGAIN: Would you describe yourself as a born-again or Evangelical Christian?
1. Yes
2. No

V10 How important is religion in your life?
1. Very important
2. Somewhat important
3. Not too important
4. Not at all important

V11 How often do you attend religious services?
1. More than once a week
2. Once a week
3. Once or twice a month
4. A few times a year
5. Seldom
6. Never

V12 Present religion is
1. Protestant
2. Roman Catholic
3. Mormon
4. Eastern or Greek Orthodox
5. Jewish
6. Muslim
7. Buddhist
8. Hindu
9. Atheist
10. Agnostic
11. Nothing in particular
12. Something else

V13 Children under 18?
1. Yes
2. No

V14 Do you follow what's going on in government and public affairs . . .
1. Most of the time
2. Some of the time
3. Only now and then
4. Hardly at all

V15 Family income over past year
1. Less than $10,000
2. $10,000–$19,999
3. $20,000–$29,999
4. $30,000–$39,999

5. $40,000–$49,999
6. $50,000–$59,999
7. $60,000–$69,999
8. $70,000–$79,999
9. $80,000–$99,999
10. $100,000–$119,999
11. $120,000–$149,999
12. $150,000–$199,999
13. $200,000–$249,999
14. $250,000–$349,999
15. $350,000–$499,999
16. $500,000 or more

V16 Do you own or rent?
1. Own
2. Rent
3. Other

V17 You or immediate family member serve/served in military
1. Yes
2. No

V18 Immigrant/citizen status
1. Immigrant citizen
2. Immigrant non-citizen
3. First generation
4. Second
5. Third

V19 General health is . . .
1. Excellent
2. Very good
3. Good
4. Fair
5. Poor

V20 Do you have health insurance?
1. Yes
2. No/not sure

V21 In the past 12 months, did you not see a doctor because of costs?
1. Yes
2. No

V22 Over the past year, the nation's economy has . . .
1. Gotten much better
2. Gotten better
3. Stayed about the same
4. Gotten worse
5. Gotten much worse

V23 Over the past four years, your household annual income . . .
1. Increased a lot
2. Increased somewhat
3. Stayed about the same
4. Decreased somewhat
5. Decreased a lot

V24 Over the next year, the nation's economy will . . .
1. Get much better
2. Get somewhat better
3. Stay about the same
4. Get somewhat worse
5. Get much worse

V25 Who bears most responsibility for the current state of the U.S. economy?
1. Barack Obama
2. George W. Bush
3. Wall Street
4. World economy
5. Congress

V26 Mistake to attack Iraq?
1. Yes
2. Not sure
3. No

V27 Mistake to attack Afghanistan?
1. Yes
2. Not sure
3. No

V28 Approval of Obama
1. Strongly approve
2. Somewhat approve
3. Somewhat disapprove
4. Strongly disapprove

V29	Approval of Congress 1. Strongly approve 2. Somewhat approve 3. Somewhat disapprove 4. Strongly disapprove
V30	Approval of U.S. House member 1. Strongly approve 2. Somewhat approve 3. Somewhat disapprove 4. Strongly disapprove
V31	Vote in 2008 General Election? 1. No 2. Yes
V32	Presidential vote in 2008 1. Obama 2. McCain 3. Other
V33	Gun control should be made 1. More strict 2. Kept as is 3. Less strict
V34	View about climate change 1. Global climate change has been established as a serious problem, and immediate action is necessary. 2. There is enough evidence that climate change is taking place and some action should be taken. 3. We don't know enough about global climate change, and more research is necessary before we take any actions. 4. Concern about global climate change is exaggerated. No action is necessary. 5. Global climate change is not occurring; this is not a real issue.
V35	Grant legal status to illegal immigrants who have held jobs, paid taxes, and have no felony conviction? 1. Yes 2. No

V36 Fine U.S. businesses that hire illegal immigrants?
1. Yes
2. No

V37 Prohibit illegal immigrants from using emergency hospital care and public schools?
1. Yes
2. No

V38 Deny automatic citizenship to American-born children of illegal immigrants?
1. Yes
2. No

V39 View on abortion?
1. By law, abortion should never be permitted.
2. The law should permit abortion only in case of rape, incest, or when the woman's life is in danger.
3. The law should permit abortion for reasons other than rape, incest, or danger to the woman's life, but only after the need for the abortion has been clearly established.
4. By law, a woman should always be able to obtain an abortion as a matter of personal choice.

V40 Which is closer to the way you feel, or haven't you thought much about this?
1. Much more important to protect environment even if lose jobs and lower standard of living
2. Environment somewhat more important
3. About the same
4. Economy somewhat more important
5. Much more important to protect jobs, even if environment worse

V41 Gay marriage
1. Favor
2. Oppose

V42 If Congress were to balance the budget, you would most prefer . . .
1. Cut defense spending
2. Cut domestic spending
3. Raise taxes

V43 Support Simpson-Bowles (15% across-the-board cuts, eliminate many tax breaks, reduce deficit by 21% by 2020)
1. Support
2. Oppose

V44 Extend Bush-era tax cuts for incomes below $200,000—increase deficit by $205 billion?
1. Support
2. Oppose

V45 Extend Bush-era tax cuts for everyone—increase deficit by $405 billion?
1. Support
2. Oppose

V46 Repeal Affordable Care Act?
1. Support
2. Oppose

V47 End "Don't Ask, Don't Tell"?
1. Support
2. Oppose

For each of the following, where would you place them on a 7-point ideology scale?

1. Very liberal
2. Liberal
3. Somewhat liberal
4. Middle of the road
5. Somewhat conservative
6. Conservative
7. Very conservative

V48 Yourself

V49 Obama

V50 Romney

V51 Democratic Party

V52 Republican Party

V53 Tea Party Movement

POST-ELECTION:

V54	Did you vote in 2012? 1. Yes 2. No
V55	Method of voting 1. In person on Election Day 2. In person before Election Day (early) 3. Voted by mail (or absentee) 4. DK
V56	Presidential vote 2012 1. Obama 2. Romney 3. Other
V57	U.S. Senate Vote 2012 1. Democratic candidate 2. Republican candidate 3. Other
V58	U.S. House Vote 2012 1. Democratic candidate 2. Republican candidate 3. Other
V59	Non-voter preference 2012 1. Obama 2. Romney 3. Other
V60	If state had a budget deficit, what percent should come from tax increases and spending cuts (0–100) 0. All tax increases . 50. Equal . 100. All cuts
V61	Did you put up a political sign in the last year? 1. Yes 2. No
V62	Make a political donation? 1. Yes 2. No

V63 — Contributions made to all candidates and committees actual value from $0 to $1 million

V64 — Were you contacted by a candidate or political organization?
1. Yes
2. No

V65 — The Irish, Italians, Jews, and many other minorities overcame prejudice and worked their way up. Blacks should do the same without any favors.
1. Strongly agree
2. Somewhat agree
3. Neither agree nor disagree
4. Somewhat disagree
5. Strongly disagree

V66 — View of Tea Party
1. Very positive
2. Somewhat positive
3. Neutral
4. Somewhat negative
5. Very negative
6. DK/no opinion

STATE NUMBERS

1 Alabama
2 Alaska
4 Arizona
5 Arkansas
6 California
8 Colorado
9 Connecticut
10 Delaware
11 District of Columbia
12 Florida
13 Georgia
15 Hawaii
16 Idaho
17 Illinois
18 Indiana
19 Iowa
20 Kansas
21 Kentucky
22 Louisiana
23 Maine
24 Maryland
25 Massachusetts
26 Michigan
27 Minnesota
28 Mississippi
29 Missouri
30 Montana
31 Nebraska
32 Nevada
33 New Hampshire
34 New Jersey
35 New Mexico
36 New York
37 North Carolina
38 North Dakota
39 Ohio
40 Oklahoma
41 Oregon
42 Pennsylvania
44 Rhode Island
45 South Carolina
46 South Dakota
47 Tennessee
48 Texas
49 Utah
50 Vermont
51 Virginia
53 Washington
54 West Virginia
55 Wisconsin
56 Wyoming

B7: CROSSNAT CODEBOOK

From International IDEA (Institute for Democracy and Electoral Assistance) (latest year data exists 2010–2014) http://www.idea.int/uid/.

idea_esf — Electoral System Family
1. Proportional
2. Plurality/Majority
3. Mixed
4. Other

idea_esnl_lh — Electoral System for National Legislature-Lower House
1. List Proportional
2. First Past the Post
3. Single Non-Transferable Vote
4. Single Transferable Vote
5. Alternative Vote
6. Block Vote
7. Party Block Vote
8. Mixed Member Proportional
9. Parallel Systems
10. Two Round System
11. Other

idea_esnl_uh — Electoral System for National Legislature-Upper House
1. List Proportional
2. First Past the Post
3. Single Non-Transferable Vote
4. Single Transferable Vote
5. Alternative Vote
6. Block Vote
7. Party Block Vote
8. Mixed Member Proportional
9. Parallel Systems
10. Two Round System
11. Other
12. Appointed or Indirectly Elected

idea_esp — Electoral System for President
2. First Past the Post
10. Two Round System
11. Other
12. Non-presidential System

idea_pt	Parliament Type 1. Bicameral 2. Unicameral
idea_swlh	Percentage of Seats Held by Women in Lower House
idea_swuh	Percentage of Seats Held by Women in Upper House
idea_dpfp	Provisions for Direct Public Funding to Political Parties 1. Yes 2. No
idea_fmp	Provisions for Free or Subsidized Access to Media for Political Parties 1. Yes 2. No
idea_fmc	Provisions for Free or Subsidized Access to Media for Candidates 1. Yes 2. No
idea_lps	Limits on Party Spending 1. Yes 2. No
idea_lcs	Limits on Candidate Spending 1. Yes 2. No
cvote_l	Compulsory Voting-Legislature 1. Yes 2. No
cvote_p	Compulsory Voting-President 1. Yes 2. No
idea_vtr_pa	Percentage Voter Turnout Registered Voters—Parliament
idea_vtvap_pa	Percentage Voter Turnout Voting Age Population—Parliament
idea_vtr_pr	Percentage Voter Turnout Registered Voters—President
idea_vtvap_pr	Percentage Voter Turnout Voting Age Population—President

From the World Bank's WDI: 2012 data
http://data.worldbank.org/data-catalog/world-development-indicators/wdi-2012

wdi_dr Death rate per 1,000 People
wdi_lebm Life Expectancy at Birth, Female
wdi_lebm Life Expectancy at Birth, Male
wdi_lebm Life Expectancy at Birth, Total
wdi_65f Survival to Age 65, Female (% of cohort)
wdi_65m Survival to Age 65, Male (% of cohort)
wdi_imf Mortality Rate, Infant, Female (per 1,000 live births)
wdi_imm Mortality Rate, Infant, Male (per 1,000 live births)
wdi_imt Mortality Rate, Infant, Total (per 1,000 live births)
wdi_litf Literacy Rate, 15+, Female
wdi_litm Literacy Rate, 15+, Male
wdi_litt Literacy Rate, 15+, Total
wdi_ef Employment to Population Ratio, 15+, Female
wdi_em Employment to Population Ratio, 15+, Male
wdi_et Employment to Population Ratio, 15+, Total
wdi_lff Labor Force Participation Rate, Total (% of total population ages 15+, female)
wdi_lfm Labor Force Participation Rate, Total (% of total population ages 15+, male)
wdi_lft Labor Force Participation Rate, Total (% of total population ages 15+, total)
wdi_ex Exports of Goods and Services (% of GDP)
wdi_imp Imports of Goods and Services (% of GDP)
wdi_gdp GDP per Capita (constant 2005 US$)
wdi_gni GNI per Capita (constant 2005 US$)
wdi_gs Gross Savings (% of GDP)
wdi_up Urban Population (% of total)
wdi_me Military Expenditure (% of GDP)
wdi_he Health Expenditure per Capita (current US$)
wdi_int Internet Users (per 100 people)

From Freedom House (total scales run from least to most free) 2012 data
http://www.freedomhouse.org/report/freedom-world-aggregate-and-subcategory-scores#.U-fj035EPwY
http://freedomhouse.org/report-types/freedom-press#.U-flIH5EPwY

fh_af Total Freedom Score (0–100) = fh_pr +fh_cl
fh_pr Political Rights Total Score (0–40)
fh_cl Civil Liberties Total Score (0–60)
fh_pf Press Freedom Total Score (0–100)

From the Heritage Foundation (scales run 0 through 100, from least to most free)*
http://www.heritage.org/index/explore?view=by-region-country-year

hf_ov	Overall Score
hf_pr	Property Rights Freedom
hf_fc	Freedom from Corruption
hf_ff	Fiscal Freedom
hf_gs	Government Spending
hf_bf	Business Freedom
hf_lf	Labor Freedom
hf_mf	Monetary Freedom
hf_tf	Trade Freedom
hf_if	Investment Freedom
hf_fif	Financial Freedom
hf_ctr	Corporate Tax Rate
hf_tb	Tax Buden as %GDP
hf_ge	Government Expenditure as %GDP
hf_gdp5	5 Year Growth in GDP
hf_gdppc	GDP per Capita
hf_unemp	Unemployment %
hf_inflate	Inflation %

*Data mainly covering period from 2012 to 2013. For full explanation of data and scales, see http://www.freedomhouse.org/reports#.U-FPRxFEPwY http://www.heritage.org/index/about.

Appendix C

An Example of a Term-Wide Set of Computer Exercises—ANES2012A

EXERCISE 1: TRIAL RUN—OPENING A DATA SET

COMMANDS NEEDED:

- **svyset**
- **tabulate**

Task 1: Open your **ANES2012A.dta** data set.
Task 2: Either by way of syntax or graphical user interface (GUI) commands:

- Weight the data by *PW2012*.
- Run a simple frequency distribution for *V1* (gender).

Data check:

You should have produced a table with 48% classified as males and 52% as females (*N* = 2,056).

EXERCISE 2: VISUALIZING DATA

COMMANDS NEEDED:

- **svyset**
- **generate**
- **tabulate**

Reasoning: Before we can even start to examine tests for our hypotheses, we need to understand how and if we are correctly measuring our properties. "Massaging" data in a theoretically responsible way is a key tool for analysis (and one that is marketable). Visualizing data is also a helpful tool for presenting our findings to others.

Task 1: Open up the **ANES2012A** Stata data file (as you did in the Trial Run). As before, use *PW2012* as your weight.

Task 2: Run a simple frequency distribution for one of the following dichotomous variables. They will be used in Exercise 3:

V46 Favor/oppose death penalty
V47 Make buying a gun more difficult or not
V22 Does one have health insurance?

Instructor's note: Although these exercises are broken into three alternative possibilities for your students to choose, you can actually break these down into nine possible combinations of independent and dependent variables. This may be most helpful for those of you with large classes with multiple discussion sections.

Task 3: Display and describe your findings. "Display" by showing the frequency distribution table.

A note on "feeling thermometers": A rating of "0" indicates that one has the most negative feeling possible toward a candidate; a 100, the most positive; and 50, completely neutral.

Task 4: Generate three (3) new variables comparing feeling thermometers toward the Democratic Party and its candidates with those thermometers for Republicans.

presdiff (*V16–V17*)
partydiff (*V18–V19*)
vpdiff (*V71–V72*)

1. For each, what does a positive number mean?
2. For each, what does a negative number mean?
3. For each, what does "0" mean?

Task 5: Display, with three separate bar charts, these three feeling thermometer differences. Use the **graph bar** command with manual survey weights. From the chart produced, what is your general impression or assessment of the differences produced for *each* of those distributions?

Task 6: Quickly make a general claim about the similarities/differences among those three difference measures. Which one seems to be most skewed toward the Democratic Party or candidate?

EXERCISE 3: SUMMARY STATISTICS

COMMANDS NEEDED:

- **svyset**
- **generate**
- **table**

In the second exercise, you were asked to use several Stata commands to transform, create, and visualize certain variables in your **ANES2012A** data set. In this exercise, you will continue the analysis with a more formal statistical summary of the data.

Task 1: Open up the A**NES2012A** Stata data file (as you did in the Trial Run). As before, use *PW2012* as your weight.

Task 2: Create the variables *presdiff*, *partydiff*, and *vpdiff* as you did before.

Task 3: Use the variable you chose in Exercise 1 as your independent (explanatory) variable:

V46 Favor/oppose death penalty
V47 Make buying a gun more difficult or not
V22 Does one have health insurance?

Using the **table** command, generate the mean and standard deviation, range, and raw count (*N*) for your computed variables *presdiff*, *partydiff*, and *vpdiff* for each (2) of your independent variable categories. Use Example 4.2.5 as your guide, *BUT CHANGE* the dependent variables (*not* V72) and independent variable (*not* V1). I'll leave this part up to you.

Task 4: Compare and fully interpret the differences between your two independent variable categories in terms of their means, medians, standard deviations, and ranges of your three dependent variables.

Task 5: Using information about the means and medians, does your analysis confirm/disconfirm the following hypothesis (choose the one that goes along with your independent variable)?

Individuals who favor the death penalty are more likely to lean Republican than those who are opposed.

Individuals who believe it should be more difficult to buy a gun are more likely to lean Democratic than those who believe the rules should stay the same or be made easier.

Individuals with health insurance are more likely to lean Democratic than those without.

Task 6: Compare the results you obtained with *presdiff*, *partydiff*, and *vpdiff*. Which one does your independent variable (*V46* or *V47* or *V22*) seem to have a greater effect on? Verbally interpret that difference and what you think may be going on with the 2012 electorate.

EXERCISE 4: T-TESTS

COMMANDS NEEDED:

- **svyset**
- **generate**
- **mean**
- **test**

In the third exercise, you were asked to compare the differences between the means of your two independent variable categories *descriptively*. This time, however, you will use the set of **mean** and **test** commands to conduct inferential hypothesis tests of differences on those variables. Use the examples in Section 4.3 (Form 2) for examples of syntax, GUIs, and interpretation.

Task 1: Open up the A**NES2012A** Stata data file (as you did in the Trial Run). As before, use *PW2012* as your weight.

Task 2: Create the variables *presdiff*, *partydiff*, and *vpdiff* as you did before.

Task 3: Using the **mean** and **test** procedures, determine whether you can *confidently reject* the possibility that, in the population from which the ANES sample was drawn, there is no difference in mean feelings toward the presidential candidates (*presdiff*), the parties (*partydiff*), and the vice presidential candidates (*vpdiff*). Set *testval* to 0. Explain why or why not.

Translation: Is there truly a difference in the population between your two independent variable categories on each of those difference scales, or may the difference you computed be attributed to the random luck of the draw? Is the sample mean thermometer differences calculated significantly different enough from "0" degrees (no mean difference between the two presidential candidates and/or parties and/or vice presidential candidates) to confidently reject "0" degrees as a possibility?

Relevant findings: Refer to the following from your output to answer that question: t-value, significance of the t-test value, and the 95% confidence interval values.

Data check: Make sure that the *sample means* calculated with the mean procedures are as follows:

presdiff = 8.8294 (*N* = 2,021)
partydiff = 8.1373 (*N* = 2,013)
vpdiff = 2.4803 (*N* = 1,701)

Task 4: Use the variable you chose in Exercise 1 as your independent (explanatory) variable:

V46 Favor/oppose death penalty
V47 Make buying a gun more difficult or not
V22 Does one have health insurance?

Using the **mean** command with the **over** option, compare and interpret the presdiff means of your two independent variable groups: categories 1 and 2. Are those mean differences significantly different from each other in the sample to confidently reject the possibility that the mean difference in the population between your two groups equals 0 degrees? Why or why not?

Translation: Is there truly a difference in the population between your two groups, or may the difference we computed be attributed to the random luck of the draw? Is the sample mean difference calculated between your two sample groups on *presdiff* significantly different enough from "0" degrees (no mean difference between the groups) to confidently reject "0" degrees as a possibility in the population from which the sample was drawn?

Data check: Make sure that the sample means calculated with this mean procedure are as follows:

	Group 1	Group 2
V46	-1.1900	30.0833
V47	30.8872	-8.3796
V22	6.1178	24.4452

Relevant findings: Refer to the following from your output to answer that question: t-value, significance of the t-test value, and the 95% confidence interval values. Use the more conservative "Equal variances not assumed" figures.

Task 5: Using the **mean** and **test** procedures, determine whether you can *confidently reject* the possibility that, in the population from which this ANES sample was drawn, there is no difference in the mean values of *presdiff* and *partydiff*. Explain why or why not.

Translation: Is there truly a difference in the population between these two variables' means, or may the difference we computed be attributed to the random luck of the draw? Is the sample mean difference calculated between *presdiff* and *partydiff* significantly different enough from "0" degrees (no mean difference between the variables) to confidently reject "0" degrees as a possibility in the population?

Data check: Make sure that the sample means calculated with this mean procedure for *presdiff* = 9.2304* and for *partydiff* = 8.0082.

*The means are different from what you should have found in task 2.

Reason: In task 2, all 2,021 respondents for whom there was a difference in evaluation between the presidential candidates were included, as were all 2,013 who responded to *partydiff*. In this step, only those for whom a difference could be included for *both presdiff* and *partydiff* are included (N = 1,992).

Relevant findings: Refer to the following from your output to answer that question: t-value, significance of the t-test value, and the 95% confidence interval values.

Task 6: Perform a similar analysis for the differences between *presdiff* and *vpdiff* and between *partydiff* and *vpdiff*.

EXERCISE 5: CROSSTABS

COMMANDS NEEDED:

- **svyset**
- **generate**
- **recode**
- **tabulate**

In the third and fourth exercises, you were asked to compare the differences between the means of your two independent variable categories *descriptively* and then *inferentially*. This time, you will use crosstabs to conduct a similar test of differences on those variables, but you will first collapse your interval-level thermometer difference scales into three ordinal categories. Use the examples in Sections 3.1 and 4.1 for examples of syntax, GUIs, and interpretation.

Task 1: Open up the **ANES2012A** Stata data file (as you did in the Trial Run). As before, use *PW2012* as your weight.

Task 2: Create the variables *presdiff*, *partydiff*, and *vpdiff* as you did before.

Task 3: Recode each of those three variables (separately) into three new variables:

pres3, party3, vp3

Collapse your three original variables into just three categories:

- Leans toward the Republicans (–1): –100 thru –1
- Same feeling thermometer rating for both parties (0): 0
- Leans toward the Democrats (+1): +1 thru 100

Data check: Before you go any further, make sure that your frequency distributions for *pres3*, *party3*, and *vp3* are as follows:

pres3

		Frequency	Percent	Valid Percent	Cumulative Percent
Valid	-1.00	778	37.9	38.5	38.5
	.00	159	7.7	7.9	46.4
	1.00	1,084	52.7	53.6	100.0
	Total	2,021	98.3	100.0	
Missing	System	35	1.7		
Total		2,056	100.0		

party3

		Frequency	Percent	Valid Percent	Cumulative Percent
Valid	-1.00	716	34.8	35.6	35.6
	.00	366	17.8	18.2	53.7
	1.00	931	45.3	46.3	100.0
	Total	2,013	97.9	100.0	
Missing	System	43	2.1		
Total		2,056	100.0		

vp3

		Frequency	Percent	Valid Percent	Cumulative Percent
Valid	-1.00	665	32.4	39.1	39.1
	.00	269	13.1	15.8	54.9
	1.00	767	37.3	45.1	100.0
	Total	1,701	82.8	100.0	
Missing	System	355	17.2		
Total		2,056	100.0		

Task 4: Using the **tabulate** procedure, create a 3 × 2 table with *your* previously chosen independent variable (*V46*, *V47*, or *V22*) as your independent variable (columns) and *pres3*, *party3*, and *vp3*, individually, as your dependent variable (rows). Ask for column percentages, chi-square, and Cramer's V.

Task 5: Answer the following questions:

- Which of your two independent variable groups is more likely to lean toward Democratic candidate Obama? By what percentage point difference?
- Which of your two independent variable groups is more likely to lean toward the Democratic Party? By what percentage point difference?
- Which of your two independent variable groups is more likely to lean toward the Democratic vice-presidential candidate Biden? By what percentage point difference?

Task 6: Using Cramer's V, how strong is the correlation between your independent variable and your dependent variables?

Task 7: Using chi-square (Pearson), given the differences in this sample, can you confidently claim that some leaning difference between your two independent variable groups on each of your dependent variables (difference >0%) also exists in the population from which this sample was (randomly) drawn? Why or why not?

Task 8: Compare your results from Exercises 4 and 5. Does the type of analysis and the reclassification of categories make any difference in how you respond to the hypotheses listed in Exercise 3?

Individuals who favor the death penalty are more likely to lean Republican than those who are opposed.

Individuals who believe it should be more difficult to buy a gun are more likely to lean Democratic than those who believe the rules should stay the same or be made easier.

Individuals with health insurance are more likely to lean Democratic than those without.

EXERCISE 6: USING REGRESSIONS

COMMANDS NEEDED:

- **svyset**
- **generate**
- **regress**

You will finish this set of exercises by employing a linear regression model to test for the relationships between a new variable and your three dependent variables.

Task 1: Open up the **ANES2012A** Stata data file. As before, use *PW2012* as your weight.

Task 2: Create the variables *presdiff*, *partydiff*, and *vpdiff* as you did before.

Task 3: Using the **regress** command, test the linear relationship between the *partydiff* (this will serve as your independent variable) and, separately, each of your other two dependent variables (*presdiff* and *vpdiff*). For which dependent variable is *partydiff* a better explanatory fit?

Task 4: Interpret both the intercepts and slopes of your two regression equations.

Task 5: Use *your* chosen independent variable (*V46*, *V47*, or *V22*) as a dummy variable and add it to the equation. Reinterpret your intercepts and slopes.

Task 6: Is your dummy variable more or less important in explaining the variance of *presdiff* and *vpdiff* than *partydiff*? Does it add anything to your explanation?

Task 7: Using an "if" statement in conjunction with the **regress** command, produce two regression equations (one for each of *your* independent variable choices). Answer the following:

- For which of your two categories is *partydiff* a better explanatory fit for *presdiff*?
- Interpret the intercept and slope for each of your regressions.

EXERCISE 7

Using the results and interpretations produced in Exercises 2–6, summarize your findings.